T0090020

Shacking Up

Stacy Whitman and Wynne Whitman

Broadway Books
New York

Shacking Up

The Smart Girl's Guide to Living in Sin Without Getting Burned

This book is not intended to take the place of legal or financial advice from a lawyer or other trained professional. Readers should consult an attorney or other qualified professional regarding their legal and financial problems. Neither the publisher nor the author takes any responsibility for any possible consequences to the reader's financial or legal status from any action taken as a result of the information in this book.

Visit our website at www.broadwaybooks.com

First edition published 2003.

Book design by Caroline Cunningham

Library of Congress Cataloging-in-Publication Data
Whitman, Stacy.
Shacking up: the smart girl's guide to living in sin without getting burned / Stacy Whitman and Wynne Whitman.—1st ed.
p. cm.
1. Unmarried couples. 2. Single women—Life skills guides.
I. Whitman, Wynne. II. Title
HQ803.5.W55 2003
306.73'5—dc21 2002026078

ISBN 978-0-7679-1040-8

146122990

For Mom, Dad, and Ted.
With gratitude and love.

Contents

cohabit, vi 1 : to live together as or as if a married couple
2 a : to live together or in company **b :** to exist together

Introduction

Think back to when you were a little girl. Even if you were a tomboy or young feminist, you probably had the fantasy of dressing up in an exquisite white gown and pledging everlasting love to the man of your dreams. You'd have a fairy-tale wedding, with flowers, cake, and all of your best friends as bridesmaids, before riding off into the sunset and living happily ever after. It all seemed so simple. If you're anything like me, you didn't picture yourself moving in with your boyfriend, bumming out your parents, and fighting with your spousal equivalent about everything from furniture to finances. But that's what ended up happening less than a year after I met Ted.

I'm not someone who had planned on shacking up. Unlike some of my friends and loved ones, I didn't have a strong opinion about it. In theory, it sounded like a good idea to test the waters before tying the knot. But I'd never really thought about it in terms of *myself.* So when Ted proposed that we move to

San Francisco and get an apartment together after just eight months of dating, I didn't know what to say. Part of me was excited beyond belief. After kissing countless frogs, I had finally found my prince: a guy who was cute, athletic, funny, and fastidiously neat. Like me, he loved waking up early, reading the *New York Times,* running on the beach, hiking in the mountains, trying new restaurants, eating coconut gelato, and watching the *English Patient.* He had an appreciation for fine art, hated cell phones, and understood the value of a cashmere sweater set. He seemed to fit in with my family and had passed the "friend test" with flying colors. I had never felt so right about anyone in my life.

But while my heart told me, *Yes!,* my mind said, *Whoa!* After all, Ted and I hadn't known each other all that long. My older sister, Wynne, was against the idea—she had two close friends whose live-in relationships had ended disastrously. I instinctively knew that my parents would be less than happy with the cohabitation notion. Then there were my question marks about commitment. Eventually, I knew I wanted to get hitched. Ted came from a family of multiple divorces. Would I be moving in with someone who had a tainted view of marriage? I wasn't going to be one of those women who moved three thousand miles only to get dumped with a capital "D." Then again, I'd never been able to hold down a long-term relationship myself. Maybe I would be the one who couldn't handle it.

Despite my concerns, I decided to take the plunge—and in retrospect, I'm glad that I did. In doing it, I discovered that Ted loved me even after finding out that I didn't balance my checkbook or seeing me on the baddest of all bad hair days and deathly sick with the flu. I was able to make sure that he wasn't hiding anything like erratic mood swings, an addiction to porn, or a secret life as a male prostitute. We found that we were able to cope with clashes over everything from cooking to closet space. We learned how to talk things out and forgive one another for less-than-perfect behavior. We had fun hanging out, folding laundry, fixing up our apartment, experimenting with new recipes, throwing dinner parties, watching "must-see" TV, and keeping each other warm (or, rather, keeping *me* warm) on chilly Bay Area evenings. (And in case you're wondering, roughly eighteen months later, I ended up earning my M.R.S. degree.)

But before you get fired up about following in our footsteps, there's something that you ought to know. Our "trial run" wasn't the perfect love affair that I'd always imagined. At times, it was the mother of all roller-coaster rides as we struggled to adjust to each other's rituals and habits. Going in, I wasn't prepared for the turmoil and, for the first six months or so, wondered whether our arguments were a sign that we weren't going to make it. I had no idea how much effort went into a live-in relationship and, on more than one occasion, wanted to run away rather than deal with it. I didn't know how much my family's quiet disapproval would eat at my heart. Sure, I was an independent, thirtysomething woman with a mind of my own. But they were my *parents,* and I felt as though I could hear the disappointment in their voices every time we spoke on the phone. (Call me crazy, but at this age, I no longer get secret pleasure from pissing off my family.)

The purpose of this book isn't to scare you or talk you out of anything—I swear. But as someone who has been there, done that, it's my objective to give you the *real* inside story. You see, shacking up is like being a contestant on the reality TV show "Survivor." It can be incredibly rewarding, but it isn't always easy or enjoyable. That's why you need to be careful about whom you form an alliance with and how you go about playing the game.

If I had to do it all over again, there are definitely things that I would do differently. There are also a lot of things I know

now that I wish I'd known when I moved in. After talking to friends and acquaintances who had also shacked up, I found that many of them had faced similar trials and tribulations—and most of them agreed that they weren't terribly prepared. Which made me think: Was there a helpful how-to guide on living together for real, twenty-first-century women like us? After searching countless bookstores and websites, I got the surprising answer: *No.* So I teamed up with my sister, who just happens to be a legal and financial genius, to fill the void.

Ten months and countless glasses of Chardonnay later, *Shacking Up: The Smart Girl's Guide to Living in Sin Without Getting Burned* was born. (Don't worry—not out of wedlock!) Using extensive interviews with researchers, psychologists, financial planners, legal experts, and dozens of couples who have shacked up, our new-millennium relationship handbook explains the potential pitfalls of living together—and how to avoid them. From deciding where to live to setting a time line for getting married, you'll get all the information and support you need to make the right decisions and develop a healthy domestic partnership that will last a lifetime.

Now that it's become less taboo, many of us are entering into cohabitation casually. A lot of us are also unaware of the legal and financial risks (which are greater now that we girls have more to lose!) or how to protect ourselves. In *Shacking Up,* you'll find important advice on managing household finances, setting up joint bank accounts, and making joint purchases. Our manual explains your legal rights as a cohabitor and provides valuable information on cohabitation agreements, leases, wills, and other important legal matters.

Shacking Up is the one-stop guide for anyone who answers "Yes" to the "Will you move in with me?" question. From decorating disasters to privacy problems, you'll get helpful tips on handling sticky domestic issues, straight from the lips of enlightened twenty- and thirtysomethings. (Note: Names in the book have been changed to protect the innocent.) This manual is also for those of you who are trying to decide whether or not cohabitation is for you. We'll explain the pluses and minuses of live-in relationships and lead you through the decision-making process. Whether you're itching to get hitched, want to take your relationship to the next level, or simply interested in spending more time together, you'll find out what it takes to be successful.

And for those of you who *do* decide to go for it, I want to leave you with this last slice of sisterly advice: Whenever you start to panic about the topsy-turvy state of your union, or wonder "What the heck am I doing?" open up your copy of *Shacking Up* and remind yourself that you're *normal*. We all have doubts, insecurities, imperfections, disagreements, and periodic freakouts. If you don't believe me, keep reading. A lot of women and men have been in your shoes and made their share of mistakes. Listen to their true-life stories, helpful hints, and smart suggestions, and accept the fact that things aren't always going to go perfectly. Shacking up is a wild, wacky, and unpredictable adventure. So fasten your emotional seat belt and enjoy the ride.

—*Stacy Whitman*

CHAPTER 1

You're Thinking of Doing WHAT?!?

Yes, the unthinkable has happened. After all those years of dating hell, you've found a man who appears to be a candidate for a long-term relationship. (We'd say "Mr. Right," but we don't want to jinx it.) At this point, you're spending almost every night with the object of your affection. You've become a pro at commuting across town with a change of clothes in your shoulder bag (thank goodness for microfiber!). But you're growing tired of the commute and forking out dough for an apartment that's little more than a walk-in closet. Then, as if he's reading your mind, the guy in your life pops the question. No, not THE question, but the other question: "What do you think about moving in together?"

Your heart skips a beat. Your head spins with visions of cozy home-cooked dinners for two and shopping together at Pottery Barn for new slipcovers and matching silverware. *Oooh,* yes, you can picture it. A place of your own. A real apartment with *real* furniture. No more schleping back and forth or paying double rent. But then, before you can finish your celebration dance, you feel a sinking sensation deep in your stomach. Is moving in with Mr. Possibility really a good idea? Would it be a step toward marriage or simply a means of saving money? Can you live 24/7 with someone who leaves empty pizza boxes lying around his apartment? What in heaven's name would you tell your parents?!?

Welcome to the wonderful world of twenty-first-century relationships. Gone are the days of formal courtship and living with Mom and Dad until you're hitched. Today, for many of us, shacking up has become a new step in the mating process. But that doesn't mean it's right for you, right now. Oh sure, some people say it can help you determine whether your relationship is marriage-worthy. Others claim that it will set you up for a huge disappointment. Yada, yada, yada. There are lots of opinions, views, and misinformation floating around out there that can be a bit confounding for smart, conscientious girls like us. Fear not: We're here to help. From this point forward, you'll have a couple of savvy sisters to guide you through the muck.

To a bunch of you, shacking up may seem the natural choice. But even if you're already convinced that moving in together is the way to go, we urge you not to skip ahead. You see, there *can* be downsides to bucking tradition. Plus, the research is fuzzy as to whether living together is a good test drive or a freeway wreck waiting to happen. For goodness' sake, we wouldn't want you to lease the car only to find out it's a lemon. So you need to tread carefully and truly understand what you may be getting yourself into. As they say, only fools rush in! In this chapter, we'll present all of the pros and cons of shacking up with your mate, so you can weigh them before reaching a final verdict. Hey, the last thing you want is to become a serial live-in chick or wind up in Heartbreak Hotel, right?

The Case for Cohabitation

In case you've been too busy climbing the corporate ladder to notice, shacking up is the thing to do these days. In the past ten to fifteen years, this once daring move has become as common as Internet dating and Kate Spade bags. The number of lovebirds sharing nests in the United States jumped by 72 percent in the last decade, according to the 2000 Census. University of Michigan sociologist Pamela Smock, Ph.D., estimates that as many as six out of ten couples now live together before getting hitched.

Why are so many of us moving in without ceremonies and rings? Are we fun, fearless females? Wild and crazy gals? Rebels without a cause? Uh, hardly. We all have our own reasons, which almost always start with a romantic spark and an intense physical attraction. We are in *love* and want to spend more time with our best friend, sidekick, and paramour. Some of us are interested in cutting down on living expenses. More important, for many of us, shacking up is a way to shift gears forward in our relationship. We want to get closer to our significant other and share our life beyond late-night dinners, sleepovers, and weekend trysts.

Granted, not all of us shack up with the "M" word in mind. But for the majority of us twenty- and thirtysomethings, the ultimate goal is a walk down the aisle. Which brings us to the big, underlying reason so many of us have for moving in: to help us decide whether our mates are the right ones for us. If we're going to take our relationships to the legal level, some of us think it would be nuts to do it without knowing what it's like to live together day in and day out. "I would never consider marrying someone without living together first," attests Megan, twenty-six, of Berkeley, California. "This way, I already know what will drive me crazy and in which ways we're really compatible, and we've already got practice working on the things that we need to work on."

Here's an APB for the matrimony police: Despite their grave fears, most of us aren't thumbing our noses at the institution of marriage. Really, we're not. Deep down, we want lifelong memberships to the Husbands and Wives Club. But we're petrified of divorce, and it's no wonder. Many of us have witnessed the painful collapse of our parents' marriages or lived through the excruciating breakup of our own. We're all too aware of the divorce rates, which have been appallingly high since the early 1980s. So we're choosing to stick our big toes in the water before diving into anything permanent. "Living together was what my husband, Jake, needed before getting married," says Kristy, thirty-five, of Portland, Oregon, who cohabited for two-plus years before tying the knot. "His dad is now on his fourth marriage, so Jake sees divorce as 'failure.' He didn't want to fail and make the same mistakes as his dad."

We don't know about you, but there are a lot of people who like the idea of having a dress rehearsal. Set aside any romantic notions you have for a sec. Let's talk practicalities. By shacking up, you get to test out what marriage would be like. It's sort of like sampling a flavor of frozen yogurt before ordering a dish or a Hollywood screen test without the hair and makeup. "Every woman should live with her significant other before taking the plunge," says Beth, thirty-two, of New York City, who lived with her boyfriend for three years before saying "I do." "How else can you see exactly what you're signing up for?"

As most of us know from college or postcollege roommate

situations, some people can be tough to live with. "Shacking up allows you to experience your partner's habits in action," says Leslie, thirty, of Jacksonville, Florida. Does he drink out of the milk carton? Leave filthy clothes all over the floor? Clip his fingernails at the kitchen table? You can find out these things and much more. For instance, you can discover whether your man pays his bills on time, gives you enough space, and respects your privacy. You can see how he copes with stress or reacts when your hair clogs the shower for the *umpteenth* time. You can determine just how patient, understanding, and considerate he really is. "We've only been living together for a week, and I'm already learning how Kevin handles pressure, what really bugs him, what he can compromise on, and what he can't," says Liz, thirty, of St. Louis.

Shacking up can also be a way to make sure your partner isn't keeping any secrets, says Kelly, thirty-three, who lived with her husband prior to marriage. "It's pretty easy to hide stuff when you're on a date or off on a weekend together, but it's hard to keep things under wraps when you're living in close quarters," she explains. "When you live together, you really begin to learn what a person is all about." Amanda, thirty, of Morristown, New Jersey, is a good example. She dated James for two years before he moved into her condo. "I knew that he could be a little moody and always seemed to be short on cash," Amanda says. "But I didn't understand the extent of his problems until after he moved in." As it turned out, James was deeply in debt and had anger management issues. "If we hadn't lived together, I'm not sure I would have learned the truth," she claims. "When you cohabit, you see everything, from his mail to how he acts after a rotten day at work. It quickly became evident that James wasn't the person I thought he was."

Don't forget, ladies: Once you shack up, the fantasy ends

and real life begins. "Typically, when you're dating, you don't have a whole lot to argue about," says Jordan, twenty-nine, who has been living with her boyfriend for a year. "It isn't until he starts taking over your closet or insists on keeping his wagon-wheel coffee table that things can start to get touchy." Like it or not, conflict is a part of any close, committed relationship. Living together gives you the opportunity to discover and resolve these points of disagreement before you're legally wed, points out Jane, twenty-seven. You can find out just how adept the two of you are at compromising, communicating, and negotiating sticking points. Like our friend Colleen, thirty-two, you may be delighted to learn that you get along even better than expected.

To Mia, the best thing about shacking up is that you can hash out your problems (toilet seat up versus down and who pays for what) without the pressure of having a ring on your finger. "I didn't have to feel like 'Oh my God, we're fighting and we're already married. This is it—we're doomed!' " the twenty-nine-year-old Chicago resident says. Ann, thirty, of San Francisco agrees that it can be better to tackle the tough stuff prior to the nuptials: "People talk about how the first year of marriage is *so* hard. If you live together first, you get all those issues—however big or small they may be—out of the way."

Living together can also help you eliminate any lingering question marks about your mate. "It's another piece of evidence to verify that you're right for each other," says Colleen. "I love getting the confirmation that I can trust him," adds Kate. "So far, we've had tests, but no failures." Can you learn all the important details if you date each other long enough? Well, perhaps. It depends on your relationship and how much time you've spent together in continuous spurts. Still, for some of us, living together is the final litmus test we need to be absolutely sure. Even if you're 99 percent certain that you're compatible before moving in, shacking up can give you that extra one percent of confidence when taking your vows, Kelly says.

And let's not forget the joys of sharing your life with another person. From ordering pizza to painting the living room, everything can be more fun when you have a partner in crime. "I really enjoy building a life together and making a home with someone I love," says Jane. Teaming up with your significant other can provide a sense of comfort and security. "I love knowing that he'll be there when I come home—playing computer games, making cookies, or watching TV," says Kate. "I feel more connected to him, knowing that he trusts me enough to share everything." "I hadn't had a roommate for five years, so I was concerned about how I would do living with Doug," confesses Jennifer, who shacked up eleven months ago. "But it's really been wonderful. I relish the companionship, whether we're eating breakfast, watching movies, decorating, or doing laundry together. I sleep easier knowing that he's there."

Even if your "trial run" is a bust, some shacking-up vets maintain that the experience can be worthwhile. Sophie, for one, has no regrets about moving in with her ex. "I was undecided about marriage before I lived with Garrett," the thirty-five-year-old says. "Living together helped me reach a decision *fast.* I panicked as I saw a future with a man I didn't love. I chose to get out and pursue the guy I'd always been secretly in love with"—her now-husband, Jeff. Ira, thirty-four, was less than thrilled when his live-in relationship with Janet didn't work out. (Doubly so because they had already purchased real estate together.) Still, he's thankful that he found out the truth before he sealed the deal. "I actually wish Janet and I had moved in together earlier," he says. "That way, issues would have come to a head sooner, before we put a down payment on a reception site or bought a house."

Many experts, including Pamela Smock, agree that cohabitation can weed out incompatible couples. Smock speculates that the divorce rates might be higher if so many of us weren't moving in prior to marriage. Then again, the breakup of a live-in relationship can be *extremely* painful. A number of the men and women we interviewed for this book said they would never put themselves through the agony again. So don't start packing your suitcases until you've finished reading Chapters 1 and 2. By being informed, you can increase your odds of having a happy ending.

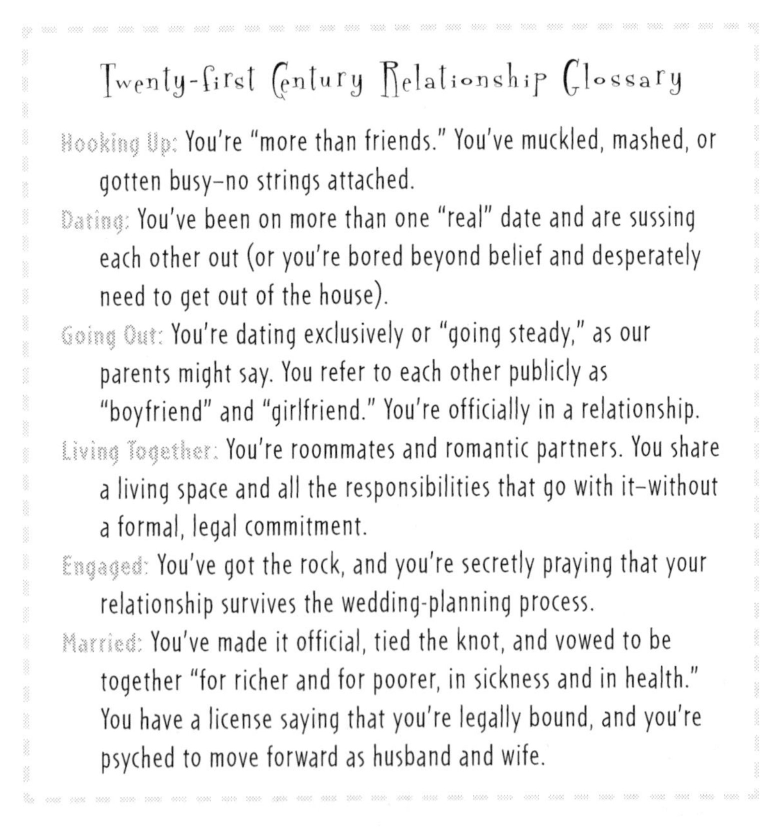

Twenty-first Century Relationship Glossary

Hooking Up: You're "more than friends." You've muckled, mashed, or gotten busy–no strings attached.

Dating: You've been on more than one "real" date and are sussing each other out (or you're bored beyond belief and desperately need to get out of the house).

Going Out: You're dating exclusively or "going steady," as our parents might say. You refer to each other publicly as "boyfriend" and "girlfriend." You're officially in a relationship.

Living Together: You're roommates and romantic partners. You share a living space and all the responsibilities that go with it–without a formal, legal commitment.

Engaged: You've got the rock, and you're secretly praying that your relationship survives the wedding-planning process.

Married: You've made it official, tied the knot, and vowed to be together "for richer and for poorer, in sickness and in health." You have a license saying that you're legally bound, and you're psyched to move forward as husband and wife.

It's Your Life—So Go Ahead and Ruin It!

One of the first things you realize when you start contemplating cohabitation is that not everyone thinks it's such a brilliant move. On the one hand, you'll have girlfriends who support the idea wholeheartedly. On the other hand, you could have parents, grandparents, aunts, uncles, or godparents—you know, the over-fifty crowd—who aren't so keen on it. Then there are people like Dr. Laura Schlessinger, the radio talk show host who lists cohabitation as one of the "Ten Stupidest Things Women Do to Mess Up Their Lives" in her book of the same title. (Funny, we think one of the ten stupidest things that you can do is listen to Dr. Laura. But who are we to judge? Our own mother likes to tune in!)

At any rate, when you're excited about the thought of moving in with your boyfriend, it can be frustrating to learn other people don't share your enthusiasm. "What's their problem?" you may ask. "Are they still living in the Stone Age?" You have to remember that it hasn't been that long since shacking up was completely taboo. To show you what we mean, let's take a superfast look at history. As recently as the 1960s, living together was something that good girls just didn't do. People back then tended to be more religious, and for many, shacking up was considered a date with the devil—hence the expression "living in sin." Cohabitation was not only considered morally wrong, it was actually illegal in every state in the nation. When you consider it that way, you can understand why many older Americans don't understand or approve of our nontraditional lifestyles.

Judging by our conversations with dozens of cohabitors, we women get a lot more flack for living in sin than our boyfriends do. As one might expect, it usually comes down to the whole S-E-X issue. Here's how the logic goes. If you're living with a man, you're sharing a bed with him. If you're sharing a bed with him, then you're having sex with him. If you're having sex, you could end up with a bun in the oven and ruin your life forever. What our elders don't always understand (or want to admit) is that most of us are getting busy with our boyfriends anyway. Blame the sexual revolution and the fact that, these days, many of us remain single well into our thirties. Can we really be expected to stay chaste until we're hitched? Please! So if you ask us, the premarital sex thing is a bit of a nonissue. (Of course, you can't tell your parents or grandparents that!)

Next, there is the old "Why buy the cow when you can get the milk for free?" argument, which quite a few women get from their mothers. In other words, how are you going to get this guy to marry you if he's already getting everything that he wants (i.e., sex and free laundry service) without a formal commitment? This line of thinking dates back to the days when women needed to wed for financial reasons and suggests that we'll be taken advantage of by our mates. For any of you who are eager to walk down the aisle, the cow argument may have some relevance. (That's why you need to make your expectations about marriage clear before moving in—more on that in the following chapter.) For the rest of you for whom shacking up isn't primarily about matrimony or "getting the ring," it's pretty much a *moooot* point. Obviously, life isn't the same as it was forty or fifty years ago. Today, women are kicking serious butt in the workplace, so we don't need spouses to support us. Despite what Mom may think, many of us are moving in with our mates to determine whether we want to marry *them*—not the other way around. So as you can see, the suggestion that we (as the cows) could be put out to pasture is a little outdated. In fact, maybe it's the *guys* who should be concerned.

Now, despite what we said earlier about shacking up being widely accepted by our generation, a few of you may have friends or siblings who, for whatever reason, tell you, "No, no! Don't do it!" Perhaps they lived with a significant other and got burned, or know some other poor soul who did. Or perhaps they have fervent religious beliefs, as in the case of Jocelyn's younger brother. "No one really cared that I was moving in with my boyfriend except my brother Michael, who gave me a religious argument against it," the thirty-seven-year-old says. "As a devout Catholic, he believed that living together was sinful and anyone who did it would (no joke) burn in hell." That didn't stop Jocelyn, who doesn't attend church regularly or share her brother's views, from shacking up with her honey. Apparently, it didn't stop Michael, either. "A few years later, Michael proceeded to move in with his now-wife," Jocelyn says. "I guess he decided that shacking up wasn't immoral as long as you plan to spend the rest of your life with that person." Talk about the pot calling the kettle black!

For some of you, all the conflicting attitudes and views are likely to cause some confusion. Who should you believe? We say, none of them! Our *Shacking Up* advice is this: You should take a hard look at yourself, your mate, and your relationship, then form a conclusion based on those factors, not what anybody else says. "It's important to be aware of your own feelings and needs, and not be too swayed by others' opinions," agrees Heidi, thirty-four, of San Francisco, who lived with her boyfriend for two years before getting engaged. "Everyone is going to have an opinion of what you should do, but only you and your partner know what is right for your relationship." That said, even if you aren't particularly religious or old-fashioned, you *do* need to be sensitive to your loved one's feelings on these matters. On pages 73–77, we'll explain how to deliver the "We're moving in together!" news to disapproving family members and friends in a conscientious manner.

Shacking Up Success Story

Mia, twenty-nine, of Chicago

How they decided: "I was living in New York and Peter was just finishing business school. We'd been long-distance dating for about two years. He ended up getting a job offer in Chicago, so we decided to move there together. It was Peter's idea to share an apartment. At that point in our relationship, he thought it made sense to live together."

What the 'rents said: "My mom was supportive of my decision (she just prayed it would end in marriage). My dad looked the other way. I don't think he wanted to think about it. In fact, for the first year, he pretended that I had female roommates and left messages on our answering machine saying, 'Hi, girls, just checking in to see how everyone is doing.' "

The big move: "After I arrived in Chicago, it was a little touch-and-go for a while. We fought about a lot of things (the toilet seat sticks out in my mind). I was in a new city and didn't have a job or many friends, which added to the stress. But I loved Peter and still thought he was "the one," so I didn't panic. It took about six to nine months for us to get into a groove. By then, we were starting to get used to each other and had managed to hash out most of our problems."

What happened next: "About a year after we moved in together, we started talking about getting engaged. We didn't set a time line, but we talked about it openly. From then on in, it wasn't a matter of 'if,' it was about 'when-how-where.' "

In retrospect: "I'm so glad we moved in together. My parents are divorced and I needed to know what living together was going to be like. If it hadn't worked out, I would probably live with another person. It would depend on the circumstances. But fortunately, it did work out. And now, with the pressures of a pending wedding gone, we cohabitate beautifully!"

Her advice: "Only move in with someone you intend to spend the rest of your life with. You should move in together because you have a common goal–not because it is cheaper than living apart."

Status at press time: Celebrating her second wedding anniversary.

Those Sobering Stats

By now, some of you may have heard about the studies that paint a not-so-pretty picture of shacking-up relationships. If you haven't caught wind of them, here's the scoop. According to a horde of scientific literature, cohabiting relationships tend to be much less stable than marriages. By that, we mean there's more arguing, hostility, hitting, and general malaise. Women who cohabit are also at much higher risk of depression, domestic violence, and being cheated on by their partners. And here is the icing on the cake: Research doesn't support the notion that a "test run" can up our chances of having a good marriage. In fact, people who cohabit prior to tying the knot have rockier marriages and are roughly 50 percent more likely to get divorced—whether they marry their cohabiting partner or someone else entirely.

"But how on earth can this be?" you may be thinking. "Why are so many of my friends moving in together if it's such a horrendous idea? And why are a lot of them now wearing wedding bands and looking totally blissful?" We had the same reaction when we heard the dismal news. It made no sense! So we put our heads together and did a little sleuthing. As it turns out, the most popular explanation for the higher breakup rates is that individuals who live together outside of marriage tend to be inherently different from those who make a beeline for the altar. How so? Generally speaking, cohabitors are less traditional, less religious, less educated, and less well off financially. These happen to be the same traits that strongly predict instability and divorce, says University of Virginia sociologist Steven L. Nock, Ph.D. (We may also be more adventurous, progressive, and fun at parties, but those things haven't been studied.) To put it another way, folks with liberal attitudes are more apt to shack up, and we're also more likely to bail on our relationships if the going gets tough.

A second but less widely accepted theory is that there is something about cohabitation itself that alters our views about marriage, thereby making us more likely to find ourselves in divorce court. "The more [young people] live together before matrimony, the more eroded their sense that marriage matters or is special over time," explains Scott M. Stanley, Ph.D., codirector of the Center for Marital and Family Studies at the University of Denver. "Basically, the suggestion is that cohabitation weakens respect for marriage as an institution." Another possible explanation is that people who shack up may learn to run away from their problems rather than tackle them. Consequently, we don't develop the communication and conflict resolution skills needed for a happy, lasting relationship.

What a buzz kill! But don't freak: The situation may not be as dire as it sounds. First of all, evidently not all shacking-up couples fall into the "high risk" category. In fact, experts have concluded that lovebirds who plan to be together "till death do us part" should be in the clear. "There is good reason to believe . . . that people who start cohabiting with a clear commitment to get married are entirely different and are likely not at any statistically greater risk than those who move in after getting married," Stanley says. "Psychologically and relationship-wise, I really do think they will look like those who don't cohabit." If you and your man are officially engaged or definitely thinking "marriage," this should be comforting news.

There's also reason to believe that the statistics cited earlier may be a bit overblown. You see, much of the research was conducted more than a decade ago, back before shacking up was a mainstream practice. In most cases, the studies don't take into account the wide range of people who are living together these days. "We need to be aware of where the numbers are coming from," says Susan Brown, Ph.D., a professor of sociology at Bowling Green State University in Ohio who has studied cohabitation. "Many of the studies are based on data from the 1980s that was based on relationships in the 1970s. The people who are cohabiting now are much different than they were twenty or thirty years ago." Sociologist Pamela J. Smock also concedes that the studies conducted a decade back may not be an accurate reflection of what's happening at present. "Things have changed a lot since the late eighties," she says. "I'm not sure you would get the same results today."

If you look at the very latest research, it does appear that the link between cohabitation and divorce may indeed be shrinking. However, social scientists maintain that more long-term studies are needed before we'll have a definitive answer. In the meantime, "Divorce isn't anyone's destiny, and there are other, more important things that predict whether or not your marriage will last," Smock points out. "Premarital cohabitation has a smaller effect on the risk of divorce than many other variables, including age at marriage, income, and education level."

So don't abandon your plans to shack up just yet. The bottom line is we can't make gross generalities, because every cohabiting couple is different. Plus, the cultural framework within which we make this decision has continued to evolve over the years. We're certainly not telling you to disregard the research—that would be foolish. We're simply saying that it might not apply to all of you. When it comes to statistics, we think it's better to evaluate your own circumstances and reasons for living together, then use the data to prevent history from repeating itself.

The Perils of Playing House

Now that we may have appeased some of your fears, it's our duty to remind you of the harsh realities. No doubt, many of you sweet, innocent shacking-up virgins are envisioning an idyllic living situation—you know, something that Martha Stewart would dream up. In your instant flash-forward, you only see yourselves smiling, laughing, and getting along splendidly. But the truth is, sharing a living space with *anyone* is never a bowl of cherries. Even the best live-in relationships come with their share of pits. This can be especially true in the early stages, when you're adjusting to each other's quirks, routines, moods, and schedules. If you and your mate move in together, there will be tons of decisions to make, and you'll have to share everything from utility bills to bathroom time. In other words, you'll have many of the same challenges as married life. On top of those basic hassles, as a cohabiting couple, you could face other obstacles that make your love shack as turbulent as a 747 in a hailstorm.

OK, maybe we're exaggerating. But then again, maybe we're not. As we mentioned earlier, some shacking-up relationships don't go so smoothly. Without a hidden camera in every household, it's impossible to say exactly why certain couples have so much trouble. But after talking to top researchers, relationship counselors, and our shacking-up cohorts, we've made some educated guesses, which we will outline in a moment. Keep in mind that if you have any of the potential risk factors that we're about to discuss, you're not doomed to failure. However, your live-in relationship could be bumpy, particularly as it takes flight.

Moving In Too Fast

Let's begin with the fact that some people shack up without giving it a whole lot of thought. Not *you,* of course. We're talking about all those *other* twenty- and thirtysomethings who jump into their live-in relationships within a few months or even weeks of dating. What the heck are they thinking? In many cases, they're not. Some are blinded by love, so they dive in without the blink of an eye. Others figure that shacking up isn't a big deal and can be easily undone (a.k.a. "you can always move out"). Still others rush the decision because of extenuating circumstances—perhaps one or both is relocating and it doesn't make sense to get two apartments. In any event, when they set up house, they don't always know their new roomies well enough or have a deep level of trust.

Uncommitted Attitudes

Certainly, you don't need a ring on your finger to be 100 percent devoted to your partner. However, it's fairly safe to say that a large number of shacking-up couples aren't fully committed to their relationships. Think about it: The reason many of us live together is because we're not prepared to make the type of commitment that we traditionally associate with marriage. Some of us aren't ready for or interested in that kind of legally binding relationship. We're not completely sure about what we want, so we choose to take a wait-and-see approach and keep the legal system out of it.

Needless to say, all of this uncertainty about "tomorrow" can really work against us. First of all, it can make us feel flustered and insecure and totally neurotic. We may question our mate's feelings about us or worry that they'll walk out if things don't go perfectly. Thus, we may not make our relationships a top priority or have the gumption to work through our problems. "Couples without a strong commitment tend to be less tolerant of their differences," says David Steele, a relationship coach in San Jose, California. "They often don't realize how much work a relationship takes. They think, 'It should just work, right?' If they're not getting along, they're apt to think something's wrong with their partner or their relationship. If your attitude is one of commitment, there are no exits. You're going to work things out no matter what. It's a very different attitude than 'If it doesn't feel good, I'm gone.' "

Family Disapproval

These question marks about the future can also weigh heavily on our loved ones. Take your mom and dad, for example. They may be concerned about the "impermanence" of your shacking-up relationship. (This is the main argument we got from our own folks.) They're apt to wonder where your "friendship" is going and whether it will end in matrimony. Even if you and your mate are very committed to each other, your family members and others may not see your relationship as a long-term thing. As a result, they may treat your partner more like a flash in the pan than a future family member.

Of course, some of you may have hip, open-minded parents who would be fully supportive of your move-in decision. Lucky girls! But for those of you whose near and dear ones are decidedly unenthused about it, even if you think their disapproval doesn't matter, you may find that it takes a psychological toll. "It's hard enough to build a relationship without having family members nay-saying or causing problems," says our friend Tricia, who shacked up a few weeks ago, to her mother's dismay. First, you may have to deal with constant negativity or pangs of guilt. Second, you could lose a valuable source of support. This may not be a problem when you and your beau are happy and hitting it off. But when you're annoying each other or duking it out, you may find yourself questioning your relationship or feeling isolated and lonely.

Just ask Nadine, thirty-three, of Miami. Her parents are very traditional and, as she puts it, the shacking-up concept didn't register on their mental radars. When she told them she was moving in with her boyfriend, Ed, they were very upset and tried to talk her out of it. "I felt terrible, but I knew living with Ed was the right move for me," Nadine says. "So I went for it." A year later, Nadine says her live-in relationship is going strong but her folks are still acting distant. "They barely ever ask about Ed, almost like they're trying to pretend he doesn't exist. There's always an undertone of 'You're doing something wrong.' It makes me feel like I can't be myself around them. I don't feel like I can talk about Ed or tell them what's really going on in my life. It makes me sad."

Uncharted Territory

Married or unmarried, none of us know exactly what to expect when we cross the threshold for the first time. But unlike matrimony, there are no unspoken rules or codes of behavior for living together. "While we may not have the same view about marriage, we often have assumptions about what the commitment means and what our rights and responsibilities are," says Nock, author of the book *Marriage in Men's Lives.* "But with cohabitation, there aren't any norms, laws, traditions, or conventional assumptions that can be made." Generations of women haven't shacked up before us, so we can't look to our elders for reassurance or guidance. When it comes to figuring out the dynamics of this living together stuff, we're more or less on our own.

For some of us, shacking up can be a gray area that's vague and undefined. With so much ambiguity, we're not always sure how to behave. At times, you may feel like a wife, but you're still wearing the "girlfriend" title. Like our friend Liz, some of you may find yourselves walking on eggshells or wondering how many liberties to take. "When Kevin and I moved in together, he said that he thought our relationship was moving toward marriage," Liz explains. "I knew I wanted to marry him. But I couldn't quite assume that's what would end up happening. So I didn't feel like I could say everything that was on my mind. I couldn't say, 'Should we spend Christmas with your family or mine?' or 'Honey, what room will we put the kids in?' As much as I wanted to be confident about the future, I didn't want to assume something and then be proven wrong."

Relationship Limbo

Some couples like Susan Sarandon and Tim Robbins are what we call "lifetime shackers." But for most of us, living together is an in-between stage that leads to one of two places: marriage or a breakup. According to researcher Larry L. Bumpass, Ph.D., a sociologist at the University of Wisconsin, about half of opposite-sex cohabitors end up tying the knot and 40 percent split up in the first five years. The other 10 percent continue living together. Besides the potential pitfalls we already talked about, this in-between stage can get very sticky if you and your mate can't decide where to go next.

Here's a disturbing statistic: About 25 percent of couples who move in together don't agree about whether they expect their live-in relationships to end in marriage. As you might guess, it is usually we women who are left hanging. Thankfully, this little "miscommunication" can be prevented by making your desires known prior to signing a lease. Otherwise, like our friend Becky, you might find yourself waiting, waiting, waiting for a proposal that never comes. "When I moved in with Tim, I thought it would be a stepping-stone to marriage," Becky says. "He thought of it as having a roommate with privileges. Unfortunately, we didn't talk about it until we'd been living together for almost a year. The entire time, I kept thinking that he was going to pop the question." When he didn't, Becky finally asked Tim about it and was horrified to learn that he didn't see marriage in their future. She moved out less than a week later.

Of course, not all of us know how we feel about matrimony before we shack up with our mates. After all, for some of us, isn't that the point of moving in? To find out whether or not our relationships are meant to be? For some mismatched couples, the problem with this mind-set is that they end up stuck in what we call "relationship limbo." In other words, they continue living together for years without making a decision. If neither one has a burning desire to get hitched or start a family, this may not be a big deal. But for Vicki, thirty-two, of Nashville, it amounted to a lot of wasted time. "I was twenty-four when I moved in with Kyle," she says. "We thought we were too young to get married, so we lived together instead. For the first couple of years, it was an OK living arrangement. Then we started to drift apart." By the time they finally ended their relationship, Vicki was twenty-nine. "I was like, 'There go my late twenties!' Now, at thirty-two, I'm still single. I've always wanted to have a big family, and I'm worried that I might not meet anyone in time to have lots of kids."

The main reason why many ill-suited couples get stuck in limbo is that breaking up can be a daunting proposition. Face it: It's *much* easier to call it quits when you aren't sharing a residence. The split-up of a shacking-up relationship can be costly and disruptive. For example, you might have to break a lease, find a new apartment, pack your belongings, rent a moving van, and face up to anyone who disapproved of your relationship in the first place. The process could take weeks, months, or even years, if you really drag it out. And that's not even mentioning all of the emotional upheaval that you'd have to endure. In a nutshell, it can be nearly as traumatic as ending a marriage. Staying together, even if it's not right, can become the path of least resistance.

Last, but certainly not least, because breaking up is so hard, you could end up saying "I do" when you should be saying "I don't!" Stanley, who coauthored the book *Fighting for Your Marriage,* calls this the inertia theory.

"Once a couple moves in together, inertia becomes involved," he explains. "In other words, the relationship may be driven forward based on constraints (i.e., it's difficult to move out). Because of this, some cohabiting couples with strong risk factors for divorce end up getting married. Essentially, the theory is that a lot of people in this boat would have broken up and moved along if they had NOT chosen to live together." In some cases, the "inertia" is compelled by pressure from your partner, loved ones, or own internal time clock to "make it official."

That's exactly what happened to Brad and Kerry of New York City. "When Kerry and I moved in together, I knew that she wanted to get married," explains Brad, thirty-four. "So after about three months of living together, I proposed. I didn't want to have the marriage issue become a bad seed in our relationship. So I guess I rushed it a little bit." Less than four years later, their marriage ended in divorce. Looking back, Brad now thinks shacking up was a mistake. "Living together puts a subtle pressure on you to get married that you might not have otherwise," he says. "If marriage is your ultimate goal, I think it's important to be ready for that next step before you move in. Clearly, Kerry and I weren't there yet."

Shacking Up Horror Story

Maddie, thirty, of São Paolo, Brazil

How they decided: "After four months of dating and commiserating over everything wrong with our lives in New York, Karl and I decided to leave our problems behind and take off for a new start together in a new place."

What the 'rents said: "My mom cried and my dad was disappointed. They both thought it was a huge mistake."

The big move: "We moved to South America, where Karl had friends and spoke the language. I felt completely alone and couldn't make friends because I barely knew a word of Portuguese. About two months after we moved, I was shocked to find out that Karl had a ten-year-old son from a prior relationship. I couldn't believe that he hadn't told me. Because of his child support obligations, he couldn't contribute as much financially to our home. Worst of all, I was disappointed in his failure to be a part of his son's life (they have no contact). It made me question everything about him."

What happened next: "I thought about leaving–going back to New York. But I was too embarrassed. I didn't want to admit that I'd made a mistake. About six months later, I ended up getting pregnant. We decided to have the baby."

In retrospect: "This is the hardest thing I've ever done. After two years together, my relationship with Karl is still pretty shaky. I honestly don't know whether we'll make it. I'd like to move back to New York, but I doubt Karl will go for it. If the baby and I go without him, I won't have a job or any way to support us. It's a difficult situation."

Her advice: "Listen to your gut. Mine told me it wasn't right, that it was too early in the relationship to move. But I didn't listen. I got swept up in the moment. I definitely should have waited until I knew more about Karl before totally uprooting my life."

Status at press time: Living together with a seven-month-old son.

To Shack or Not to Shack?

Ahhh . . . so here we are, back to the original question. Obviously, there are things that can go wrong in a live-in relationship. But there are a lot of things that can go right, too. The fact of the matter is, there are always going to be upsides and downsides, no matter where you're living. The key is to be aware of the risks and evaluate your chances for success based on those factors. In our opinion, happily-ever-after relationships aren't a matter of luck. In most cases, they're within our ability to control. Knowledge is power, as the saying goes. By picking up this book, you've already taken a huge stride to ensure that you end up winning in this little thing called love.

At this time, some of you may still be pumped to give shacking up a try. Some may be feeling a bit wary. Still others may be wishing that someone would just tell you what to do. No such luck, sister! There simply is no one-size-fits-all answer. It all depends on your personal situation—what your goals are, whom you're dating, and where you are in your relationship.

So let's move on to Chapter 2, where you'll learn how to take a closer look at your own circumstances and figure out whether shacking up is the right thing for you.

A Quick History of Shacking Up

Colonial America: The ***Mayflower*** lands at Plymouth Rock, bringing Pilgrims with strong religious views about marriage. Colonies institute laws requiring the presence of an official and witnesses in order to tie the knot. But as settlers spread out across our vast continent, not everyone is able to fulfill the lawful requirements for matrimony. Common law marriage becomes prevalent.

1780s: Premarital pregnancies and illegitimate births are on the rise, even though premarital sex is scorned by most Americans. Historians consider the spike in knocked-up singles a revolt of the young against familial controls over marriage. Since most women have no way to support themselves financially, they have no choice but to get hitched.

1870s: Many states pass laws making "living together" and fornication illegal, some of which are still on the books today!

1920s: Women (finally!) earn the right to vote, inching us closer to equality and independence. Go, suffragettes!

1940s: WWII begins and women join the battle on the home front, many working in factories and manual labor positions. For the first time, women are an integral part of the workforce. Who needs a man to bring home the bacon?

1960s: The sexual revolution begins with the introduction of the Pill. The Equal Pay Act is signed into law. Women are now competing in the job market and becoming less and less dependent on men for financial security.

1970s: Bell-bottoms. Bee Gees. Bad hairdos. It's the seventies, man! ***Roe v. Wade*** assures women the legal right to choose. Meanwhile, live-ins begin to gain legal rights. With ***Marvin v. Marvin,*** contracts regarding live-in relationships (i.e., cohabitation agreements) are deemed legal. Thanks to legislation changes, cohabitation is no longer a crime in many states. While shacking up still isn't conventional, more and more American sweethearts are choosing to move in together.

1980s: Cohabitation makes it to the big screen in movies like ***About Last Night*** and ***Baby Boom.*** Credit card companies start replacing "spouse" with "co-applicant" on sign-up forms. In the early eighties, divorce rates hit an all-time high. Marriage rates begin to fall. Women are working more, making more, and the glass ceiling is beginning to shatter. We've come a long way, baby!

1990s: Living together has become as mainstream as Gap stores and energy bars. The 1990 Census begins tracking "unmarried partner" households for the first time. According to one nationwide survey, 62 percent of young men and 55 percent of young women agree "it's usually good for a couple to live together before marriage." More than 55 percent of all first marriages are now preceded by cohabitation.

2000s: From Oprah and Stedman to Monica and Chandler, it seems like everyone is shacking up! What once was a no-no is now the norm from Hollywood to Hicksville. With 5.5 million couples living together in the United States, it can't be all wrong.

CHAPTER 2

Making the Decision

If, like us, you have trouble with simple decisions such as what to wear to yoga class, then you may be nervous about making a choice that could affect the rest of your life. After all, you know that there's a lot riding on this one. You'd hate to jeopardize your relationship by moving in under the wrong circumstances. You don't want to get stuck in a nightmare living situation that's difficult to get out of. Plus, if it doesn't work out, you'll feel *really* stupid, and you'll have gotten your parents' panties in a twirl for nothing.

Go ahead and consult your Magic 8-Ball, but what you really need to do is some serious thinking. "Before moving in with someone, it's important to know your own goals, your reasons for wanting to live together, and what you want out of your partner," says Wes Patterson, Ph.D., a Miami-based licensed psychologist. "Then you must ask yourself, does your mate possess the things that you want?" If your answer's "Yes," you'll need to find out where your boyfriend stands on certain key issues and make sure that you're headed in the same direction."

In this chapter, we've put together a three-step program to guide you through the soul-searching process. You'll be given a list of questions to ask yourself as well as three quick tests to help you figure out if your man-of-the-moment is everything you're looking for. Then, you'll be able to gauge your relationship's long-term outlook with our *Shacking Up* Chemistry Quiz. Finally, we'll tell you what discussions you need to have with your man before making your final decision, plus offer tips for getting a gun-shy guy to open up.

Before you get started, however, there are a few things that we want to make crystal clear. Moving in together is a big step that shouldn't be taken lightly. Right now, you may be caught up in the moment, but you've got to keep your mind on the future. "Don't let 'convenience,' financial or otherwise, be a factor at all in your decision," advises Janine, twenty-three, of New York City, who has been living with her boyfriend for more than a year. Cindy, thirty-five, of Los Angeles, couldn't agree more. "I tried living with two different guys, and neither time worked because we weren't ready to really commit on a deep level," she says. "It was great in the beginning, but as the passion ebbed and everyday life set in, I found myself wanting more and eventually left to find it."

If your relationship is still in the early stages, we seriously recommend waiting until you know each other better before making the leap. Believe us: You don't want to find out about his run-ins with the law, obsessive-compulsive behavior, or fondness for wearing women's panties *after* you've totally uprooted your life. "Don't cohabit if you don't already know each other's personalities inside and out," says Daniel, twenty-seven, of Hoboken, New Jersey, who dated his girlfriend for four years before moving in with her—and has been happily cohabiting for more than a year now. "Wait until you *really* know a person before you move in," seconds Andrea, thirty-three, of Twin Falls, Idaho, who shacked up with Dale after two months of long-distance dating. "Otherwise, it can set you way back. It took two long years for me to have Dale move in, realize he's a jackass, have him move out, and heal emotionally."

Shacking Up Heaven-sent Hint

"Don't move in only because you're poor and his refrigerator is full of food and he has cable and he lives in a nicer neighborhood. The sad truth is that if and when you break up (and the odds are you will, if you shack up for monetary reasons), you'll end up spending an obscene amount of money getting a new apartment ASAP."
–Beth, thirty-two

No doubt, there are couples who have shacked up without knowing all these intimate details and ended up happily hunkered in long-term relationships. But they are the exceptions to the rule. If you don't mind the thought of moving in and moving out again, then by all means, go for it! However, if you're seeking a forever-type deal, we beseech you to think twice about your reasons for wanting to live together. Our *Shacking Up* creed: You must go into your live-in relationship with the intention of giving it your all and building a future together, not seeing how things pan out. "I don't think living together should be looked at as a 'trial period' because that only adds to the pressure," says our pal Ann. "I believe that problems arise when one or both people use cohabitation as an endurance test of the relationship," adds Cindy. "If you're going to live together without marriage, you should make sure that you have a strong partnership first."

By holding off, you'll also get a chance to discover how the two of you handle the ups and downs of your relationship—a strong indicator of whether you'll make it as a couple, says Steven M. Sultanoff, Ph.D., a licensed marriage and family therapist in Malibu, California. Plus, you'll have time to build confidence in each other, which will help keep your tiny love boat from capsizing. "You should wait long enough to know what happens in a relationship over time, so you're not shocked or scared when difficult times arise," Cindy says. If you already have some serious relationship problems—you fight like cats and dogs, you have major trust issues, or you feel like your boyfriend doesn't respect you—you've got to deal with them NOW, before going anywhere near your suitcases. There's a chance that you can work through your differences, but there's also a decent probability that you can't. You wouldn't sink money into a car that wasn't running smoothly, so why put your happiness on the line for a relationship that needs major fixing?

At this point, despite our earlier warning, some of you may still be picturing your live-in relationship like an episode of "Will and Grace," with the two of you bantering playfully as you share everything from shopping expeditions to home-cooked meals. If you do move in, there are bound to be lots of magic moments when you and your man feel completely in sync. But you'll also have disputes over normal roommate stuff, like paying bills, sharing closet space, and cleaning the shower. You may wonder why he can't remember to fill up the ice cube trays, how his running shoes could smell so ungodly, and how he could possibly think farting is funny. He may get on your case for leaving globs of toothpaste in the sink, misplacing the remote control, and constantly gabbing on the phone with your girlfriends. There will be foul moods, gross habits, silly misunderstandings, and emotional baggage to cope with. In general, you'll have more to fight about, and you won't have the option of retreating to your own places.

As we explained in the last chapter, sharing a living space with *anyone* can be difficult. But it can be particularly stressful when you and your roommate are romantically involved. Take it from us: You'll be more apt to take things personally and let disagreements get blown out of proportion. OK, we know what you're thinking. *Not us! We're different! We're great together—we hardly ever argue!* We hate to burst your bubble, but you ain't seen nothin' until the two of you have dealt with chores, finances, and the unedited versions of each other. We're not saying that your living-together experience wouldn't be positive and prosperous overall. We're just trying to prepare you for the possible challenges so you can be certain that your relationship is resilient enough to withstand the pressure.

Remember, the things that bother you about your partner now won't—*poof!*—disappear after you move in together. If anything, they'll be magnified and joined by a small marching band of other grievances. That's why you must be completely honest with yourself about what you're getting yourself into and whether you can live with it—because his all-nighters with the boys, refusals to spend time with your family, and inattention to hygiene aren't likely to end after you shack up. "Don't assume that because you're sharing a place, you can change his way of life," says Amber, thirty-two, of Boston. "You'll be moving out before you know it."

To prevent a major miscommunication, you need to be totally up-and-up with your mate before you make a move. Be totally clear about your expectations of him and the relationship, and don't make *any* assumptions. "Make sure he wants to live together as much as you do and that you're both doing it for the same reasons," says Janine. "If you're hoping to tie the knot, you don't want to find out later that he has no plans of marrying you—or vice versa." "Talk things to death," Cindy adds.

The material on the upcoming pages will help ensure that you leave no stone unturned. After you've gathered the vital data and spent hours hyperanalyzing it with your friends, you should be as ready as you'll ever be to make a smart decision. Even if you're 99 percent sure that living together is the best thing for you, we urge you to spend a few minutes reviewing this chapter. In it, you'll find valuable info that will help you start your living arrangement on the right foot.

If you still have some minor question marks in your mind at the end of the chapter, don't be too worried: With any big decision, it's natural to second-guess yourself to a certain degree. "If about 80 percent of the time you think, 'I want to be with this person,' and the other 20 percent of the time you're not really sure, you're probably experiencing normal cold feet," says Michelle Gannon, Ph.D., cofounder of Marriage Prep 101, a premarital relationship skills workshop in San Francisco. But if you have major doubts—let's say, you feel a big pit in your stomach or can't sleep at night—you'll want to take heed. "If you're more 50–50, then you need to stop and figure out why you're reluctant or afraid," Gannon adds. Says Jenny, twenty-eight, of New York City, who has been shacking up for five months: "If it's right, then it feels natural. If it doesn't feel natural, think twice."

Personally, we believe that the right answer lies deep inside all of us. The problem is, we can't always "see" it because our X-ray vision is blurred by love and hormones. Sometimes we want to be in a relationship so badly that we can convince ourselves of anything. So if all the practical decision-making strategies to follow still leave you questioning, LISTEN TO YOUR GUT INSTINCT!!! Your female intuition was given to you for a reason, and if you ask us, that funny, little feeling in your stomach is usually right on the money.

Ask the Magic 8-Ball . . . Will Your Love Shack Last?

According to social scientist Lynne Casper, Ph.D., coauthor of *Continuity & Change in the American Family,* your motive for moving in can have an impact on the outcome of your live-in relationship. We've identified three main reasons for living together and asked Casper and other experts (disguised as our trusty Magic 8-Ball) what the chances are that your love shack will stay intact.

The Practical Shack: Your primary objective is to save money or cut down on your commute time. You're looking for Mr. Right-Now, not necessarily Mr. Right. You're all about stashing some cash or making day-to-day life easier, not investing in a long-term relationship.
The Magic 8-Ball says: "Don't count on it."

The Test Shack: You're uncertain about the future of your relationship as well as your partner. You want to test the waters to help you make a decision.
The Magic 8-Ball says: "Outlook not so good."

The Committed Shack: You're 99 percent sure of each other and the prospect of spending the rest of your lives together.
The Magic 8-Ball says: "Signs point to 'Yes.' "

Your Inner Dialogue

What the ?#@! Are You Going to Do?!

Next time you're in the car, turn on the tunes. Listen closely to the words. Almost every other song (unless you're into gangsta rap) is about love found, love lost, and the anguish of heartbreak. In any relationship, when you put your heart on the line, you take an emotional gamble. But hey, life is full of risks. When you think about it, we take a chance every time we step outside of our front doors. If we weren't willing to take any chances whatsoever, we'd probably still be living with our parents, working at our local libraries, and hiding our hard-earned money under our mattresses.

Now, let's not forget that there are good risks and bad risks. A good risk is one in which you don't have a lot to lose or the odds are stacked in your favor. Examples: striking up a conversation with a boy-next-door type, investing in government bonds, or asking your boss for a well-deserved raise. Alternatively, a bad risk would be accepting a dinner invite from a married man, boffing a coworker in the office (does the name Monica ring a bell?), or extending your credit limit to go on an emergency shopping spree at Barney's.

Obviously, you're the last one who wants to take a bad risk that could leave you apartmentless and emotionally crippled. So how do you determine whether you'd be taking a good or bad risk by shacking up with your man? Answer: By doing a thorough risk analysis. In other words, you need to take a long, hard look before you leap. After quizzing top relationship experts, we came up with the following three-step plan for self-enlightenment.

Step #1: Know Thyself

If you'd spent the last few years marooned on a tropical island like Tom Hanks in the movie *Castaway,* you might have had time to figure out exactly what you want out of life. Instead, you've been too busy trying to get your career off the ground, stay in shape, and have a social life. You may have some vague idea of your own basic needs and desires. But as you contemplate this next step in your relationship, it's important to clarify them as much as humanly possible. Otherwise, how the heck will you get where you want to go in life? And how will you know whether your current flame is the right one to go with you?

Life is like a river, and knowing yourself gives you a steering device and a paddle, so you don't just drift along. Fear not: This intriguing bit of self-analysis should take no more than ten to fifteen minutes, and it can be done on your commute to work or while riding a stationary bike at the gym. Just grab a piece of paper and write down your answers to the following seven questions.

1. What are the most important qualities in a life partner?
2. What are your reasons for wanting to move in together?
3. Do you think marriage could be the next step?
4. Do you feel ready to be in a serious, committed relationship?
5. Are you prepared to be flexible and make sacrifices?
6. What are your relationship "nonnegotiables" (i.e., anything that you absolutely, 100 percent can't tolerate, such as lying, smoking, poor personal hygiene, cats, etc.).
7. Where do you see yourself in five years? Ten years? Twenty years? Fifty years?

Reality Checkpoint #1

Unless you're psychic, it can be difficult to visualize yourself years down the road. Who can predict exactly what will happen or where life will take you? That's OK: You don't have to have a crystal-clear image of a house with a white picket fence or a round-the-world voyage on a sailboat. We're just trying to get you to think in future terms. Can you maybe imagine a turbo-powered career? A husband? Kids? A Range Rover? What about living in a small town? City life? Missionary work? Travel?

If you have trouble with questions one through six, then you've got some work to do. In our opinion, you're not ready for a live-in relationship until you know how you feel about this stuff! You can take a chance and who knows?—maybe the two of you will somehow grow together and end up happy. You could be that lucky. You could also win the lottery. But do you really want to take that kind of gamble? Hold it—before answering, try a visual of yourself waking up a few years from now, looking over at the hairy blob sleeping next to you, and thinking, *This isn't where I want to be or what I want to be doing!* Yikes.

If you were able to come up with concrete answers to all of our questions, congrats: You passed your first test. Now that you're tuned into your own needs and desires, you have a much better shot at getting what you want. By putting your feelings into words, you've also prepared yourself to express them to your partner. Keep in mind, however, that knowing yourself is only half the battle. Before you move in together, your boyfriend must be clued in to what he wants, too, and be willing to share those viewpoints with you.

In "Talking It Over with Your Man" (pages 59–68), we'll assist you with the fun-filled task of finding out what your boyfriend is thinking. Meanwhile, if he's the type who enjoys self-reflection, you may want to give him a copy of the seven getting-to-know-yourself questions from page 35 so he can start gathering his thoughts. Or, if that approach seems forced, you can try posing the questions verbally in a more casual way. (More on that later in the chapter.) But before you start having a heart-to-heart, there are two more steps to complete.

Nine Very Bad Reasons to Move In with Your Mate

If you find yourself thinking along the following lines, we suggest putting the brakes on your shacking-up plan:

- "I have no idea where our relationship is going, but we're together practically every night. It seems crazy to pay for two apartments."
- "I was unsure of how my partner felt until he asked me to move in with him. Now I know that he really is serious about 'us.' "
- "I can't stand my nightmare roommates. I need to find a new place to live *pronto,* and I can't afford to live alone."
- "Moving in together is the only way I'll ***ever*** get him to commit."
- "I'm afraid that he'll break up with me if I don't move in with him."
- "We're so in love! Sure, I've only known him for a couple months, but it feels right. Why wait?"
- "He's moving three thousand miles to be with me. I can't exactly ask him to get his own apartment."
- "My parents are ***so*** controlling. This will show them that they can't rule my life!"
- "Our relationship may be a little rocky, but I can't stand the dating scene anymore. I'm ready to settle down!"

Step #2: Rate Your Mate

Back in the old days (and still in some traditional cultures!), marriages were arranged by the bride's and groom's parents. These days, thank goodness, we get to pick our own partners. However, with that freedom of choice comes the difficult and, at times, agonizing challenge of figuring out who we're supposed to (gulp) spend the rest of our lives with.

At this stage in your dating history, you may be (quite understandably) starting to question your own judgment. After all, you've made mistakes in the past. You've fallen in love with the wrong guys and dated losers who you'd like to have stricken from the record books. We've all done it! The important thing is that you've seen the error of your ways, and you now have a better idea of what and who will make you happy.

Based on our own choosing-a-life-mate experiences, we'd say that two basic things are needed to make you feel certain about someone: time and challenges. Time gives you the opportunity to discover how your partner acts when the new-relationship lust wears off and he starts letting his guard down. Challenges allow you to see him at his worst and learn how he deals in times of crisis, such as when the power goes out during the NBA finals, his car breaks down on the freeway (and you're driving), or (God forbid) a close family member falls ill.

Unfortunately, there's no foolproof method for determining whether he's "the one." As we've already established, it isn't easy to see the truth about a guy when he's on his best behavior. Plus, when you're madly in love or desperate to be in a relationship, you're apt to rationalize or ignore your partner's less-than-savory traits and behaviors. How can you be sure that you're not deluding yourself now? Here are three quick tests that can help you peel off your love goggles and see the light:

Test 1

Phillip McGraw, Ph.D. (a.k.a. "Dr. Phil"), author of *Relationship Rescue* and a regular on "Oprah," suggests making a list of pros and cons to determine how your man is measuring up. Start by writing down all his "pluses"—personality traits that you appreciate and admire (i.e., he's hardworking, generous, and trustworthy). Next, write down his "minuses"—what you consider to be negative characteristics (examples: he's moody, perpetually late, or not completely honest). When you're done, sit down and analyze your list. If the pluses outweigh the minuses, you should be in the clear. If you're heavier on minuses, then beware. Warning: Maybe you saw the episode of "Friends" in which Rachel discovered the less-than-flattering pro-and-con list that Ross had made for her. Learn from Ross's mistake: If you want to save yourself a lot of grief, be sure to destroy your list or put it in a place where you-know-who definitely won't find it (underwear drawer not recommended).

Test 2

Here's another exercise to help you identify your mate's best and worst characteristics. On a scale of 1 to 5 (1 = *"el stinko"* and 5 = *"par excellence"),* rank your boyfriend on the character traits listed below. (Note: In Step #1, we asked you to name the most important qualities in a potential life partner. Add these to the list on the left if they aren't already on it.) If you record mostly 4s and 5s, your boyfriend is in the top percentile and well worth hanging on to. If you have a lot of 2s and 3s, he isn't living up to your expectations and probably never will. If you get any 1s at all, he simply doesn't have what it takes to make you happy.

THE TRAIT	HOW HE RATES
Honesty	
Loyalty	
Kindness	
Humility	
Sense of humor	
Responsibility	
Self-confidence	

Attentiveness	....
Patience	....
Sensitivity	....
Communicativeness	....
Maturity	....
Even-temperedness	....
Generosity	....
Adaptability	....
Open-mindedness	....
Energy	....
Intellectual curiosity	....
Motivation	....
Reliability	....
Happiness	....

TEST 3

Finally, there's the "friend" test—our personal favorite. Even if you're in denial about your boyfriend's misconduct or the fact that he makes you clam up à la Julia Roberts in *Sleeping with the Enemy,* you can usually count on your close friends to pick up on the negativity. If you haven't gotten any solid feedback from them already, ask your most trusted pals what they *really* think. (Not surprisingly, your intuitive female friends are best at predicting the outcome of a romance, according to a recent study published in the *Journal of Personality and Social Psychology.)* Tell them not to spare your feelings, and don't get defensive if they tell you something that's painful to hear. They're only trying to help! After you've had a chance to think about it, you might recognize that they're right. "If only my friends had been honest with me before the move-in—instead of after the breakup—it might have saved me years of heartache," says Yvonne, thirty-six, who purchased a home with Kurt before coming to terms with his commitment issues. Feel free to get a second opinion, but remember: The point of this exercise is to discover the truth about your partner. If you're determined to keep fooling yourself, leave your well-intentioned friends out of it.

Red Flags: Four Signs Your Stud May Be a Dud

Ever look back at the end of a failed relationship and realize that the red flags were there from the beginning? But, foolish, lovesick girl that you were, you chose to ignore the signals or made excuses for your boyfriend's undesirable behavior. "The things that you deny are problems early in the relationship often become your reasons for breaking up," warns David Steele, M.A., M.F.T., a relationship coach in San Jose, California.

A red flag is a sign that trouble could be ahead in your relationship. If you come across one, it doesn't guarantee that your ship will sink like the *Titanic*. But you may be in for very choppy waters and should proceed with caution. Here are four red flags to watch out for at this stage of your relationship–and advice on what to do if you're dating one of these iffy characters.

- **He's a serial cohabitator.** If he's had two or more live-in relationships, he may be more interested in saving money on rent or having someone to wash his dishes than building a future together. To keep from getting caught in his revolving door, do some probing. "Ask him how he got into his other living situations and why they didn't work out," advises Kelly, who was live-in girlfriend number three for Ben (now her husband). If he claims to have learned from his mistakes and is eager to make a real commitment, then he's worth a second look, she says. Steer clear if he acts nonchalant or refuses to discuss his relationship history.
- **He's traumatized by his parents' divorce.** If the poor guy

doesn't believe that a satisfying, long-term relationship is possible, he's apt to follow in his parents' footsteps, says psychologist Scott M. Stanley, Ph.D. If, on the flip side, he's determined to find the right person and settle down for life, he should have the right mind-set for a lasting commitment.

- **He never wants to get married.** OK, maybe you don't, either–in which case, you can ignore this little tidbit. But if you do dream of tying the knot someday, you should probably start looking for a new love interest. "My research shows that male preferences drive the outcome of most relationships," says sociologist Susan Brown, Ph.D. Translation: If your boyfriend has no interest in getting hitched, it's extremely unlikely to happen. Don't assume that living together will change his mind–it almost certainly won't.
- **He's cheated on you.** We're not saying that it's impossible for a cheater to clean up his act. But history *does* tend to repeat itself (just ask Hillary Clinton). In all likelihood, his infidelity is a sign that there's something major missing in your relationship or, at the very least, that he has commitment issues. Before investing any more of yourself in a losing proposition, Stanley suggests getting to the root of the problem via therapy or couples counseling.

Reality Checkpoint #2

If you got favorable results on all three minitests, you've found yourself a good guy (yes, they do exist!), and you can proceed to Step #3. As for the rest of you, we ask you to take a step back and level with yourselves. Do you really want to move in with someone who doesn't have much, if any, long-term potential? We don't want to sound like your mother (lovely woman though she is). We're simply trying to prevent you from wasting your time or winding up in a living situation that you'll regret.

Now, it's possible that you're still thinking that your boyfriend can be trained, or that he'll suddenly wake up one day and want to be a better man like Jack Nicholson in *As Good As It Gets.* If so, you deserve credit for being an optimist. It's true that you may be able to break him of some less appealing habits, such as drinking out of the milk carton and peeing in the shower. However, don't expect to change his personality or values. He's had several decades to become the man he is today; it probably would take several decades of intense therapy to reform him. Even then, there are no guarantees. Remember, it's a tag sale buy-as-is deal.

Perhaps the real question is, can you really see this guy, who is overly possessive, flirts with other women, spends half his time playing video games, or (scary thought) lashes out at you in verbally abusive ways, as the father of your unborn children? If you ask us, this is what it all boils down to, even if you can't imagine having a baby anytime in the near future. For argument's sake, we'll say it's fine to waste your own time with a selfish jerk or unreliable loser, but is that the kind of man you want to be influential in the lives of your future offspring? We don't think so.

We know what you're about to say: But it's so hard to find a guy whom you connect with, whom you find attractive (and vice versa), and who isn't gay! You can't bear the thought of returning to the dating scene, and if you wait any longer for Mr. Right, you'll still be single when you're spending your afternoons in a nursing home playing Bingo. There may be plenty of fish in the sea, but you're tired of fishing! We understand completely, but let us offer one reminder: It's better to be alone than to hook up with the wrong fish, which will only leave you with a bad taste in your mouth and a smelly apartment.

Let's talk about self-esteem for a minute. As a gender, we seem to be lacking in the self-worth department. Thus, we're at risk of taking what we can get and selling ourselves short. In case you've forgotten, you have a lot going for you. When we say a lot, we mean a *lot*. You've got a great job, lots of friends, and a cool apartment. You're a catch! Therefore, you need a man who will help you reach new heights, not drag you down. *Merriam-Webster's Collegiate Dictionary,* Tenth Edition, defines "settle" as "to sink gradually or to the bottom." Be honest: If you take the plunge now, will you be settling for less than you need and deserve?

One final warning: There are a few crazy women out there who say, "What's the big deal? See whether you like living with him and, if not, you can always move out." Not to sound ageist, but these women tend to be young and inexperienced, and they generally don't have parents who would kill them for being that irresponsible. Almost anyone who has shacked up with a significant other will tell you it isn't that easy to "just move out." As we stated earlier, dissolving a domestic partnership can be almost as hard as getting a divorce, and it can set you way back financially as well as emotionally. All in all, moving in with the wrong guy can be a costly mistake. Do yourself a favor, and hold out for a man who will make you truly happy!

More Relationship Red Flags

- **You haven't known each other very long.** It takes time to build intimacy and trust. Before shacking up, we recommend dating for at least a year so your relationship has enough time to grow and develop.
- **You're young or inexperienced.** "Live and learn" is how the saying goes. If you haven't taken a few laps around the block or kissed a frog or two, how will you know who and what you want?
- **You have different religious views.** You celebrate Christmas

and he does Hannukah–what's the big fuss? Unfortunately, it could become a deal breaker if you're talking about marriage and/or having a family.

- **One of your families strongly disapproves.** If the parentals are having a cow, you or your partner may feel guilty or conflicted, which is apt to put excess strain on your relationship.
- **You're having communication problems.** Good communication is essential to a strong, healthy relationship. If you can't say what's on your mind or you both avoid touchy issues, you'll be in for trouble when you're sharing a residence–and all the problems that come with it.
- **One of you is still married.** Until the divorce is final (and we're talking signed on the dotted line), your relationship will consist of three people: you, your partner, and the not-quite "ex." Sound a wee bit crowded?
- **One of you has a kid.** Unless you're in a very stable relationship that's likely to be permanent, it will be stressful for you and bad for the child.

Step #3: Evaluate Your Relationship

You may be wondering how to tell whether you're in a good relationship if (1) you've never been in one, or (2) it's been so horrifyingly long since you've been in one that you've forgotten what it's like. All we can say is it's kind of like your first orgasm—when you have one, deep down, you just know. You may keep thinking "Is this it? Is this what it's supposed to feel like?" But somehow, instinctively, you know that it's the real deal.

If you're not feeling butterflies the way you have with past boyfriends or old crushes, don't take it as a bad sign. Based on our interviews with happy, longtime couples (and our own experience), a healthy relationship makes you feel strong and steady, not nervous or neurotic. If your relationship is solid, you shouldn't be consumed with fears about it ending or have panic attacks about the future. You should feel good about yourself and comfortable speaking your mind. You should believe that your partner knows and loves the real you. All in all, you should feel calm, confident, and content.

Researchers from all over the country have done studies to try to determine why some couples stick together and others don't. By looking at their work and talking to some real-life "success stories" (couples who have been happily hitched for ten-plus years), we've come up with our own formula for a lasting relationship. We call it the Seven C's, and it's made up of these ingredients: commitment, closeness, consideration, compatibility, confidence, communication, and conflict resolution skills. If you and your boyfriend have all seven, then you should have the right couple-chemistry. If you're missing any of the essential elements, you could have an explosive mix. Take our *Shacking Up* Chemistry Quiz to discover what your relationship is made of.

The Seven C's Glossary

Commitment: Being fully invested in your relationship and determined to work through any problems.

Closeness: Having an intimate knowledge of each other's backgrounds, values, goals, expectations, hopes, fears, likes, dislikes, strengths, and weaknesses.

Consideration: Being thoughtful and concerned about each other's needs and feelings.

Compatibility: Having similar interests, activities, habits, likes, and dislikes.

Confidence: Having complete trust in your partner and his feelings for you.

Communication: Being able to express your thoughts clearly and calmly as well as listen carefully and compassionately.

Conflict resolution: Knowing how to discuss problems openly and effectively, keep arguments from escalating, and resolve disagreements constructively.

Shacking Up Chemistry Quiz

Commitment

1. When you talk about the future, you speak in terms of "we" or "us"
   A. all the time. We're definitely in this relationship for the long haul.
   B. sometimes. I hope we'll be together forever, but I don't want to make too many assumptions.
   C. almost never. I'm taking it one day at a time.
2. The best part about shacking up would be
   A. being together and merging our lives.
   B. finding out whether he's "the one."
   C. saving money.
   D. getting the hell away from my annoying roommates.
3. Are you the top priority in your man's life?
   A. Yes, definitely. He always puts me first.
   B. Most of the time. If I'm not number one, I'm definitely number two or three.
   C. Hardly! His job, workouts, golf games, poker nights, etc., always seem to take precedence.
4. When you bring up the subject of your relationship, your partner
   A. is always happy to discuss it.

B. is sometimes willing to discuss it.
C. cringes, clams up, and heads for the gym.

5. If you and your man got in a huge blowout, you'd probably think
   A. fighting sucks, but I know we'll work through it.
   B. oh no—does this mean we're going to break up?
   C. if he ever acts like that again, I'm outta here.
6. Your boyfriend's company is downsizing, and he may lose his job. Your initial thought is
   A. I'll do anything I can to help, from helping him update his résumé to networking.
   B. if he's out of work, I hope I won't end up paying for everything.
   C. I can't date a loser on unemployment!

Closeness

7. How long have you been dating each other?
   A. More than a year.
   B. Six to twelve months.
   C. Less than six months.
   D. A week—but it feels like an eternity.
8. How would you describe your comfort level in the relationship?
   A. Totally comfortable. I'm 100 percent "me" when we're together.
   B. Pretty comfortable. There's still a tiny bit of awkwardness between us.
   C. Not very comfortable. He makes me nervous, but boy, is he a hottie!
9. If your boyfriend ordered dinner for you, would he pick something you like?
   A. Yes, definitely. He knows me like the back of his hand.

   B. Possibly. But I wouldn't want to risk it.
   C. Doubtful. The last time he ordered for me, I got a corn dog.

10. Can you name your beau's favorite sports team?
   A. Definitely—as well as the players and season stats.
   B. Possibly—I just need a quick peek at the sports section.
   C. I think I know the uniform color—does that count?

11. You're at a party, and you get cornered by someone you dislike. When your boyfriend sees the "Help me!" look on your face, he
   A. reads the SOS signal and initiates a search and rescue operation.
   B. senses something's wrong and mouths, "What?!?"
   C. has no idea there's a problem and continues talking to his buddy.

12. Do you know each other's lifelong career goals?
   A. Yes, definitely.
   B. Possibly—not 100 percent sure.
   C. Nope—too unmotivated to discuss them.

13. Can you name each other's greatest fears?
   A. Yes, definitely.
   B. Possibly—not 100 percent sure.
   C. Nope—too scared to find out.

Consideration

14. Your boyfriend has promised to meet you at 8 P.M., but he's running behind schedule. He
   A. calls at 7:30 to say he's going to be late.
   B. calls at 8:10 to say he's en route.
   C. just shows up—late again!

15. You slave over a pan of homemade brownies for your guy, but they're a little well-done. He
    - A. thanks me profusely—he *loves* brownies!
    - B. eats a couple and doesn't say anything.
    - C. takes a bite, says, "You're no Mrs. Fields," and tosses his half-eaten brownie in the trash.
16. You and your beau have a special Saturday-night date at the hottest restaurant in town. At the last minute, he's invited on a ski weekend with the guys. He
    - A. tells his buddies, "Sorry, I can't go. I already have plans."
    - B. asks whether I'd mind if he goes and promises to make it up to me.
    - C. calls from the chair lift to say he needs to cancel dinner.
17. If your boyfriend needed a ride to the airport, you would
    - A. drive him, even if it meant missing my favorite Pilates class.
    - B. drive him, as long as it didn't mean missing my favorite Pilates class.
    - C. give him the number of a good cab company.
18. You're a Diet Coke fiend. Your partner is picking up drinks for the beach. What does he bring you?
    - A. Diet Coke—the 20-ounce bottle.
    - B. Water—and says, "It isn't healthy to drink so much Diet Coke!"
    - C. Mountain Dew—*his* favorite beverage.
19. You're both famished after a six-hour hike, and there's one piece of leftover pizza in your fridge. You
    - A. say, "It's all yours!" and offer to heat it up for him.
    - B. ask if he'd be interested in splitting it.

C. suggest flipping a coin for it.

D. gulp it down and ask what he's going to eat.

Compatibility

20. You and your partner are
    - A. birds of a feather. We have a lot in common.
    - B. an interesting mix. We have our differences, but we seem to complement each other.
    - C. polar opposites. Think Ozzy Osbourne meets Martha Stewart.
21. After spending a long weekend together, you're usually
    - A. sad that it's over and amazed at how well we get along.
    - B. feeling good but definitely ready for a little space.
    - C. at each other's throats, especially if there's a long car ride involved.
    - D. don't know. We've never spent a long weekend together.
22. When it comes to money, you and your mate are
    - A. very alike. We feel the same way about spending and saving.
    - B. somewhat alike. We occasionally disagree on dollar issues.
    - C. very different. One of us is a penny-pincher, the other constantly pushes the platinum card.
23. You and your partner are
    - A. the same religion. Thank God!
    - B. different religions. But it isn't an issue for either one of us.
    - C. different religions. And I'm praying it won't be a problem.

D. different religions. And I hope he's joking when he talks about me converting.

24. You ask him to come to your parents' house for the weekend. He

    A. happily accepts and says he loves my family.
    B. gives an excuse about having to work, but adds, "Maybe next time."
    C. says, "Sorry! I just can't spend that much time with your family."
    D. says, "I'm not ready to meet your parents yet."

25. It's Saturday morning and

    A. we both wake up at the same time and start the day together.
    B. one of us gets up early while the other sleeps in, but it isn't a big deal.
    C. one of us wakes up early as usual, then starts getting on the other's case for being such a slug.

26. In terms of neatness, you and your partner are

    A. very similar. We're both either neat or sloppy.
    B. somewhat similar. One of us is a little neater than the other.
    C. totally different. Just like Felix and Oscar.

27. Your mate thinks your jokes are

    A. funny. He usually laughs his butt off.
    B. sometimes funny. Sometimes I get that fake, little laugh.
    C. not so funny. He often doesn't get them.
    D. stupid. He typically rolls his eyes or pretends he didn't hear me.

28. Your sex life is

    A. stellar. No complaints whatsoever.
    B. so-so. Definitely room for improvement.
    C. What sex life?

Confidence

29. How sure are you that your boyfriend would be there if you *really* needed him?
    A. 99 percent certain.
    B. 80 to 99 percent certain.
    C. 50 to 79 percent certain.
    D. How the devil should I know?
30. If your man had a problem at work, would he come to you for advice?
    A. Yes. He respects me and values my opinion.
    B. Possibly. He'd probably call his family or friends first, then try me if they weren't around.
    C. Are you kidding? He doesn't give a rat's ass what I think.
31. Your beau gets an e-mail from an ex-girlfriend. He tells you he's not going to respond. You
    A. don't think twice about it. I trust him implicitly.
    B. feel a twinge of jealousy and wonder whether I should be concerned.
    C. start trying to figure out his computer password so I can read the e-mail and see if he responded.
32. If you moved in together, would you trust your partner to pay the bills?
    A. Yes, definitely. He's very responsible and would never be late on a payment.
    B. Possibly. He's fairly responsible, but I'd probably feel more comfortable doing it myself.
    C. Forget it! His middle name is "late fee."
33. If your boyfriend found a wallet containing $2,000, would he give the money back?
    A. Absolutely. The guy's a saint!

B. Maybe. He's usually pretty honest, but it's hard to say for sure.
C. Extremely doubtful. He's got the moral fiber of an Enron executive.

Communication

34. You're on an eight-hour car ride—just the two of you. You
    A. fill the time easily with anything from casual chatter to talk of serious life matters.
    B. talk for a while but start to run out of conversation after a few hours.
    C. spend most of the time sitting in silence and staring out the window.
    D. try not to open my mouth in fear of starting an argument.
35. You get into a big fight with a coworker. You call your boyfriend wanting to talk about it. He's most apt to
    A. listen patiently and offer sympathy.
    B. listen for thirty seconds, then start giving his advice.
    C. tell me to stop being such a baby and change the subject.
36. If something's bugging your boyfriend, he usually
    A. tells me about it—he's good about talking about his feelings.
    B. doesn't say anything, but will spill the beans if I ask what's up.
    C. acts grumpy, mopes, and refuses to explain what's wrong.
    D. drinks Jack Daniel's until he passes out.

37. If you had a "girl" problem such as a yeast infection, you'd
    - A. tell him the whole icky scoop—I can talk to him about *anything.*
    - B. hint that I've got a minor health issue but refuse to go into specifics.
    - C. avoid having sex with him until the problem clears up.
38. How often do the two of you have misunderstandings?
    - A. Almost never. We speak the same language.
    - B. Occasionally. We're not always totally clear with one another.
    - C. Frequently. Sometimes I think he's talking Swahili.
    - D. Constantly. He really *does* talk Swahili.
39. Your boyfriend is rambling on about something dull like his car engine. What do you do?
    - A. Listen and act interested, even though I couldn't care less.
    - B. Stare at him with a blank look and hope that he'll stop talking.
    - C. Let out a fake "snore" so he knows that he's boring the you-know-what out of me.
40. You and your man have deep conversations
    - A. all the time. We *love* talking about things like art, politics, and the meaning of life.
    - B. sometimes. But not nearly as much as we did when we were first dating.
    - C. almost never. Unless the World Wrestling Federation and celebrity gossip qualify as "deep."

Conflict Resolution

41. In general, how would you describe your arguments?
    A. Constructive. We're both able to stay calm and hash out our problems.
    B. One-sided. One of us gets mad and the other withdraws.
    C. Nasty. Lots of mean comments, raised voices, and door-slamming.
    D. Nonexistent. We've never had a fight.
42. You think disagreeing is
    A. normal. It's part of every relationship.
    B. a bad sign. It probably means that the relationship isn't meant to be.
    C. something to avoid at all costs. I hate conflict!
43. Your man makes a comment that hurts your feelings. What do you do?
    A. Tell him that it bothers you and calmly explain why.
    B. Give him the cold shoulder until he asks what's wrong.
    C. Get pissed and lash back at him—the jerk!
44. Your mate gets things his way
    A. about half the time. We're both good about compromising.
    B. more than half the time. He's stubborn as a mule, so it's usually easier to give in.
    C. less than half the time. He knows who wears the pants in this relationship!
45. You're dying to go to a party, and he wants to stay in and watch videos. You're most apt to
    A. look for a win-win solution. We'd agreed to spend an hour at the party before coming home and hitting the couch.

B. decide to do our own thing. It isn't worth arguing about!

C. fight about it until one of us caves in or storms off in a rage.

46. If you and your mate weren't seeing eye-to-eye on something, you'd probably try to

A. listen to and acknowledge his point of view.

B. change the subject or leave the room before it got ugly.

C. keep trying to prove my point until he admitted that I'm right.

47. After an argument with your boyfriend, you tend to feel

A. closer to him than ever. We have a better understanding of each other.

B. slightly rattled. I can't help but question our relationship.

C. totally depressed. I feel miserable, alienated, and alone.

D. Don't know. We've never had an argument.

48. The car has a flat. You

A. work together as a team (just like Lucy and Ethel) to change the tire.

B. are instructed to wait in the car until he's done fixing it.

C. end up screaming at each other and standing in a huff until AAA arrives.

Scoring

Count up all your A's, B's, C's and D's. Record the totals below.

Total A's: ______

Total B's: ______

Total C's and D's: ______

Reality Checkpoint #3

While our *Shacking Up* Chemistry Quiz can help you take an honest look at your relationship, we want to remind you that it isn't scientific. Even if you aced it, please use your best judgment. If your gut is telling you something's off-kilter, you should follow your instincts. People whose live-in relationships have failed often say that they sensed from the get-go that moving in was a mistake. So if you're feeling queasy, be certain to listen up.

If you got mostly A's: Go to the head of the chemistry class! Like Tarzan and Jane or Batman and Robin, it sounds like the two of you are a solid match, a compatible pair, and a dynamic duo. You gel on many levels and seem to have the right ingredients for "happily ever after." As long as you and your honey are sailing the Seven C's, your relationship should be able to weather any storms. But remember that there are no money-back promises. No doubt, your partnership could use a little work in certain areas. So look back at your answers to see where your weakest links are and which C's you can improve on. Keep trying to make your relationship the best that it can be, and you should remain at the head of the class indefinitely.

If you got mostly B's: There are some kinks in your relationship that must be straightened out before you move in together. With some effort (and perhaps the help of a good coach or therapist), it may be possible to fix the problems, says David Steele, Ph.D., founder of LifePartnerQuest in San Jose, California. Or your relationship may just need time to evolve. Either way, we suggest staying put for now. Don't take a leap of faith until you're a little closer to the landing pad! If your relationship lacks commitment, wait and see if your devotion grows. If you're missing closeness or confidence, you may be able to build these over time. If consideration isn't there, you're definitely in trouble. Good communication and conflict resolution skills *can* be learned (we'll tell you how in Chapter 7), but you should make sure they're in place before placing both of your names on one mailbox.

If you got mostly C's and D's: *Sorry,* sister. It looks like a chemistry experiment gone awry. Your knight in shining armor may be a dud on a stud. Or maybe you and your man are like oil and water—you simply don't mix. We're not saying that the situation is completely hopeless. But at the moment, you don't have the necessary elements for a peaceful and satisfying coexistence. Before going any further, we urge you to be straight with yourself. Yes, there's a chance that you can salvage this relationship. However, it isn't going to happen overnight or without a fair amount of sweat and tears. So forget about putting a deposit on that U-Haul for the time being.

Talking It Over with Your Man

We think the "Will you move in with me?" question is a pretty huge deal. But when we asked our pool of shacking-up couples how the subject of living together came up, many of them drew a blank. Oh sure, some remembered whose idea it was. But exactly *when, where, how* the issue was raised? They tended to be a bit fuzzy on those details. That's because, unlike a diamond ring, down-on-one-knee proposal, there usually isn't any big celebration or fanfare to accompany it. In fact, it doesn't always come in the form of a question, either. Often it's more of a hint or suggestion.

If your boyfriend is the one doing the "suggesting," you'll probably feel an initial surge of excitement. But if you're like many of the women we talked to, it may be followed by a feeling of anxiety. You may have concerns about how the two of you would get along as roommates or what the whole living together thing would mean. As we said before, shacking up is a major step up on the relationship ladder, and it's not easily reversed. That's why you need to iron out a few important points with your significant other prior to making your decision. "Before moving in together, couples should be explicit about their expectations and hopes for the future," says relationship expert Michelle Gannon, Ph.D. "You both need to be clear about what you want and communicate it to one another," says Nicole, thirty-one, of San Francisco. "False expectations will end in tears."

"Awkward" is the way many women describe these what's-the-deal conversations. Unless you've been dating for a long time or are just incredibly comfortable with each other, there's a good chance that you'll find yourself walking on eggshells or dancing around the tough issues like Fred Astaire and Ginger Rogers. Fear is often the underlying reason. "Part of me worried that I wouldn't be able to put my money where my mouth was," says Kristy, who dated her boyfriend for four months before moving in with him. Other shacker-uppers like Amber, thirty-two, of Boston, say that they feared rejection and didn't want to rock the boat. "I wanted to raise the marriage issue before moving in with Bruce, but it seemed too premature," she explains. "I thought it would scare him."

Like Amber, you may be thinking it's too soon in your relationship to bring up heavy subjects like marriage and kids. But if it's a matter that's important to you (even if it's a few years down the road), you need to talk about it before moving in. Let's put it another way: Do you really think you should be shacking up with a guy with whom you can't share your hopes and dreams? If you're not ready to discuss your deepest feelings, our *Shacking Up* advice is to put the move on hold until you're able to discuss your deepest feelings. If an outstanding circumstance such as a job relocation prevents a relationship holding pattern, you can try using a more subtle tactic to determine your boyfriend's modus operandi (see page 68 for tips). But from two certified wusses to another, it's *always* much better to be direct.

It's possible that a few of you are reluctant to pop the tough questions because you're secretly afraid of what you'll discover. This is almost as crazy as not seeing a dermatologist when you have a funny-looking mole that you're concerned could be cancerous. If you and your beau want different things or are headed in opposite directions, it's time for you to move on, not move in! As painful as this realization may be, you're much better off coming to grips with it before you start disrupting your life and digging yourself deeper into the relationship. Trust us—you'll save yourself a lot of time and agony in the long run.

Even if you're almost positive that you know how your man feels about the serious life issues, we still suggest getting some verbal confirmation. It'll make you feel good to hear his visions of your future together coming from his lips, and it's the best way to make sure that you don't get blindsided by his lifelong desire to join the Peace Corps, points out Janine, of New York City. "Never assume that you know what your partner is thinking," warns Kate, twenty-eight, a fellow New Yorker.

Now that we've convinced you to hash things out with your honey, we're going to help you do it. On the upcoming pages, we'll explain what conversations you need to have and the kinds of questions you should ask. Hopefully, you're able to talk openly and honestly with your man. If not, we have advice (from both guys and girls) on how to go about it. It's not always easy to initiate these discussions, but lots of women have done it—and so can you. Here are three talking-it-over tips from the trenches to consider as you march forward.

1. **Take it slow.** Give yourselves plenty of time to hammer out the important issues. Elaine, thirty-three, of Boston,

suggests spreading your discussions out over a period of weeks or, better yet, months. "Do it in baby steps," she says. "Don't go by an unrealistic timetable," adds Kristy. "If your lease is up in two weeks and the two of you haven't talked things out, talk to your landlord and see if you can go month-to-month."

2. **Play it cool.** Bring up stuff when it's comfortable and appropriate, like on a long car ride or hike, says Kelly. Avoid the "We need to talk" line—it'll make him sweat bullets. To get the conversation flowing, try telling him how you feel first, then allow him to respond. Don't just start pummeling him with questions. "You don't want to make him feel like he's a guest on 'Larry King Live,' " Kelly adds.
3. **Be honest.** Spilling your guts can be frightening when you're not sure what your partner's reaction will be. But no matter what you unearth, you're better off finding out now rather than later, notes Naomi, twenty-five, of New York City, who has been in two live-in relationships—the first of which ended badly. There's always a chance that he shares your feelings, in which case you can stop wondering and worrying. So buckle down and lay it on the line. If necessary, try role playing: Pretend you're a no-nonsense woman like Oprah or Madonna. It may sound silly, but it could help you overcome your stage fright.

Ten Crucial Topics to Cover

When you're in love, it's easy to get swept up in the romance. Everything feels *soooo* right. You're like two peas in a pod. You just want to go with it! Honestly, the last thing we want to do is rain on your parade. But the reality is, a live-in relationship is like building a house or starting a business—it requires careful research and planning. Think of it this way: You wouldn't take a new job without learning what's expected of you, the health benefits, the 401(k) plan, and the future growth potential. And that's just a job!

We realize that not all of you have the same reasons for wanting to live together. Some of you may view it as a "trial run." For some, it may be a prelude to marriage. Others may want to take their relationship to the next level or spend more time together. In any case, you wouldn't be moving in with him if your relationship didn't have some future potential. Thus, it makes sense to discuss day-to-day practicalities as well as bigger issues like religion and family to make sure the two of you are totally simpatico. *Sí?*

After talking to the experts (licensed psychologists, relationship coaches, and dozens of men and women with firsthand experience), we've compiled a list of ten topics to discuss before shacking up—as well as sample questions that can be used as conversation starters. Not all of these questions may apply to you, but that's OK: This isn't meant to be a script, simply a guide. No matter how you go about it, the point is to get a clear idea of each other's views and expectations on each of these topics.

What if you and your partner don't see eye-to-eye on every issue? No biggie: You're normal. "Every couple has their differences," says therapist Steven M. Sultanoff, Ph.D. "You can't expect to agree on everything." But you do need to come to some sort of resolution on those sticking points before moving in together. "The question is, can one of you tolerate and even accept not getting what you want?" Sultanoff asks. If both of you feel strongly about an issue and are unwilling to bend, you may be at an impasse. But if one or both of you is willing to compromise, then you should be in the clear.

1. Moving In

What are your reasons for wanting to live with me? Do

you see this as a temporary or long-term arrangement? Have we known each other long enough? Is the timing right?

2. **Lifestyle**

   How do you see our relationship changing if we move in together? Where do you see us living? Would we spend every night together? What about weekends? Holidays? How would we deal with household chores like cooking and cleaning? Will you be able to handle my anal retentiveness/sloppiness? What about my dog/cat?

3. **The "M" Word**

   Do you believe in marriage? Do you think it can last forever? Do you think it's in your future? Do you think that you and I are headed in that direction?

4. **Children**

   Do you like kids? Can you picture yourself as a dad? How many kids can you see yourself having? When do you see yourself having them? If we were to have kids, would both of us keep working?

5. **Religion**

   How important is religion to you? Do you see yourself ending up with someone with the same religious views? How will our religious differences be handled on special occasions and holidays? If we were to get married, would our religious differences become a problem? If we had children, in what faith would they be raised?

6. **Career**

   Do you see your career dictating your life or your life dictating your career? Is there a chance our career goals could conflict? If so, what would we do?

7. **Money**

   What are your basic values, goals, and priorities when it comes to finances? Do we have similar spending/saving habits? Do we have similar money management styles? Would we want to open a joint bank account or keep all of our money separate? (Note: Finances are a major part of a live-in relationship.

Therefore, before making a final decision about shacking up, you may want to discuss all the specifics of how your household expenses would be handled. At the very least, you should have an in-depth conversation before signing a lease. In the beginning of Chapter 5, we lead you through this all-important money chat. You may want to peek ahead to see what subjects you'll need to cover.)

8. **Family and Friends**

   For you, is family every day, most weekends, once a month, or only on certain holidays? Are you cool with seeing my family just as much or more? What about our friends? Will we spend as much time with my friends as we spend with yours—or vice versa?

9. **Geography**

   Do you plan on staying here or have dreams of moving somewhere else? Do you want to be free to pick up and move at any time or are you anxious to establish roots? Where do you see yourself living in five years? Ten years? Twenty years? Fifty years? City or small town? House, condo, or apartment?

10. **Personal History**

    Is there any important part of your personal history that you've neglected to tell me? What about any psycho ex-girlfriends, arrest records, former marriages, children from previous relationships, sexually transmitted diseases, or financial, legal, drug, alcohol, or gambling problems?

The Marriage Question

This is the big one—the "M" word. We realize that not all of you know how you feel about tying the knot at this point. After all, for many of you, the point of moving in together is to see if you're compatible and find out if he's "the one." For others, it may simply be the next logical step in your relationship, and who knows what will happen next? For still others, getting hitched may not be part of your master plan. But for those of you who *would* like to walk down the aisle someday, we think you owe it to yourselves (and your mates) to raise the issue before setting up house.

Broaching the topic of wedded bliss isn't always a piece of cake. In fact, we'd almost rather tell our men their lovemaking is miserable than mention the dreaded of all words—"marriage." Nothing seems to put guys on the defensive faster than talk of taking vows. But as we said earlier, any reluctance on your part to raise the subject is probably a sign you should postpone shacking up. Remember: If you can't tell your boyfriend how you *really* feel, the two of you will have a tough time negotiating the trials and tribulations of a live-in relationship. Your discussion doesn't have to get overly specific. No need to tell him about the *perfect* reception site or exquisite bridesmaid dresses you recently spotted. However, you should make sure that you're both thinking "marriage" and have the same basic time line for approaching the altar. "I've seen too many of my friends move in with guys without discussing marriage first, then end up finding out they're not even close to being ready or sure that they'll ever be," says Emily, twenty-nine. "One of them waited three years for a proposal, and then her boyfriend told her he couldn't do it. She was *crushed*." If you can't be totally open and honest with your mate, you can try raising the topic in a casual way, suggests couples therapist Michelle Gannon, Ph.D. "You can say something like, 'Do you want to get married someday?' or 'Do you see it in our future?' " she adds. "See what he says and let him freak out if he needs to."

According to Gannon, age may be a factor in whether or not your guy flinches at the idea of tying the knot. "Most men in their twenties don't want to talk about marriage," she says. "Men in their thirties tend to be more open to it—or at least not so surprised that you'd suggest it." Other factors such as financial instability, a family history of divorce, or a devastating breakup with an ex-girlfriend or ex-wife may also come into play. If that's the case, you can wait it out and see if his circumstances or his feelings change. "He just may not be ready," says Bruce, thirty-three, of Boston. "Not everyone has the same time frame for settling down."

If your boyfriend responds negatively or shuts down, it doesn't necessarily mean that he has zero future potential. "There's a certain category of guys who will try to avoid making a full commitment for as long as possible," says Bruce, who waited four-plus years to propose to his live-in girlfriend. "Ultimately, they may commit, but they'll do whatever they can to dodge the bullet." His advice: Be persistent. "Follow through on forcing him to talk about it, but don't be threatening," he says. Gannon concurs. "Allow him to have his feelings, then try probing a little further." If it's an appropriate point in the relationship to bring up marriage (say, you've been dating exclusively for a year-plus), then he should look at it as a legitimate question, Bruce adds. If not, then he may not be ready to make the kind of emotional commitment that living together requires.

Of course, there's always a chance that his unwillingness to discuss marriage means that he'll never step up to the plate (or, in this case, the altar). So it's up to you to decide how important the marriage license is to you. Could you live happily ever after, devoid of any doubt, without one? Whatever happens, we advise against trying to pressure him into it. "You might be able to talk a guy into proposing to you, but do you really want to marry him under those circumstances?" Gannon asks. "It's better to be with someone who wants the same things as you."

If your guy is gung ho to swap vows but you're not ready to take the plunge, you also need to level with him. If the roles were reversed, you'd want him to come clean, wouldn't you? It might hurt his feelings, but hopefully he'll appreciate your honesty in the long run. If you think that there *is* a chance that you could marry him someday, ask him to be patient and come up with a plan that will satisfy both of you. "Agree to sit down and talk about it again in a few months or set a time line for getting engaged," Kelly suggests. But if you can't see yourselves *ever* getting hitched, do the honorable thing and cut him loose.

Doing Detective Work

Say your mate isn't as good at sharing his feelings as you? Even though you're not 007, some basic investigative work can help you uncover his thoughts on marriage and kids. However, we must add a *Shacking Up* disclaimer: If you're hoping to tie the knot or start a family in the near future, you owe it to yourself (and your boyfriend) to be up front about it. If, on the other hand, you're not positive what you want or you don't mind playing Russian roulette, you can try one of these two suss-him-out strategies:

1. **Be observant.** How does he talk about the "M" word? Does he refer to it with respect? Or does he call it the stupidest thing a guy could ever do? Does he like spending time with other couples? Or would he prefer to hang out with his single friends? Does he break out in hives whenever you go to a wedding? Is he good with children? Does he seem engaged and interested? Or does he act uncomfortable or call them "good birth control"?
2. **Talk in theory.** Raise the marriage question not in terms of "us" but in a general, nonspecific way. Ask him whether he believes in marriage as an institution. Does he think that we're meant to be with one person our entire lives?

The Final Deliberation

You've gotten to know yourself, measured your chemistry, and talked until you're blue in the face—whew! You're almost done. Now, you're in the final stage, with only a few question marks to go.

Is the Timing Right?

As previously noted, shacking up with your boyfriend can be loads of fun (did someone say cozy evenings cuddling on the couch?), but it can also be nerve-racking, especially in the beginning. Finding an apartment, dealing with landlords, packing and unpacking boxes . . . hey, you know what a nightmare it can be. You'll also have to adjust to your new roommate situation. Suddenly you and Mr. Wonderful will be sharing, well, pretty much everything and making important decisions together, which means you'll be more apt to butt heads. You're going to need as much poise, patience, and self-confidence as possible. Therefore, you'll be better off doing it when you're both feeling on top of your games.

If other areas of your lives are in a state of disrepair—let's say, you just got laid off from your dot.bomb job, your parents just announced they're getting a divorce, or one of you is coping with a serious health problem—it may not be the best time to make a move. We realize waiting isn't always easy, especially when you're dealing with leases and such. But doing so will benefit you in the long run. So you spend a little extra money on rent for a while. Big deal. It will be a lot less expensive than the relocation expenses and therapy sessions that you'll need if you move in prematurely and your relationship buckles under the strain.

Eek–What Will My Parents Think?

Most of you really don't even have to ask this question. Consciously or subconsciously, you already know the answer. And as much as our formerly rebellious selves would like to say "Who cares? It's your life!," we know that, deep down, you *do* care. Otherwise, the question wouldn't have popped into your head in the first place.

Your family's feelings are definitely something you need to consider for two reasons. First, any strong objection on their part may be a sign that you are, in fact, thinking about making a bad move. We're not suggesting that your parents know what's better for you than you do. But if they're freaking because they think your boyfriend is a boar, you may want to listen. Our suggestion: Talk to your family and try to find out what their specific issues are. Then, ask yourself whether their criticisms are valid, and try to be objective. Ultimately, this *is* your decision, but you're also the one who will have to live with the consequences. That's why you can't be too careful.

Second, if your parents or other family members are going to have a huge problem with your living arrangement, you must decide if you want to put yourself through that sort of agony. Making the adjustment to living with someone can be challenging enough—doing it without the support of your loved ones is another ball game altogether. "How your family views you has a lot to do with how you feel about yourself and your life," says relationship coach David Steel. "Family disapproval may make it extra hard on you and your relationship."

If you and your mate have thought it through and strongly believe that cohabitation is right for you, then you're going to have some explaining to do. In the next chapter, you'll find tips on how to break the news to your loved ones without starting World War III.

What If We Break Up?

On the good news side, you'll have found out that you're incompatible before saying "I do!" in front of a roomful of people. The bad news? Whether you're the dumper or the dumpee, take our word: Breaking up will *suck*. You'll have to deal with the emotional trauma, which our sources say can be pretty intense. (According to a study published in a 2002 issue of the *Journal of Marriage and Family,* the end of a cohabiting relationship can be just as distressing as a divorce.) Then there are the other gory details: You'll have to divide your stuff—not an easy task if you haven't been making separate purchases or keeping track of who bought what. One or both of you will also be stuck trying to find a new place to live pronto, which could compromise your standard of living and set you back financially. Finally, there could be some financial consequences if your boyfriend is a real ass and you didn't take proper precautions (more about that in Chapters 5 and 6). Again, we're not trying to scare you. We're simply trying to remind you to think long and hard before making your choice.

What If I'm Still Not Sure?

Remember what we said earlier about listening to your gut instinct? Now is the time to tap into that trusty inner voice. As we told you earlier, it's normal to feel a little nervous when you're making a decision of this magnitude. But if you're seriously shaky, losing sleep, or experiencing that telltale pit in your stomach, then it's a warning sign that you should pay attention to. Our advice: Hold off on making a move until your gut says "Go!" "People always say when you know, you know," says Tara, thirty, of Mill Valley, California. "If you don't know, then give it some time. The answer should come to you."

Shacking Up Readiness Checklist

- ____ I feel confident that living together is the right move for me/us.
- ____ We have the same reasons for wanting to live together.
- ____ We totally trust and believe in each other.
- ____ We're both equally committed to the relationship.
- ____ We know that it won't always be easy and we won't always agree.
- ____ We've talked about the big issues–marriage, family, religion, finances, etc.
- ____ We feel that the timing is right.
- ____ We've factored in how our families' feelings will affect us and our relationship.

CHAPTER 3

Ten Things to Do Before Packing Your Bags

You did it. You made the decision. You're going to take the plunge and move in together! You feel relieved, excited—OK, you can admit it—thrilled to death!!! It's hard not to smile to yourself as you make mental plans for your new abode, which, in fantasyland, looks like something straight from the pages of *Elle Decor.* But hold on: You're getting a little ahead of yourself now. Before you sign a lease or begin picking out paint samples, here are ten important items to add to the top of your to-do list.

1. Break the News to Friends and Family

One fun part of this premove period will be spreading the joyous news to your friends—presuming that they like your boyfriend, you're not rushing in, and he isn't the third guy you've lived with in the past three years. Naturally, your closest friends will be delighted for you and not a bit surprised. They may even suggest a girls' night out to celebrate. Other more casual acquaintances are apt to offer their congratulations, then ask the big question: "So, do you think that you two will get married?" (On page 243, we discuss different ways of dodging this bullet.) You'll already be thinking about throwing a housewarming party (after you're all settled in), so you can have your buddies over and show off your place.

Alas, as we warned you in Chapter 1, your announcement may not be met with warm wishes from everyone—particularly your parents. Fact is, unless you grew up in a hippie commune or your folks are just supercool and laid-back, you may experience anything from cautious concern to unspoken disapproval to a full-on freak-out. Not that you need reminding, but your parents are from a different era. When they were your age, living together outside of marriage may have been a major no-no. Their religious beliefs could also be a factor. Perhaps they think that shacking up is improper or immoral. Or, they may be worried that you'll get strung along, taken advantage of, or just plain hurt. "My mom disapproved because she thought there should be some kind of stronger commitment (i.e., marriage) before I became further invested in the relationship," says Jane, twenty-seven, of Santa Barbara, California. "Essentially, she was afraid that, if we broke up, I'd be even more devastated because we'd lived together."

Besides your mom and dad, there may be other near and dear ones who oppose your shacking-up decision. They could include a friend who had a disastrous live-in relationship, an overprotective sibling, or relatives who are very traditional or religious. "The ones who were most upset were my grandparents," says our girlfriend Ann. "After we moved in together, my grandfather called me to tell me how upset he was and that it was making him depressed. It was terrible!"

At this stage, some of you may feel like shouting "Why don't they trust me?" or "Why can't they just be excited?" Keep in mind that these naysayers really do have your best interests in mind. You're their little girl, granddaughter, sister, or best friend, and they want you to be happy. Just because your loved ones don't approve of your choice of lifestyle doesn't mean that it's a mistake or you're a bad person. The important thing is that you believe in yourself and your decision. It's great that you care about them and their feelings. You want to do the right thing. The only problem is, in this particular case, your notion of the "right thing" isn't the same as theirs.

Depending on how far away you live, you may be tempted to try to keep your live-in relationship a secret from your family. We advise against the stealth approach for several reasons. First of all, it's unfair to your boyfriend. How would you feel if he asked you to remove every trace of yourself whenever a family member came to visit? Second, it can be stressful—watching every word you say so you don't "slip" and praying your friends from home don't run into your parents and unintentionally spill the beans. Last, but not least, it's high time that you started developing a healthy, adult relationship with your family. This means learning how to communicate, establishing boundaries, and respecting one another's opinions and choices.

No one likes to be the bearer of bad news. The last thing you want to do is upset anyone. Unfortunately, there's no easy way around it. In their book *Difficult Conversations: How to Discuss What Matters Most,* coauthors Douglas Stone, Bruce Patton, and Sheila Heen compare delivering a difficult message to throwing a hand grenade. "Coated with sugar, thrown hard or soft, a hand grenade is still going to do damage," they say. "Try as you may, there's no way to . . . outrun the consequences."

Anyway, if you're like us, your chief concern is how your folks will react. It may drive you batty that they can't let go or trust you to make your own decisions (and mistakes). But you still love and respect them, and they'll be a part of your life after you shack up. You don't want to start things off on a bad foot. Thus, you need to be careful about *how* you tell them. Bottom line: What you say (or don't say) could impact their response—so think before you speak. Prior to pulling the pin on the grenade, be sure to study these six tête-à-tête tips from the pros.

Drop the bomb (with respect). Start by acknowledging the fact that you may not see eye-to-eye on this issue, and that the purpose of the conversation is to understand how all of you feel about it. "Treat the conversation as an exploration of thoughts and feelings," Heen suggests. Let them know if you're still mulling over the decision and seeking their opinion or advice. Or, if your decision is final, tell them in a way that is firm and respectful. "Say something like, 'Scott and I have made the choice to move in together' instead of 'Scott and I are *thinking of* moving in together,' " Stone says. Otherwise, they may think there's a possibility of talking you out of it.

Show that you care. Before explaining your rationale, give them an opportunity to express their feelings. "At this point, your parents are full of thoughts and can't take in the details of [your] reasons," Stone says. "It's better to work to understand their reactions." That doesn't mean you have to agree with them, he says. "You can say 'I can see that this is really hard for you. I know that you think this is immoral.' That's different from saying 'I agree that it's immoral' or 'I think you're wrong.' " "The fact that you listened [and empathized] will make a big difference . . . even if you ultimately make a decision that they disagree with," adds Heen.

State your case. When the time comes to present your side, take what Stone and Heen call the "and" stance. "We often treat our conversations as debates," Heen says. "Either your parents are right and moving in is foolish, or you're right and your relationship will flourish and grow." When you adopt the "and" stance, you accept that both viewpoints are valid. "Remembering that you don't have to agree enables you to listen to your parents' perspective and share your own," she adds. Stone suggests saying something like "I understand why you think this is immoral and why it's so hard for you. Let me say a few things about how I see it." Our advice: Tell them how happy you are to have found someone whom you love and truly believe could be "the one." Explain that you've thought long and hard about this decision and why you believe that it's right for you.

Discuss your concerns. If you have any qualms about your decision, share them with your parents. Make it clear that you're aware of the possible downsides and complexities of living with your boyfriend. This will invite them to help you think through the issues in a supportive way rather than spending their time arguing that you don't know what you're getting yourself into, Heen explains.

Don't try to win them over. Trying to persuade your parents to feel something other than what they feel is a waste of time, Heen says. "Don't think that you can convince them that you're doing the right thing or expect them to be happy," she says. However, they are more likely to change their views over time if they feel like you understand and care about their feelings.

Give it time. Remember that your news may be a shock, and your parents may not know how to respond or act. They may be unsure about their role in your new life. Are they becoming in-laws? What will they say to their friends? How will they introduce your boyfriend—as their daughter's "special friend," "roommate," or "significant other"? Realize that they'll need time to adjust, and try to keep the lines of communication open.

He Said/She Said: "How Did Your Family React to the News?"

"When I told my mom that Phil and I were moving in together, she stood up and left the room without saying a word. It wasn't until the next day that I got up the nerve to tell her we were also planning to buy a house together. That's when she started screaming, 'Oh my God! Are you *crazy?*' " *–Zoey, thirty-six*

"My mother was concerned that it would be too easy for us to simply continue living together and not get married. His parents were OK with it, but I think it took them a while to adjust to the idea and be able to tell their friends about our living arrangement."

–Amber, thirty-two

"My mom said, 'I hope it leads to something more permanent.' "

–Nate, thirty-three

"No one called and said, 'Congratulations on moving in together!' Instead, they said, 'How is it? Is everything OK?' If I'd gotten a ring instead of an apartment, they would have been celebrating instead of questioning it." *–Isabelle, twenty-five*

"I never told my family that we were living together, knowing that they would disapprove." *–Suzanne, thirty-six*

2. Talk About Finances

You're probably getting tired of talking by now, and a few of you may be tempted to hightail it through the financial drivel. After all, if you're like us, money isn't your favorite topic, especially when there are more exciting (or less depressing) things like apartment hunting or decorating to discuss. But the reality is, to avoid an ongoing financial fracas, there are wads of dollars-and-cents details that must be sorted out. For instance, prior to moving day, you and your mate will need to decide how much you're each going to chip in for basic monthly expenses, who's going to write the checks, and whether to open a joint bank account. And that's just the very beginning.

Relationship experts say that money is the leading source of conflict for couples, both married and unmarried. Why? Many of us have different views, values, priorities, and habits when it comes to finances. People generally fall into two basic categories—spenders and savers. If you and your partner aren't the same breed, you can count on more ups and downs than the Dow Jones. The two of you may also run into problems if you have vastly different income levels or financial obligations. That's why it's absolutely essential to talk it all over and agree on how to handle your household expenses and other monetary details from here on in.

But we never fight about money! some of you may be thinking. When you're living under separate roofs, finances may not seem like a big issue. Like many couples, however, you could find that pecuniary conflicts surface after you start cohabiting. After you shack up, you'll be mutually responsible for things like rent or a mortgage, utility bills, insurance payments, and so on. You may feel upset when you discover that he spends a fortune playing golf but won't help pay to reupholster the sofa. He may clue into your equally hefty clothes budget and get miffed when you refuse to chip in for DIRECTV. Or, you may not agree on how to split expenses, especially if one of you makes three times more than the other.

As you can see, finances are a subject that you shouldn't gloss over. In Chapter 5, we cover everything from household budgets to the dos and don'ts of joint bank accounts. At this point, we strongly urge you and your partner to read this chapter and come up with a solid financial game plan. If you've talked about spending the rest of your lives together, you may want to go ahead and talk about longer-term issues such as savings accounts, investments, IRAs, and 401(k)s. If you're not so sure about the future, at least be sure to cover the nuts and bolts of your daily finances, as outlined on pages 119–142.

Remember, talking about what you *don't* have is just as, if not more, important than talking about what you *do* have. In other words, you should both be sure to address any concerns that you have about the other's financial background. Because once you're living together, you won't be able to hide the "past due" notices or the telephone calls from creditors. And let's not forget that most landlords run a credit check on prospective tenants. No doubt you'd rather hear about any financial skeletons such as a defaulted loan or astronomical credit card debt from each other, not a real estate broker.

Thinking of merging your money before marriage? We advise against it and can't say enough about reading pages 133–135 before you start placing all of your assets in one basket. Pooling all of your funds is a major financial decision with serious potential risks. So read ahead and don't forget—a fool and her money are soon parted.

3. Figure Out Where to Live

OK, enough of the tedious, ulcer-inducing stuff. Finally, it's time to think about something cheery. We're talking about your love shack—the place that you and your man are going to call "home, sweet home." If one of you owns a house or condo, the where-to-live question may be a no-brainer. But if you're both renters, you'll need to make a choice: Should the two of you move into his place, your place, or find a new place altogether?

If one of you already has a fabulous flat, the answer may seem obvious. However, there are also potential drawbacks to shacking up in a place that feels like "his" or "mine." If you move into his pad, for example, you may always feel like a guest. Plus, where will you put all of your belongings? Does your boyfriend have any clue as to the extent of your wardrobe? If, on the other hand, your beau moves into your place, you may be nervous about how you'd handle it. Relinquishing your turf could be tough, especially if your space is fixed up *perfectly.* Add his golf clubs, big-screen TV, and God-awful "Frasier"-esque recliner, and the hair on the back of your neck may start to bristle.

To minimize this territorial stress, we recommend ditching your current digs and getting a new place that feels like it belongs to both of you. By starting fresh, you'll be able to work together to create a mutually pleasing living space. You can also look for a pad that has loads of closet room, more than one bathroom, and enough space in general so you can each be alone when you need to be.

One final note: Shopping for an abode can be a blast, but it can also be stressful and frustrating. As you tour prospective pads, you'll quickly discover whether you and your beau have similar wants, needs, and priorities in terms of living conditions. You may find that he's focused on parking, water pressure, and cable-readiness, while you're fixated on the beautiful molding and track lighting. This will be a good test of your compatibility as well as your ability to communicate and compromise. *Shacking Up* maxim: Decide what's most important to you and fight for it, but don't expect to get everything your way.

In Chapter 4, we'll talk about leases and why you should both sign one if you're renting an apartment. You'll also find out why you should draw up an informal lease agreement for the nonowner if one of you owns the place where you'll be living. If you're thinking of buying a house or condo together, refer to pages 136–140 for more on ownership options and the potential pitfalls of making such a huge purchase together.

4. Agree on a Common Courtesy Code

Anyone who has shared close quarters with a roommate knows that it can be extremely irritating. One postcollege experience stands out in our friend Laura's mind. "It began with my roommate, Penny, borrowing clothes without asking," the thirty-one-year-old says. "Then, there were the missed phone messages and blaring music. The capper was one weekend when my mom was visiting. Penny came home with a total stranger and proceeded to have extremely vocal sex in the room next to where my mother was sleeping." To Laura, it all seemed impossibly inconsiderate. Didn't Penny know better? But as she sadly discovered, not everyone has the same unwritten rules of conduct.

It's hard to know what roommate grievances you'll have after you and your man move in together. (Hopefully nothing along the lines of the Penny scenario.) But you can try to head off a few likely suspects by establishing a "common courtesy code." The code is a list of basic household dos and don'ts that you and your partner should talk about and agree to. Some of the potentially touchy areas that you'll want to cover: calling home if you're going to be late; picking up after yourselves; inviting friends over; overnight guests; paying bills on time; relaying telephone messages; and borrowing each other's stuff without asking. You'll also want to discuss household chores, after you've read pages 95–96.

5. Set Ground Rules for Handling Conflicts

By now, you've probably been dating long enough to get into one or two (or possibly three) little scuffles. If you haven't, it's time to put on your boxing gloves, because the action is about to begin. Fighting is never enjoyable, but it can actually be good for your relationship if you can prevent your arguments from getting ugly. In Chapter 7, we'll explain why it's so important to keep a lid on your temper. You'll also learn how to address your differences in a healthy, productive manner. Meanwhile, until you have a chance to peruse that entire section, we recommend establishing a few "rules for the ring" (see pages 193–194 for details). These ground rules can help keep your altercations from taking on a nasty tone, which would be upsetting and possibly damaging to your relationship. So talk about the dos and don'ts for fighting fair *now,* before the opening bell.

6. Protect Yourself Legally

Protect yourself? Protect yourself from what? Is it really necessary? Doesn't it seem a little, well, paranoid? First, take a deep breath. We're not sending you to People's Court or a three-hundred-dollar-per-hour attorney. What we're talking about is taking a few easy precautions to safeguard your savings account and prevent a lot of headaches in the event of a breakup—no lawyers required.

Protecting yourself is simpler than it may sound, and it's a smart move if you have *anything* to lose (such as your life savings and worldly possessions); you'll be depending on your mate for financial support; or you plan on purchasing any significant assets together. Despite what you may think, it doesn't mean that you lack faith in your partner or your relationship. No siree! In fact, the legal avenues that we're talking about are designed to protect both you *and* your man. We like to think of them as tools to make the transition from singleton to coupledom smooth and worry-free.

The first thing to consider is a shacking-up contract, which is like a prenup for live-ins. This is essentially a written document that spells out the sharing of expenses and any special financial arrangements you make. In your agreement, you can specify who owns what (including favorite pieces of furniture and beloved pets) and how joint property would be divided if the two of you were to split. "It's good to talk about what you would do if you decided to break up," attests Dave, thirty-four, of Boston, who lived with his girlfriend for nine months before getting engaged. "After discussing what would happen if our relationship went up in smoke, we felt as though there was nothing left to worry about. It helped relieve some of the pressure."

Aside from a shacking-up contract, there are other short-form written agreements to consider if you're planning on making any significant purchases (such as furniture, electronic equipment, or appliances) together. We've provided details on both types of legal protection in Chapter 6 ("Legalese for Live-Ins").

7. Sign Up for a Couples' Education Class

A lot of couples undergo some type of relationship "training" before tying the knot. (With certain religions such as Catholicism, it's a premarital must.) But since living together poses many of the same challenges as married life, we say why wait until you're engaged? Jane backs us up: "Prior to getting married, we participated in a couples' education course that we both found very helpful," she says. "In retrospect, I think doing something like that when we *first* moved in together would have helped us both and made things easier."

From one-day classes to multiweekend workshops, there could be a variety of options depending on where you live. For the most part, the point of these types of education courses is to discuss your expectations and learn basic skills such as communication and resolving conflicts. Jill, thirty-eight, a couples' counseling grad, likens it to a career training seminar. "You do it to learn the things that will help you be more successful in your relationship," she says. Michelle Gannon, cofounder of Marriage Prep 101 in San Francisco, explains that by developing strong relationship skills, a couple can avoid unhealthy relationship patterns and nip potential problems in the bud.

One nationwide skills-building program known as PREP (Prevention and Relationship Enhancement Program) has a proven success rate. The research-based program was developed by two top psychologists at the University of Denver. Their studies show that PREP couples have "about half the likelihood of breaking up or divorcing [and] have . . . greater relationship satisfaction . . . than control couples up to five years following training," according to the PREP website. "PREP is not therapy," it continues. "It is education. It is coaching very much like learning to play tennis or golf." Says PREP cofounder Scott M. Stanley, one of the chief goals is to teach couples how to "protect the fun and friendship . . . that bonds them together."

All the experts we talked to agree that the best time to start working on your relationship is before there are problems. "Many couples make the mistake of waiting until they have serious issues to seek support," says David Steele, a relationship coach in San Jose, California. "Education courses and counseling are most effective when you approach them from a positive, empowering standpoint." If you decide to go the couples' education class or workshop route, be sure that the folks running the particular course are cohabitation-friendly. (Remember, these relationship-skills workshops are often geared toward engaged or married couples. They don't always take kindly to premarital fornicators!) For more information about PREP or to find a PREP instructor near you, click on www.prepinc.com. You can also find a directory of couples' education programs in the United States on www.smartmarriages.com.

If you and your partner feel weird about attending a group workshop or have specific issues that you'd like to try to work on, we suggest signing up for private counseling sessions with a licensed relationship coach or couples' therapist. To make sure you hook up with the right professional, be certain to ask about credentials, training, and experience dealing with couples' issues, approaches to therapy, and fees/billing policies before booking a session. If you don't feel comfortable with a particular coach or therapist, keep looking until you find a better fit. The last thing you want to do is waste time and money sitting on the wrong couch.

8. Set a Time Line for Getting Engaged

Right now, one or both of you may not be ready to invest (emotionally or financially) in a pair of platinum bands. But if you know that you want to walk down the aisle some time in the not-so-distant future, you may want to set a time line for getting engaged—or at least engage in a conversation about it.

As we explained a couple of chapters back, one of the pitfalls of living together is that it's easy to get caught in relationship limbo. Once you're shacking up, there may not seem like any big hurry to tie the knot. Not to perpetuate any stereotypes, but it's usually the guys who drag their feet. For a lot of men, cohabitation is a way to "buy time," agrees our guy spy, Nate, thirty-three. "Living together seems safer and easier than making a full commitment," he says. "There are some guys who will try to let things go on that way forever."

A few of you may be thinking that the time line sounds like a pathetic attempt to push a man into proposing. But we're not talking about setting a "deadline" (with a do-or-die cut-off point) or making an ultimatum. By creating a time frame for getting engaged or talking about it, you're merely clarifying your hopes and expectations—you're definitely thinking "marriage" at some point—and ensuring that your partner feels similarly. Doing so may help prevent feelings of insecurity that can make the tiny bumps in your relationship feel more like fourteen-hundred-foot peaks.

Bringing the "M" word to the table shouldn't be too difficult, assuming that you discussed it before deciding to move in together (as we suggested in Chapter 2). Then again, for some gun-shy guys, the mere mention of it is enough to make them hyperventilate. To prevent a panic attack, you can try saying something like "I'm not trying to pressure you. But as you know, I wouldn't be moving in together if I didn't think we were headed toward marriage. So it's important for me that we sit down in "X" number of months and talk about whether we're going to take our relationship to the next level."

Later in the book we'll tell you what to do when you've reached the end of your time line and no proposal has come forth. Until then, promise yourself (and him) not to bring up the marriage subject again. That means no hinting about the to-die-for ring that you saw at Tiffany's or drooling over your newly engaged pal's gorgeous three-carat rock within earshot of your beau. Samantha, thirty, of Cleveland made that mistake. All her heavy-handed innuendos about getting hitched made her boyfriend Justin feel hounded, or so he told her the day he dumped her. Granted, she's probably better off without him. But wouldn't it have been nicer if the relationship had ended on her terms? We think so.

9. Share *Shacking Up* with Your Mate

As a gender, we women tend to put a lot of effort into our relationships. That's why we're constantly picking up magazines, buying self-help books, and tuning into "Oprah." We're anxious for any information we can get our hands on to help us become better partners, lovers, and friends. While it's great that we're making an effort to become more relationship-savvy, however, there's only so much we can hope to accomplish if our partners are clueless.

So what's a woman to do? Hand him your copy of *Shacking Up,* a cold beer, and a bowl of his favorite chips. If you don't want to relinquish your book (or he won't go for it), try relaying some of the most relevant tidbits to him over dinner or while you're washing dishes. He may roll his eyes, but meanwhile he'll be processing and storing the info for future reference.

10. Prepare for an Adjustment

Any time you make a big transition—whether it be shacking up with your boyfriend, moving to a new city, starting a new job, getting engaged, or having a baby—there's apt to be some stress involved. If your living arrangement seems shaky at first, don't panic. It may take a little while to get used to each other's habits and ways of handling things. According to Richard Carlson, Ph.D., and Kristine Carlson in their book *Don't Sweat the Small Stuff in Love,* "Transitions are like speed bumps: You need to slow down while approaching them. Rather than expecting your life to be the same . . . try to be open and accepting to change."

We estimate that the typical adjustment period after shacking up is about six to twelve months. During that time, you and your mate may argue, feel insecure, and get pissed off about stupid, little stuff. At moments, you may even start to wonder whether moving in together was a mistake. Keep in mind that these feelings are common. If you recognize that your living-together experience won't be perfect, it'll be easier for you to deal with the day-to-day irritations that are a fact of life. "When you make the assumption that a transition is going to take time, it seems to take the urgency, as well as much of the frustration, out of the picture," the Carlsons write. "It allows you the time to adjust and settle in."

You and your boyfriend are off on an amazing adventure together. Like the rest of us, you're going to encounter the occasional squall and periods of choppy water. The key is to stay positive and work together to keep your love boat afloat. When you feel the wind pick up and the ship starts to rock, batten down the hatches and roll with it. If you can get through the rough patches, you should have many beautiful days of smooth sailing ahead!

CHAPTER 4

Setting Up Your New Digs

The weeks before moving in together are usually filled with gleeful anticipation. Even if you have dozens of cardboard boxes to pack or your parents are giving you the cold shoulder, you'll probably find yourself bubbling with excitement. Like the crew of the *Andrea Gale* at the start of *The Perfect Storm,* little do you know that all hell is about to break loose. OK, perhaps we're being a wee bit dramatic. But the fact is, you're embarking on a big journey, and along your highway to happiness there are bound to be a lot of wrong turns, dead ends, and potholes. "Going from the in-love stage to the day-to-day living stage can be a big shock," says Isabelle, twenty-five, of New York City, who shacked up with her boyfriend a year ago. "You're on this huge high. Then, when you start cohabiting, reality sets in, and you find yourselves fighting over little stuff."

People always say that the first year of marriage is the hardest. We like to argue that it's the first year of *living together* that they're really talking about. If the road is so rough, some of you may wonder, why does anyone bother to go down it? It's kind of like having a baby (or so we're told). If you can just manage to deal with the morning sickness, varicose veins, and pain of labor, there could be a lifetime of rewards ahead. "Living together is the ultimate yoga posture," says Cindy, thirty-five, of Los Angeles. "It's hard, but if you take your time and breathe deeply, the payoff is really worth it."

In this chapter, we'll talk about some of the things you and your partner are apt to squabble about after the moving van pulls into the driveway. But first, there are a few business matters to discuss.

Taking Care of Business

Good news: We're not about to fry your brain with a bunch of boring legal stuff. (We're saving that for Chapter 6.) But we do have a few, important FYIs regarding your new address.

If You're Renting a Place . . .

If you're renting a house or apartment, both of your names should be placed on the lease. This goes for whether you're moving into a new pad or one of you is moving into the other's digs. The reason? There are several, actually. First, you'll both be legally responsible for paying rent and keeping the place in stellar condition. Second, you'll each have a sense of ownership and feel like masters of your domain. Third, if your relationship goes by the wayside, you won't wind up on the street unless it's by choice.

For those of you who choose to ignore this advice, a word of caution: Most leases stipulate that the owner/landlord be notified and give consent if you wish to add a new tenant. Failure to do so may be grounds for eviction. Another important note: In most states, it's illegal for a landlord to refuse to rent to an unmarried couple. (The two exceptions: Utah and Georgia.) If you think that you've lost out on an apartment or been given the heave-ho because of your living-together status, contact your local tenants' rights group for assistance.

If your local utility companies allow it, we also recommend putting both of your names on the gas/electricity, telephone, and water accounts. That way, if something goes wrong, you and your mate are both responsible. Fear not: You won't need a joint checking account to pay the bills; you can issue them from your personal bank accounts.

If One of You Owns a Place . . .

If one of you is a homeowner, we suggest that you draw up an informal lease for the person moving in. In the lease, you can specify a monthly rent for the nonowner, as well as any other financial arrangements that you've agreed upon. Again, it's a matter of feeling like equal partners in your new home. Without a written agreement, one of you may feel like a houseguest while the other continues to feel like king or queen of the castle. Plus, it's always good to put any financial deal in writing in the unfortunate event that your relationship goes sour and you find yourselves on "Judge Judy."

If You're Thinking of Buying a Place Together . . .

Slow down! This is a big step with many legal and financial ramifications. Before jumping into home ownership, be sure to read pages 139–140, where we explain why it can be risky business.

Renter's and Homeowner's Insurance

If a pipe bursts or all your belongings are destroyed by fire, you'll be glad that you spent the extra money to insure your personal property. As an unmarried couple, you should have two options: You can purchase a joint policy or separate policies. (Note: Some insurance companies don't allow nonmarrieds to buy joint policies. It will be cheaper for you to own a joint policy, but be aware that if something awful does happen and you need to collect on it, the settlement check will be issued to both of you. Needless to say, this could get a little sticky if one of you owned most of the property.

Establishing Territory

Humans are territorial by nature—we like having our own turf and tend to guard it fiercely. Right now, you may not be able to imagine yourself feeling possessive. Just the opposite: You're excited about sharing a home and everything in it with your mate. Sadly, that sentiment often changes when it comes time to decide who gets which closet or whether to turn the spare bedroom into *his* office or your dressing room.

Ideally, to ensure that you each have plenty of space, the apartment or house that you choose to live in should have lots of rooms and closets. As we mentioned in Chapter 3, to avoid a major turf war, you're better off getting a new place rather than moving into his or your place. By starting fresh, you'll be able to establish a feeling of mutual ownership and control. If a new place isn't an option, all isn't lost—you may just have to work a little harder to make the digs feel like "ours." Wherever you decide to live, you both need to feel at home.

If your boyfriend's moving into your place, be sure to make

room for his belongings before the moving van arrives. Look at it as a good opportunity to clean out your closets and go through the piles of junk that have accumulated. Put some furniture into storage, take the coats you haven't worn in a decade to Goodwill, or have a garage sale. After he arrives, encourage him to add his personal touch to the place—photos, a favorite painting, or his collection of beer mugs from around the world. Go out of your way to make him feel welcome and wanted. Try to be easygoing and flexible, even if the thought of a large mounted mackerel on your kitchen wall is totally depressing.

Likewise, if you're moving into his place, you'll need to pare down. After you've weeded out your closets, go through them again and do one final purge. Chances are you're still hanging on to a lot of old clothes and shoes that will never see the light of day. (Trust us, the blazer with the superpadded shoulders, circa 1983, will never come back into style.) A fashion fundamental: If it hasn't been on your body for more than a year, give it away. In the days before the move, if your beau hasn't emptied a closet or made room for you, he better get moving pronto. Who gets the larger closet? Whichever one of you has the most clothes, of course. Once you've moved in, be sure to ask before redecorating or rearranging furniture or cabinets. In general, "respect each other's feelings and compromise where you can," advises Kate, twenty-eight.

One important thing, regardless of where you're residing, is that you each get a room or specially designated space to call your own. This is where you can put personal items, such as photos of your college pals, your collection of antique perfume bottles, and perhaps any furniture that your partner doesn't care for. It can also serve as a hiding place when you need room to breathe. Guys in particular need a quiet place to take five, says our friend Wendy, thirty-two, who has lived with two hibernating types. She calls it the "man cave." (As does John Gray,

Ph.D., in his book *Men Are from Mars, Women Are from Venus.)* Heidi, thirty-four, has a different name for it. "Chris has turned our basement into his own little lounge that we refer to as 'Manville,' " she explains. "It started as a lawn chair and our spare TV. Now, we've put the TV on a table with a lamp, and there's a rug, a space heater, and a comfortable chair. It's great. He has a place to go watch sports when I don't feel like it . . . or away from me when I'm bugging him."

If you're living in a tiny apartment or studio, of course, his-and-her "caves" may not be possible, in which case your best option may be the bathroom. So be it. Add some eucalyptus, an aromatherapy candle, and a magazine rack, and you can actually turn it into a sweet little sanctuary.

Later in this chapter we'll discuss some of the other territorial tugs-of-war that the two of you may face (see Decorating Dilemmas and Privacy, Please!). Not to worry: All this "yours" versus "mine" tension should start to die down after you get settled and accustomed to sharing everything from a medicine chest to the contents of your refrigerator.

Divvying Up Chores

According to research, a funny (but not altogether surprising) thing happens to many women after they move in with their boyfriends: They start doing more housework. In one study published in a June 1994 issue of the *American Sociological Review,* cohabiting women reported spending about thirty-one hours a week on housework—about six hours more than single women living independently. Meanwhile, cohabiting guys are getting off easy with approximately nineteen hours of weekly housework.

Judging by our conversations with scores of shacker-uppers,

there are plenty of exceptions to this rule. Some men not only pull their weight around the house, they crack the cleaning whip. But in general, it is we ladies who end up doing most of the dirty work, despite our high-powered careers and jam-packed schedules. What can you do, aside from reaching for a broom and dustpan? Reach an agreement ASAP about how you're going to divide your household chores.

Start by making a list of all the household duties that need to be done on a daily, weekly, and monthly basis. The list shouldn't be limited to cleaning. Types of tasks to include: paying bills, balancing the checkbook, taking out the garbage/recycling, vacuuming, straightening up common areas, cleaning the kitchen and bathrooms, changing the sheets, doing laundry, grocery shopping, cooking, washing dishes, watering plants, and mowing the lawn. Once you've completed your list, go over it and determine your respective job assignments. If you both despise mopping floors but don't mind doing laundry, try rotating responsibilities throughout the week or month.

Note: A "fair" division of labor doesn't have to mean splitting the chores 50–50. Certain tasks may be more demanding than others, or one of you may have more free time on your hands. What matters is that you agree on a system and each try to hold up your end of the bargain. Don't forget: You're a team, and you need to work together to keep the household running. There may be times when you have to pick up slack for each other. You should both try to be understanding. For example, if you're exhausted and coming down with a migraine, he might offer to do the laundry even though it's your turn—or vice versa.

Cleaning Crises

Shortly after Stephanie shacked up with Jay, she came up with a nickname for him: Monica. As in the TV show "Friends." "Being a Virgo, Jay tends to be very attentive to detail," explains Stephanie, thirty-three, of San Francisco. "OK, I'll say it—he's a neat freak. Fortunately, I also like having things organized and tidy. But when it comes to cleaning, I have to admit that he's got slightly higher standards."

Perhaps, like Stephanie and Jay, you and your mate have different definitions of "clean." You may have been aware of these differences before moving in together, but now you (ugh!) have to live with them. Needless to say, it can be the source of considerable tension. If you're the neatnik, you may feel frustrated or overworked. "Cleaning up after Jake is like picking up after a tornado," says Kristy. "When I come home and see the clothes explosion, I think, 'Why can't he just put it away?' " If you're the messier one, you may feel guilty, put upon, or badgered. "It's not in my genetic makeup to hang up clothes, and I just don't see the disgusting stuff that she sees in the bathroom," claims Bruce, thirty-three. "Sometimes I wonder why I should have to live up to her standards."

Hey, it's not easy being hygienically challenged. Nor is it fun when you feel forced to live in a pigsty or constantly pick up after someone. The obvious solution, of course, is to meet in the middle. "Let's say, on a scale from one to ten (ten being the neatest), you're a nine and your significant other is a six," Bruce says. "The compromise should be halfway between those numbers." Kate also shoots for a happy medium. "My boyfriend's much neater than I am and has a very high standard of cleanliness," she says. "So I try to remember to be a little neater than my natural tendency in some areas, and he tries to loosen up in others."

If your big issue is clutter, one way to cope is by trying to confine the mess to certain parts of your apartment or house. That's how Nicole and Ian managed to deal with it. "We've designated our areas of tidiness and sloppiness," Nicole, thirty-one, explains. "Basically, we have three rooms that are totally organized and one that looks like a bomb hit it." Kristy cut a similar deal with Jake. "When we first moved in together, he was using my office as his dressing room," she says. "I allowed half of the room to get messy, but the other half had to be neat."

Unfortunately, there are other, more immediate household tasks that can't be swept under a carpet or behind a closed door. They include things like doing dishes, mopping the kitchen floor, cleaning the shower, and folding laundry. The problem with leaving these tasks undone is that nine times out of ten, they'll fall on your significant other's shoulders. Again, it comes back to compromise (a recurring theme in this book, if you hadn't noticed). If you haven't done so already, you need to sit down and come up with a cleaning schedule and policies that work for both of you. Be certain to agree on what needs to be done as well as *how* and *when* it's done.

If you're less "detail oriented" than your partner (or a total slob), here's our advice: Try extra hard to fulfill your end of the bargain. Don't wait to be reminded to do your agreed-upon share of the housework. Remember, both of you need to do your part to keep the household running smoothly. If you're more of the anal retentive type, try to chill out. You can't expect your significant other to play by all of your rules. Understand that your priorities may be different, and keep reminding yourself to be more accepting and patient. Decide what's most important to you and let the other minutiae go.

It can be easy to let your mate's slovenly ways get to you, especially if you like having things *über*-clean and organized. If something's *really* driving you bonkers, raise the issue as soon as possible. Don't suck it up or let it fester. "You can't expect someone to change his behavior if you don't explain what's bothering you," Kelly points out. To prevent the problem from getting out of hand, you have to communicate your needs and expectations. But try to do it when you're feeling calm as opposed to frustrated. Here are four tips that may help get his rear in gear:

Don't bitch. Refrain from hurling daggers like "You're such a slob" or "Why is it that I have to do *everything* around here?" which are apt to get his defense mechanism up or make him resentful.

Make a request. Be very clear about what you'd like him to do. Try saying something such as "Could you do something about that pile of clothes?" or "I'd appreciate it if you put your dishes in the dishwasher." Watch your tone and don't throw him any attitude.

Give him credit. Remind him of times when he's been helpful around the house and how much you appreciated it. Be sure to factor in all the other chores that he currently does, such as paying bills, mowing the lawn, or taking out the recycling.

Offer positive feedback. Remember to pat him on the back for a job well done, especially when he goes above and beyond the call of duty. "A little positive reinforcement goes a long way," Kristy notes.

The Guy's Take: How to Get Your Man to Clean Up His Act

Three certified slobs reveal what motivates them to help around the house:

- **"Guilt.** When I see my girlfriend picking up after me, I feel really bad, and that usually gets me up off the couch (that is, unless the Red Sox game is on)." *–Bruce, thirty-three*
- **"My girlfriend's stress.** Sometimes she's OK with leaving the dishes in the sink. But when she's stressed about school or work, I know that the dishes MUST be washed immediately. I try to be sensitive to her moods and get the job done when she's under pressure." *–Rob, thirty-three*
- **"Definitely not nagging.** Nagging just creates a bigger void. Rather than demanding 'This must be done!' I would try reminding your boyfriend that you both have jobs within the house and outside of the house. The burden at home has to be 50-50. Then, you should lead by example." *–Patrick, twenty-nine*

Decorating Dilemmas

The moving boxes have arrived. You've started to unpack. You can't wait to get it all set up and start enjoying your new home. But then, *oh dear* . . . while you're unpacking, you discover a few unforeseen snags. After combining your belongings, you find that you have a bizarre mishmash of furniture. There's too much of this, not enough of that. You need to decide what goes where and how to deal with duplicate items. Then there's the question of what to do with his autographed Metallica picture and high school baseball trophies—total eyesores. Help!

Clashing Styles

If you're lucky, the two of you will have similar tastes and decorating will be a fun project that you work on together. You'll hold hands while browsing at Ikea or flipping through the new Restoration Hardware catalogue and rejoice that you have someone to agonize with over fabric swatches. If you're not so lucky, however, you and your mate *won't* see eye-to-eye, and you'll end up squabbling about everything from color schemes to wall hangings.

We can't blame you for caring. Like your clothes and your car, your home is a reflection of your personality. It says a lot about you. You want it to be comfortable and look a certain way. It's part of your identity. So when your sense of style is questioned or challenged, emotions can run wild. You may be upset that he doesn't like your colorful florals and chintzes or the antique armoire that you spent months saving up for. Likewise, he may feel insulted when you suggest chucking his striped, overstuffed sofa or hanging his prized Western landscape in the loo.

There's always a chance that your boyfriend will leave the decorating up to you. If that's the case, he either doesn't have strong feelings or he's a very smart man. Through experience or instinct, he may know how hard it is for two people to decorate. By staying out of it, he may think that he'll avoid a lot of headaches. "It's definitely easier if one person is in charge," agrees Heather Wolf, an interior designer based in Sonoma, California. The biggest drawback to this scenario is that you won't have anyone to go shopping with or debate with about the benefits of cotton versus velvet slipcovers, says Alice, thirty-five, of Atlanta, who was solely responsible for decorating the flat that she shares with her boyfriend, Kim.

More likely, however, your man *will* have an opinion and

won't want to hand you the reins. In which case, you'll have the challenge of decorating as a duo. If you have drastically different tastes, work to try to understand each other's style, advises Stephanie, who clashed with her boyfriend Jay over "pretty much everything." Accept that you're going to have to make concessions and choose your battles, suggests Cameron, thirty-one. "Think about how strongly you care about each thing, and compare it with how strongly your mate cares," she says. "Sometimes it's worth letting your mate have something that he really, really wants even if you don't love it—because, down the road, it'll be easier for him to give in when you fall in love with that crazy item that he thinks is hideous."

Of course, it's not always easy to find a middle ground. And if you try to compromise on everything, you may end up with a hodgepodge of furniture that neither one of you is really happy with. A win-win solution: You each get a room or part of a room (if you have limited space) to decorate. "In the computer room, my boyfriend has decided to paint one wall black and put up his political memorabilia. Similarly, in our small library, I'm going to paint one wall red and hang up my dance posters," says Kate. "Designating spaces where we can each do what we want helps ease the tension of disparate tastes." As far as common areas go, we recommend taking a democratic approach. Everything that goes in these shared rooms should be jointly agreed upon. Items that don't make the cut can be put in your personal spaces.

To save yourselves a lot of grief, it's best to come up with a game plan before you begin moving furniture or hanging artwork. You may also want to set some official rules of conduct. "When I moved into my boyfriend's apartment, I wanted to add a few personal touches. His rule was that I couldn't 'girl' up the place," says Sonya, twenty-nine, of New York City. "I waited until he was out of town before I hung curtains and border paper. I did have my brother check it out and he said it wasn't too girly." We suggest making a pact to discuss any décor changes or purchases before making them. As tempting as it may be, DON'T JUST MOVE EACH OTHER'S STUFF! This kind of cat-and-mouse game will only cause friction.

If there's something of his that you *really* can't live with (such as his autographed Metallica picture), tell him—in a nice way, of course. "Sometimes you just have to say 'I really hate this picture. And I know you love it. And I love you for loving it. But for now, can we find a place to put it where I don't have to look at it 24/7?' " says Wolf. If you play your cards right, you may be able to negotiate the objectionable item out of a central living area or, better yet, into a closet. But don't expect your mate to give up without a fight. "We used to have a chair that Joe didn't want to throw away because it had been in his family for thirty years, but it had a huge hole in the seat and it was impossible to sit in," says Megan, twenty-six. "It took the dog pulling a dead rat from inside of the chair before I was able to convince him to toss it!" Also, be prepared to relinquish something sacred of yours should your man request it.

One final word of advice: Take the decorating process one step at a time, and don't rush into any big decisions. "Decorating can be stressful," says Wolf. "If you just moved *and* you're moving in together, you have a lot of changes going on at once. You're already stressed out enough." Wolf suggests giving yourselves a chance to settle in before you start shopping for a new couch or hitting Home Depot. Oh, and whatever happens, be sure to measure CAREFULLY before ordering a large piece of furniture such as a sofa or entertainment console. But that's a whole, other story . . .

Duplicate Items

Two sofas. Two beds. Two duvets. Two toasters. With all the overlap, your new pad is beginning to look a bit like Noah's ark. If you had a big basement or attic, you could simply store the "extras." But you don't. So now you're faced with a quandary: Should you dispose of them or fork out for a storage bin?

It's a tricky question. If you sell them or give them away, it'll be that much harder for you to piece your lives back together if things don't work out. On the other hand, if you pay to put them in storage, you'll end up draining your pocketbook. Besides, doesn't it seem a little doomsday to hold on to the overflow in case the two of you break up? What does it say about how much faith you have in your relationship?

Laura, thirty-one, of Detroit says she pondered many similar questions. Ultimately, she and Peter decided to part with most of their duplicate items. "To me, it was very symbolic of our commitment to each other," she says. "I didn't want to look at the relationship as impermanent, and as long as I was hanging on to my old mattress and blender, I felt like I was leaving myself an out." There were, however, a few things that they opted to hang on to, such as an end table and armchair that once belonged to Laura's grandmother. "We thought that we might be able to use them if we ever moved into a bigger place or purchased a ski condo," she explains. "Plus, they had sentimental value."

Our feeling: If you're hesitant to hock your stuff, you should examine your reasons why. Are you a pack rat? Are you holding on to it because it's valuable or for possible future use? Or are you having serious doubts about your relationship? If you're questioning your commitment (or his), we urge you to reconsider or postpone the move. It's never a good idea to enter a live-in relationship with negative vibes or wondering how you're going to get out of it. Chances are, your prophecy will be self-fulfilling.

Privacy, Please!

Even if you and your partner are lucky enough to live in a place with separate bathrooms and plenty of breathing space, you're bound to suffer some lack-of-privacy issues every once in a while. Some of it may be normal roommate stuff; the rest may have to do with sharing quarters with a love interest. Here's a rundown of some of the privacy problems that you and your new roomie may encounter.

Living Under a Microscope

One of the great things about being single is freedom. When you fly solo, you have the ability to make your own choices without answering to *anyone* (unless, of course, you still live with Mom and Dad). Then, you fall in love and discover how wonderful it is to be a twosome. While you're dating, you're still able to maintain your privacy and autonomy. But then you decide to shack up together, and suddenly your entire life is on display and possibly even subject to criticism.

"When I first moved in with my boyfriend, I felt like I was on an extended job interview," says Gayle, twenty-nine. "At certain times, I felt as though I was being scrutinized or judged." In other instances, when you're reminded to put the cap on the toothpaste or call if you're going to be late, you may begin to feel like you've moved back in with your parents. "For me, the hardest part is having to answer to someone who cares about my comings and goings," says Beth. "I'm very independent and fiercely private. I like to come and go as I please. You can't do that when you live with your significant other."

Relax. These emotions are typical during the living-together adjustment period, which usually lasts anywhere from six months to a year. In the beginning, you may feel a little stifled or like your partner's science project. Things should start to mellow out as you get used to each other's habits and gain more confidence in the relationship. Once you get in a groove, you'll both start to realize that you don't have to share every little detail of your lives, and you'll begin to feel in control of your own life again.

Special Shacking Up Getting Dressed Guidance

Do not seek fashion advice from your new roomie. True, he's the only one who really needs to find you attractive, and you may not have another prospective fashion consultant on the premises; but unless his name is Georgio Armani, he's probably not the best person to determine whether your shoes match your outfit. Also, be sure to overestimate the time that you'll need to get ready. Set his expectations low, and your boyfriend will be pleasantly surprised when you're dressed and good to go in under an hour. Remember, if you lead him to believe you're a zero-maintenance, fab-in-a-flash kind of gal, he'll act impatient whenever you do feel the need to primp. Last but not least, never, *ever* ask "Does this make me look fat?" unless you're attempting to pick a fight or a glutton for punishment. Despite their infinite wisdom, guys will answer this question incorrectly 95 percent of the time.

Your Beauty Secrets Revealed

We'd all like our men to think that we're natural beauties. Yep, that's right. All this gorgeousness is totally effortless. Until now, despite all your slumber parties and weekend getaways, you've managed to keep most of your beauty secrets under wraps. He probably still thinks you're a natural blond, and he has no idea about the eyebrow tweezing, the moustache waxing, or the self-tanning. So how are you going to get the job done when you're officially living together?

Unless you're on totally different schedules, it'll be challenging. Our advice: Rather than trying to hide it, be open about the fact that you get "a little help from your friends." It may take a while, but you'll slowly stop feeling self-conscious about it. If you're like Sophie, thirty-five, you'll break him in with a face mask, then graduate to the zit medicine and deep-conditioning treatments. Then, one day, maybe you'll come clean about the highlights and waxing. (If you end up pooling your money, it'll be hard to hide the two-hundred-dollar checks to your local day spa.) Once your secrets are out, it should be comforting to know that he loves you even if you're high-maintenance and capable of looking like Lyle Lovett on a bad hair day.

At a certain point, however, you may want to draw the line. Put it this way: There are some things that even your closest girlfriends and aesthetician don't need to see. For those truly private matters, put up the "Do Not Disturb" sign and get busy. "My girly time is spent behind a closed bathroom door," says Cindy. "I don't want him to see me plucking hairs on my chin or Lord knows where. It's my way of hanging on to a shred of dignity."

Why Can't He Just Leave Me Alone?

You've had a lousy day at the office, dealing with annoying coworkers and constantly ringing phones. You're in a bad mood, and you don't want to talk to anyone. At least when you had regular roommates or lived with your parents you could go into your room and shut the door. Now that you're sharing a bedroom, however, there is no door to hide behind or, even worse, your significant other gets hurt or offended when you act quiet or withdrawn.

It's nothing personal—sometimes you just need to be alone. But that can be easier said than done when you're living under one roof with your best friend, lover, and partner. How to ensure that you get enough solo time? "Both of you should schedule activities outside of the house so that occasionally you each get the place to yourself," says Rebecca, thirty-four, of Gales Ferry, Connecticut, who had to struggle to find alone time when she first moved in with Greg. Or, try to arrange your work schedules so that you're not always leaving and coming home at the same time, she suggests.

As we mentioned earlier, it's crucial for each of you to have an "escape hatch" in your house or apartment—a room or corner that you consider yours and can retreat to when you need some privacy. Setting boundaries is also key. If one of you needs some space, you should be up-front about it instead of trying to hide, acting distant, or getting irritated. Make it clear that you're not mad—you simply need a little downtime. You may also want to create some household rules like knocking before entering or trying not to interrupt each other when you're, say, using the computer, on the phone, or reading.

"My boyfriend is very good about letting me know that he loves me and wants to spend time with me, but that he also needs some time to himself," says Cameron. "He will often ask something like 'Do you mind if I go play now?' and if I mind, I say so. But I always weigh whether having him with me at that exact moment is more important than letting him release tension." When they do head to opposite ends of the house,

Cameron says she and her boyfriend check in with each other periodically to keep the connection. "Sometimes it's on the way to the kitchen to get a drink or the bathroom, but we wave and say hello, ask how it's going, and maybe kiss briefly," which is "tremendously satisfying to both of us," she says.

Space Invaders

Sometimes it's not your roommate who cramps your style but rather a litany of friends and family members who seem to appear out of nowhere. Maybe it's your boyfriend's brother who keeps dropping by unexpectedly and (surprise, surprise) just in time for dinner. You walk in to find your boyfriend and his buddies gathered in your living room to watch the big game. Or one of his old college friends is in town and wants to crash on your couch—for a week!

Alas, not everyone has the same need for privacy. Your mate may be a social animal while you're more of a loner. Perhaps he grew up in a big family and likes having a lot of people around and you were an only child. Instead of getting upset, try having an honest conversation about it. In a nonaccusatory way, explain why it bothers you when people pop by unannounced. Make a pact to ask each other before inviting anyone over, and try to discourage friends and family from coming by without calling beforehand. "If I'm bringing a friend home on the spur of the moment, I'll call so we don't surprise Alex in his boxer shorts," says Kate. Like Alex and Kate, you may also want to make a policy about overnight guests. "If someone will be staying for a few days, or it could interfere with the other person's plans in some way . . . we always consult with each other first," she adds.

The Girl's Take: "One Thing I Wish I Knew Before Moving In with My Boyfriend"

Six girlfriends sound off on their top living-together grievances.

- "He's a pack rat, and I despise clutter. It's hard to understand why an adult needs to collect matches, stamps, coins, half a set of golf clubs (he doesn't even play golf!), a huge ball made out of rubber bands–the list goes on." *–Beth, thirty-two*
- "Both the frequency and odor of his farts are unparalleled! I knew from day one that he was a farter, but I didn't know to what extreme!" *–Kristy, thirty-five*
- "When he lived in San Francisco, there was a water shortage (so he says), and he got in the habit of never flushing the toilet. Now, every time I go into the bathroom, I'm greeted by a big bowl of urine." *–Brook, twenty-nine*
- "The minute he walks in the door, he changes into shorts and takes off his shirt. It drives me crazy when he comes to the dinner table without a shirt. There's something about staring at chest hair and nipples that kills an appetite instantly." *–Sonya, twenty-nine*
- "He's a clothes slob–not in the way that he dresses, but in the way that he discards clothing after wearing it (which is wherever it falls) or even after washing it (crumpled up in the clothes hamper)." *–Amber, thirty-two*
- "If the TV is on, he's physically unable to concentrate on anything else." *–Jenny, twenty-eight*

Feeding Frenzy

Most of us associate food with pleasure. We want it (sometimes more than sex!), we need it, we often obsess about it. We also tend to have strong likes, dislikes, beliefs, and attitudes that go all the way back to childhood. In a nutshell, we have a lot of control issues that can make sharing a kitchen, well, a little sticky. Here, we've identified four common food-related bones of contention—and sought out advice on how to deal with them.

Problem #1: You do all the cooking, he doesn't lift a finger.

Maybe your boyfriend grew up in a household where Dad brought home the bacon and Mom fried it up in a pan. Or maybe he's just out of college and hasn't developed his culinary skills, or he's a long-time bachelor whose fridge contained nothing more than Budweiser and condiments. Whatever. The point is, you've fallen into the role of chef, sous chef, prep person, and dishwasher all rolled into one.

There's always the possibility that you like reigning over the kitchen. After all, cooking has its advantages. First of all, you get to control what you eat (and exactly how much oil and butter goes into it). Second, it can be relaxing, therapeutic, and a good excuse not to hit the gym. Third, you may love the way your boyfriend drools over your stuffed chicken breasts or homemade lasagna. But as much as you enjoy creating culinary masterpieces, let's be honest: All that kitchen work is time-consuming. And the truth is, you wouldn't mind getting a little help once in a while.

As you learned earlier in this chapter, you and your mate need to divide your household chores in a way that seems fair to both of you. If you feel like you've taken on more than you bargained for, you should talk to him and figure out how to make things more equitable. Don't be a martyr! You'll only end up feeling resentful. If your boyfriend can't cook, ask him to help more with clean up or grocery shopping, or by picking up take-out during the week. If he's not already doing so, remind him that he can earn some brownie points by showering you with compliments.

Problem #2: He thinks he's Julia Child.

Once upon a time cooking was considered woman's work. Then came women's lib, and we got busy with our careers, investing our money, and managing our lives. So some men started donning aprons and learning to do more than make toast or carve a turkey. Today, a lot of guys actually *like* to cook, which is great since it takes some of the burden off of us. However, when you attempt to share a stove, a sink, and a cutting board with your significant other, it can really open up a can of worms.

You've probably heard the expression "You can't have two cooks in the kitchen." You see, for many people, cooking is an art, a skill, and a source of pride. And we all have unique ways of doing things. One of you may chop while the other juliennes. You may like to use recipes while he prefers to wing it. You may clean up along the way while he saves it all for the end. And when we develop our own methods, we don't always like it when someone meddles with our system. "My boyfriend's very territorial when it comes to preparing meals," says Jane. "He can't stand to have me interfere or be in his way."

If your man fancies himself an accomplished chef, he may also try to offer tips or critique the way you cook. There you are, innocently chopping an onion or sautéing chicken when you suddenly feel like you're tuned into the Food Network. Stephanie describes a typical interaction with her live-in boyfriend, Jay. "We'll be making dinner and he'll say things like 'Let me show you how to cut that' or 'That's not the way you do it,' " she says. "It's like he thinks that I've never stepped foot in a kitchen before and *his* way is the *only* way!"

Aaargh!!! It's hard to say why it bothers us so much to get unsolicited advice from our mates. Perhaps we think that they're questioning our skills or trying to boss us around. "I find that it only annoys me when I feel like I know something about the subject," says Laura. Stephanie concurs. "I'm a novice skier, so I don't mind getting skiing tips from him. Tell me how to cut a carrot, however, and I want to chop his head off. I don't understand why he thinks that I'm incapable of slicing a vegetable!" But according to Tom, forty, of Los Angeles, we have it all wrong. "Guys simply like to share their knowledge," he explains. "It usually has nothing to do with trust."

It took a while, but Laura says she finally got it. "When my boyfriend gives me cooking tips, he's not criticizing *me.* I know he really means well. The key is to not take it personally," she says. No doubt, that can be easier said than done, even if your name is Deepak Chopra. We're all human! So if his how-to comments start to get to you, couples therapist Steven M. Sultanoff, Ph.D., suggests saying something like "This is the way I'd like to do it. You're welcome to do it differently" or "When you say things like that, I feel hurt." Try not to get mad or defensive, which will only raise your blood pressure and inspire Mr. Smarty Pants to continue.

Another thing that you and your mate can do to keep tempers from flaring: Take turns in the kitchen. That's how Stephanie and her man ended up resolving their differences. "He'll cook one night, and I'll cook the next night," she explains. "It gets a little lonely sometimes, but ultimately it's easier." Or, if you don't mind relinquishing your wooden spoon, you can try Jane's hands-off technique: "We had quite a few arguments about cooking initially, but now I've learned that the best thing to do is let him do all the kitchen work."

Problem #3: You're dying for salad, he wants a burger.

Eating is simple when you're single. When you're hungry, you eat. When you want frozen yogurt for dinner, you eat frozen yogurt. These days, however, you're part of a duo, and the two of you don't always fancy the same foods at the same time. "As a single girl, I rarely made myself a 'real' dinner," says Cindy. "More often, I would have a scoop of cottage cheese, then a few crackers and maybe an apple or a bowl of cereal. Now, I'm expected to eat a full meal, with a pork chop or chicken breast, veggies, bread—the works." Then there's also the timing issue. "Tom likes to have dinner at eight or eight-thirty, and I don't like eating so late. It's definitely a source of conflict."

So what's a couple with yin-and-yang food tastes to do? "We compromise," Cindy says. "We still have 'real' sit-down dinners, but we've lightened up the menu—soba noodles and veggies, fewer meat-based meals." In terms of timing, they either meet halfway—dining at seven or seven-thirty—or go every man for himself. "Our neighbors Jackie and Bill never share dinners during the week because their schedules and appetites just don't gel," Cindy adds. "On weekends, they make lovely gourmet meals and have a great time." If you like dining together during the week, Kelly, thirty-three, of Boston, suggests working to find a middle ground at home, then ordering food that your partner doesn't like when dining out.

Problem #4: You're getting fat.

Weight gain is often one of the unfortunate side effects of moving in with a guy. That's what can happen when you go from the land of Lean Cuisine to junk-food central. All of a sudden, you're surrounded by temptations such as ice cream, cookies, and chips. You may also find yourself eating hearty, "man-sized" meals or heavier foods in general. Our stay-slim suggestion: Go ahead and eat what he eats, just eat less of it. Accept the fact that you're going to have trouble keeping your spoon out of the Ben & Jerry's, especially after a glass of vino. Instead of trying to deny yourself, which usually backfires anyway, resolve to exercise more. A little added activity can do a lot to counterbalance the extra calories you're consuming. While you could keep doing all that extra housework, we recommend hitting the gym or taking a bike ride. Besides keeping your girth in check, it'll do wonders for your self-esteem.

Eight Ways to Prevent Domestic Disputes

Like many first-time shacker-uppers, we assume that you're anxious for advice that will help you maintain harmony on the home front. To follow are a few of our favorite insider tips, along with one or two of our own.

1. **Get a place with his-and-her bathrooms.** Depending on your budget, this may or may not be an option. But if you *can* afford it, we highly recommend finding an apartment or flat with more than one bathroom. The perks: You won't have to fight about who showers first or how much time you spend in the bathroom. He won't get on your back about using his razor or leaving makeup and hair products all over the place. And you won't ever have to look at much less tiptoe (yuck!) through the sea of short, dark hairs on his bathroom floor. "For me, having my own bathroom made a world

of difference," says Sharon, thirty-seven, of Philadelphia. "A private place with no pee on the toilet seat—what more could a girl ask for?"

2. **Hire a housekeeper.** This one is definitely worth splurging on, especially if you can't swing a place with two bathrooms. For the cost of dinner for two at a moderately priced restaurant, you can hire a professional to do your dirty work, including washing the dishes, mopping the kitchen floor, and scrubbing the shower. Even if it's just once a month, it'll help keep things in order and prevent who-does-more-around-the-house arguments. "It really isn't that expensive, and it sure does get rid of a lot of headaches," vouches Mike, twenty-eight, of New Orleans.
3. **Potty train.** If you have your own bathrooms, this tip may not apply. But if you're sharing a W.C., take note. After dozens of interviews with shacker-uppers, we've found that the porcelain god is a big source of angst for a lot of couples. To head off arguments (pun intended), we suggest forming a special set of dos and don'ts just for the commode. Topics to cover: A regular cleaning schedule, wiping up pee, leaving the seat up versus down, and flushing after use.
4. **Get a life.** Yes, there is such a thing as spending too much time together. If you and your boyfriend hang out 24/7, you're almost guaranteed to get on each other's nerves. So schedule regular evenings out with the girls, take a class, or join a book club. It will help boost your self-confidence and fill you with positive vibes. After a short break, your boyfriend's irksome habits may not seem so annoying.
5. **Don't snoop.** Now that you have full access to his private matters, including old love letters, photos of ex-girlfriends

and whatnot, you may find yourself tempted to take a little peek. One word of warning: DON'T. "During our first few weeks of living together, I made the mistake of snooping through Jake's mementos and letters," admits Kristy. "It really set us off on bad footing. It took a while for him to trust me after that. He still sometimes harks back to it." If you're concerned or curious about your boyfriend's past, ask him about it directly. It'll be faster and less risky than rifling through his stuff.

6. **Ask before calling the Salvation Army.** You may get bummed out at the sight of his La-Z-Boy recliner or collection of plastic cups left over from his college days. But you better think twice before disposing of them. Beth, a veteran cohabitor, learned the hard way. "I've gone to the extreme of throwing out one or two (well, maybe three) of [my boyfriend's] things," she admits. "Needless to say, that wasn't a smart move on my part." Beth says her problem came to a head the day she tossed his old plastic pencil holder, which was "impossible to dust." Her boyfriend threw a fit. "He felt that I wasn't respecting the things that were valuable to him," she explains, "and he wasn't sure if he could be in a relationship with someone who didn't respect him." The take-home lesson: "I'll never, ever, EVER throw anything of his out again, no matter how tempting," she says. "It's a mistake that I will never live down!"
7. **Have a garage sale.** Here's a great way to get rid of clutter, avoid fights about closet space, and make a few bucks in the process. Before posting the "For Sale" signs, however, just be sure that the two of you agree on what's up for grabs and what isn't.
8. **Don't pick zits.** You've probably heard this beauty advice a zillion times, and right now it may seem like it's

coming from left field. But there's a reason why we're including it. As you already know, popping a zit can turn a molehill into a mountain and sometimes cause scarring. If your zit-removal strategy backfires and you're left with an ugly red mark, you'll be filled with self-loathing. Low self-esteem will put you on edge and up your chances of getting into an altercation with your man. So keep your hands off and allow nature to take its course. Or, try one of the miracle topical solutions on the market—we just can't live without Buh-Bye and Boo Boo Zap, both from BeneFit.

The Guy's Take: "One Thing I Wish I Knew Before Moving In with My Girlfriend"

- "She never flushes when she pees. She says it's supposed to 'save water.' If I did these things, my mother would have beaten me with a pan." *–Jim, twenty-six*
- "Not only does she gab on the phone with her mother, but she shares things about us that I would not share with anyone, like details of our sex life. That totally weirds me out." *–Brad, thirty-four*
- "She leaves the toilet cover up. I know this is supposed to be a guy thing, but she does it, and I hate it. It's an open invitation for my toothbrush and miscellaneous things to fall in. And it leaves germs to fester in the air." *–Keith, twenty-seven*
- "That I would have a curfew whenever I go out." *–Mike, twenty-nine*

CHAPTER 5

Money Matters

Ugh. Who wants to think about paying bills and balancing checkbooks when you could be doing something fun like climbing into bed with your roommate, eating Thai take-out for two, and watching back-to-back episodes of "Sex in the City"? We agree: On the pleasure scale, money management ranks right up there with a visit to the dentist. But like regular dental exams and cleanings, it's something you need to do to ensure a strong and healthy fiscal future for you and your mate. Why? Eliminate dollar dilemmas, and you've gotten rid of one of the leading causes of couples' combustion.

We don't know if money is the root of all evil. But finances can make or break a relationship, says David Bach, author of *Smart Couples Finish Rich.* "People often think that love can conquer all," he says. "But when you combine two people with different views or habits, it can be a recipe for disaster." In fact, research shows that lovebirds argue more about finances than anything else. What's ruffling their feathers? As we touched on earlier, money means different things to different people. Depending on your outlook, it could buy freedom, security, and retirement at age fifty, or glitz, glamour, and a closet full of shoes *now.* To add fuel to the fire, many couples have conflicting attitudes toward spending, saving, investing, and keeping records.

The good news is a lot of ugly disputes can be avoided by discussing your differences and working together to develop a financial game plan that suits both of you. "By talking and planning, you can prevent money from becoming a major source of stress in your relationship," Bach says. Violet Woodhouse, Esq., a certified financial planner and author of the book *Divorce and Money,* says that the best financial tip that she can give couples who are moving in together is "discuss *everything*!!!" A little communication and planning today will leave you with plenty of bickering-free time tomorrow.

In this chapter, we'll tell you how to discuss your dollars, what questions make sense, and help you put together a joint spending plan to prevent financial fiascoes. We'll also offer a few important heads-ups about joint bank accounts and making big household purchases together. To make it less taxing, we've divided the chapter into two parts: Day-to-Day Finances and Your Financial Future. Those of you who are taking more of a wait-and-see attitude toward your relationship should focus on the first section—at least for now. If you're engaged or planning on being housemates for life, you should definitely tackle both.

Day-to-Day Finances

Your Basic Game Plan

Some of you may be wondering how you can have an economic summit when you haven't balanced your checkbook in, well, years, you're not sure what a 401(k) is, and your idea of fiscal responsibility is to avoid bouncing checks. Or maybe your definition of financial planning is having both a checking account *and* a savings account—yippee! Fine. So you're no Suze Orman. But now that you're making a romantic merger, you have a major impetus to (finally!) get your finances in order.

You may have gotten away with your bad habits or hands-off approach as a swinging single. However, financial carelessness simply won't cut it in a live-in relationship. We believe the future of your domestic partnership is contingent on both of you being honest, organized, and responsible with your own money as well as having a common fiscal strategy. On the next few pages, we'll explain how to finagle your daily finances as a shacking-up couple with minimum stress. Just follow our five steps to start down the path to pecuniary perfection.

#1: Discuss the Meaning of Money

Before you start counting the pennies in your respective piggy banks, we urge you to have a general powwow about money. Begin by talking about what money means to each of you and the attitudes learned or formed in your childhood homes. Next, discuss your individual spending styles. Would you consider yourself a spender or a saver? How much do you like to try to sock away every month? What are your views about credit and debt? How about your priorities? What do you prefer to spend your money on—rent/mortgage, furniture, home improvements, clothes/shoes, food, car, club memberships, stereo equipment, golf lessons, exotic vacations, or trips to see the folks? If the thought of spending fifty thousand dollars on a Porsche Boxster makes you cringe, say so! This certainly isn't the time to hide your true feelings or tell your mate what you think he wants to hear.

Don't have a coronary if you and your man aren't completely monetarily compatible. Unless the two of you were separated at birth, it's unlikely that you'll have all the same habits, attitudes, wants, and needs when it comes to money. And neither of you is right or wrong for feeling the way you do. There are lots of couples with conflicting financial priorities who have learned to accept their differences and find compromises. You should be fine as long as you keep working to understand each other's feelings and trying to meet halfway. FYI: Knowing your mate's history, values, motivations, and dreams should help you be more patient when it comes to pocketbook issues. Don't forget: The best time to have this kind of conversation is *before* you move in together and the arguing begins.

How do you tell him you're a spender or a saver if you're not even sure yourself? Answer this quick question: If you won a thousand dollars in a raffle tomorrow, what would you do with it? Would you, say, buy a fabulous new outfit, finally get that DVD player, or plan a weekend at the Four Seasons? Then you're a spender. If the first thing to roll off your tongue is pay off my student loan, open a high-yield CD, or start an IRA, you're a saver.

#2: Lay Your Dinero on the Table

The next step is to talk about where you both stand financially. We realize that some of you may feel uncomfortable with the idea of discussing your finances. Money can be a sensitive subject. You may be embarrassed to tell him about your puny salary or the fact that you're up to your earlobes in student loans (especially if he has a high-flying Wall Street job or a gigantic trust fund). Or, you may have a lot of property, investments, or cash in the bank that you're not anxious for anyone (much less a prospective gold digger . . . oops, we mean husband) to know about.

So exactly how much private financial info do you need to disclose? We don't know what Miss Manners would say, but here's our *Shacking Up* rule of thumb: You should tell each other about any income (including salary, dividends, and interest) as well as any major expenses, debts, or financial obligations (such as alimony, child support, or caring for an elderly relative) that will affect your ability to pay your share of the rent and other household expenses. However, if you have any long-term investments or savings that you never, ever touch (for example, your grandmother left you a few thousand dollars that you consider your "rainy day" fund), we don't think it's necessary to share these details with your mate—that is, until you've made a firm commitment to stay together forever.

There are several reasons why we do recommend being candid about your current cash flow. First, the obvious: You need to know how much money you have to spend before deciding where to live and determining a joint spending plan. Second, if you sign a lease or open utility accounts together, you could be held liable for your partner's share of the rent and other bills. Third, when you make the commitment to share an abode, you automatically gain a small stake in each other's finances. If you take it one step further and open a joint bank account or make any large purchases together, you'll have an even deeper stake. Lastly, having a clear picture of your partner's financial situation and ability to contribute to your love nest is key to preventing misunderstandings.

If there's a chance that you and your mate might tie the knot, it's extra crucial to come clean about any money drains or financial skeletons that you have. As long as you remain unmarried, you shouldn't be held accountable for each other's debts and liabilities (unless they're incurred on a joint bank or credit card account). But if you get hitched and live in a community-property state such as California or Texas, you could become legally responsible for your spouse's past due notices, even if you opt to keep your bank accounts separate. So if your man has a gambling problem or a habit of racking up the credit card bills, you conceivably could be the one who ends up paying. What's more, if you get married, your credit ratings will be instantly linked, which means any black marks on his financial record could taint yours—and vice versa. That kind of negative credit history could end up hurting you when applying for a car loan or a home mortgage. Again, we can't stress enough that honesty is the ONLY policy. A financial foundation laid with fibs, half-truths, and little white lies is destined to collapse as quickly as a house of cards.

To get the where-we-stand-financially talk rolling, you and your partner should each make a list of your current income sources and financial obligations, suggests Woodhouse. Or, better yet, take the extra time to put together a monthly cash flow statement (don't worry—it isn't as complicated as it sounds). This little exercise can help you take stock of your personal finances and show you exactly where your money is going. We've provided a worksheet on pages 125–128 that you can use as a guide. After you've completed the sheet, Woodhouse recommends sitting down and reviewing the basic facts and figures with your mate.

While you're comparing notes, you should also talk about how much you're each able and willing to spend on rent and other daily living expenses. Notice that we used the word "willing." Before you put your name on a lease, it's important to be realistic and practical about how much you feel comfortable spending. The last thing either of you wants to do is agree to contribute more money than you want to pay or can afford. Example: You're moving into your boyfriend's condo and don't feel you should be responsible for major household repairs or the satellite TV that you have no intention of watching. We're not saying that you should nickel-and-dime these things, but if you're going to be upset about forking out for them, you should speak now or forever hold your peace.

One last point: Before you consider pooling any of your money, purchasing a major asset together, or exchanging vows, Woodhouse encourages you to "do your due diligence" when it comes to your partner's financial history. She recommends obtaining credit reports from three different credit agencies, exchanging the information, then discussing it. While it may sound unromantic, it's the only way to ensure that your fiscal future isn't tied to a financial misfit, vows Yvonne, thirty-six, who got a credit report on Kurt without telling him (although we wouldn't recommend the secrecy). Three credit agencies that you may want to try: TRW (800–392–1122 or www.trweb-credit-reports-4-free.com), Trans Union (800–888–4213 or www.transunion.com), and Equifax (800–685–1111 or www.equifax.com).

Your Monthly Cash Flow Statement

The best way to get an accurate cash flow estimate is to track your spending for two straight weeks. From taxi fares to extrafoamy nonfat lattes, write down every cent that you spend and on what. Then, use your checkbook, bank statements, and pay stubs to figure out the rest. Don't forget to factor in annual expenses (things like your car registration or holiday gifts). To come up with a monthly estimate for these items, simply divide the yearly payment by twelve. For expenditures that fluctuate month-to-month (such as dry cleaning or haircuts), tally up expenses over a six-month period and divide by six to determine a monthly average. Once you've done your estimates and added up all your monthly expenses, you should calculate 10 percent of that figure and plug the number into the line that says "Stuff You May Have Missed." Hopefully, this will allow for any incidentals that you may have forgotten to list.

PLUSES

Monthly Income After

After Taxes and 401(k) Deductions _______ *

*If you don't have taxes withheld at work, or you're self-employed, be sure to add your tax payments to the MINUS column below.

Interest _______

Dividends _______

Regular "Extra" Income (including bonuses) _______

TOTAL PLUSES: _______

MINUSES

Home

Mortgage or Rent _______

Homeowner's/Renter's Insurance _______

Association Dues/Maintenance Fees _______

Cleaning Supplies/Expenses _______

Repairs/Maintenance _______

Landscaping _______

Property Tax _______

Other _______

Utilities

Heat/Hot Water ________

Electricity/Gas ________

Water ________

Phone ________

Cable TV ________

Internet Connection ________

Other ________

Auto/Transportation

Car Loan or Lease ________

Car Insurance ________

Registration ________

Maintenance ________

Parking/Tolls ________

Gas ________

Public Transportation ________

Other ________

Health

Medical/Dental Insurance ________

Prescriptions ________

Gym Membership ________

Unreimbursed Medical/Dental (co-pays, etc.) ________

Other (massages, therapy, etc.) ________

Food and Drink

Groceries ________

Eating Out ________

Snacks/Beverages ________

Personal

Cell Phone ________

Laundry ________

Dry Cleaning ________

Entertainment (movies, etc.) ________

Clothing ______

Cosmetics ______

Beauty (hair cuts, pedicures, etc.) ______

Gifts ______

Travel ______

Postage ______

Work Expenses (dues, classes, uniforms) ______

Other ______

Miscellaneous

Credit Card Payments ______

Loan Payments ______

Work Expenses (union dues, etc.) ______

Alimony ______

Child Support ______

Investments/Savings ______

Other ______

TOTAL MONTHLY EXPENSES: ______

STUFF YOU MAY HAVE MISSED: Increase your total monthly expenses by 10 percent ______

TOTAL MONTHLY INCOME: ______

Minus

TOTAL MONTHLY EXPENSES: ______ **and STUFF YOU MAY HAVE MISSED:** ______

Equals

TOTAL MONTHLY CASH FLOW: ______

#3: Decide Who Pays What

Once you've discussed the ins and outs of your bank accounts, you'll need to decide how to split your household expenses. If you and your mate are at comparable financial levels, you may choose to split your bills 50–50. But if there's a large income gap—let's say one of you picked the big-bucks business and one of you the not-for-profit track—you may want to use a pay-what-you-can plan, like Beth and Henry. "I didn't think 50–50 was fair since Henry makes so much more than I do," says Beth, thirty-two, an editor living in New York City. So she did a mathematical formula to come up with a 70–30 ratio, which Henry signed off on.

Another option would be to split household expenses such as rent and utilities down the middle, with the higher earner picking up the tab for "extras" such as weekend getaways and special splurges. If you do choose to split expenses unequally, we suggest sleeping on it, then talking about it again the next day. It's important that you both feel 100 percent comfortable with any arrangement. If you feel taken advantage of or, alternatively, like a "kept woman," you should rethink your decision. And if your financial situations change in the future, don't forget to sit down and review your individual household contributions.

#4: Draft a Prospective Spending Plan

Yes, we know it's a drag, but a monthly spending plan (a.k.a. a budget) can pay off in a couple of key ways. First, it can help you and your partner keep tabs on your spending (so you don't accidentally rack up your credit card bills and start accumulating debt—never a good thing!). Second, if you haven't already done so, it will force the two of you to clarify your goals and priorities. Face it: Some of us would rather travel around the world than dine on lobster and caviar. For others, saving for a house is more important than designer labels. By discussing how much you'd like to spend on everything from travel to groceries to telephone bills—and explaining why you feel the way you do—you may be able to avoid numerous misunderstandings. Or you may be happy to discover that you have similar preferences. For some of you, this may also be an opportunity to examine your spending habits and confer about how you can work together to cut back. For example, during their spending-plan discussion, our friends Stephanie and Jay determined that skipping Starbucks in the morning wasn't an option, but eating at home three nights a week was an easy way to save.

Assuming that you're not planning on combining all of your money (a move we definitely don't recommend—you'll find out why in a bit), you're actually going to need two plans. The first will be a joint spending plan consisting of expenses that you intend to share, even if you aren't splitting them evenly. The second is a personal spending plan made up of expenses that you'll be solely responsible for. An easy way to do it is to go down the "minus" column of your monthly cash flow statement and mark each item with a "J" for "Joint" or a "P" for "Personal." Then, list the J's and P's separately on two sheets of paper and fill in your dollar estimates to the right of each item. *Voilà!* Your dual spending plans are complete. Here's an idea of how the whole ball of wax might look.

JOINT SPENDING PLAN

	Total	You Pay	He Pays
Home			
Mortgage or Rent	______	______	______
Homeowner's/Renter's Insurance	______	______	______
Association Dues/Maintenance Fees	______	______	______

Cleaning Supplies/Expenses	______	______	______
Repairs/Maintenance	______	______	______
Landscaping	______	______	______
Property Tax	______	______	______
Other	______	______	______
Utilities			
Heat/Hot Water	______	______	______
Electricity/Gas	______	______	______
Water	______	______	______
Phone	______	______	______
Cable TV	______	______	______
Internet Connection	______	______	______
Other	______	______	______
Food and Drink			
Groceries	______	______	______
Eating Out	______	______	______

PERSONAL SPENDING PLAN

Auto/Transportation	
Car Loan or Lease	______
Car Insurance	______
Registration	______
Maintenance	______
Parking/Tolls	______
Gas	______
Public Transportation	______
Other	______
Health	
Medical/Dental Insurance	______
Prescriptions	______
Gym Membership	______

Unreimbursed Medical/Dental (co-pays, etc.) ______
Other (massages, therapy, etc.) ______

Food and Drink

Groceries ______
Eating Out ______
Snacks/Beverages ______

Personal

Cell Phone ______
Laundry ______
Dry Cleaning ______
Entertainment (movies, etc.) ______
Clothing ______
Cosmetics ______
Beauty (haircuts, pedicures, etc.) ______
Gifts ______
Travel ______
Postage ______
Work Expenses (dues, classes, uniforms) ______
Other ______

Miscellaneous

Credit Card Payments ______
Loan Payments ______
Work Expenses (union dues, etc.) ______
Alimony ______
Child Support ______
Investments/Savings ______
Other ______

If you're unfamiliar with the budgeting process, you may be wondering how you can put together a spending plan if you have no idea what your household expenses will be. How can you predict how much you'll spend on things like food and entertainment? Don't those things fluctuate month to month? Here's the thing: The main purpose of a spending plan is to establish or clarify goals and priorities. The dollar figures are really just rough estimates to shoot for. About three months or so after you move in together, be sure to go back and review these spending plans to make sure they're on target.

#5: Put It in Writing

Imagine for a moment that you're launching an exciting, new business with one of your friends. You wouldn't agree to be business partners if you didn't trust and respect her. But you're also going to be investing a lot of hard-earned money (not to mention time and sweat) in the venture. Perhaps you're even quitting your job or geographically relocating to make it happen. You'd be insane to do it without drawing up a written agreement to protect your interests, right? Well, since the financial risks are similar, we believe that it's smart to take the same practical precaution with your live-in relationship.

Ideologically, we don't like the notion of having a written agreement, either. We know it sounds negative and distrustful. But it's also an easy move that could prevent your shacking-up experience from turning into a financial nightmare. How so? By putting your pecuniary pact on paper, you'll be able to clarify who is responsible for what in terms of expenses. This can help avoid confusion after you move in together. It will also help eliminate any "he said, she said" if things don't work out between the two of you. To help you put pen to paper, we've provided a sample financial agreement in Chapter 6, along with some other legal need-to-knows. As the saying goes, better safe than sorry!

The Business of Banking

Should You Pool Your Money?

Until you're married with the legal protection that comes with a wedding, we strongly advise against merging all of your money. Actually, there are a bunch of reasons why we're against it, but we'll begin with the bleak break-up scenarios. We know you'd rather be optimistic about the future of your relationship. We, too, like to believe that everything will turn out peachy. But we're also aware of how challenging cohabitation can be. Look, you just never know what could happen. And if your relationship did flop, there wouldn't be any laws to protect your life savings. That means the two of you could end up in a costly legal battle over how to divide your money. Or, even worse, your boyfriend could clean out your account and hit the road, leaving you with a broken heart, a mountain of bills, and not a penny to pay them with. Unless you have a brother who will serve as a bounty hunter, you could be stuck trying to track him down and collect the cash yourself, without having much of a legal leg to stand on.

Some unmarried couples feel that pooling their money is a move that symbolizes their love and commitment to each other. We think it's an unnecessary risk that can only lead to problems. Just ask Sonya, twenty-nine: "When we moved in together, we immediately combined our assets, which led to arguments about who came to the relationship with the most debt or the most money." By joining your bank accounts, you essentially agree to give up full control of your money and share it with your partner. You're each responsible for activity in the account, including bounced checks and bank charges, notes Elizabeth S. Lewin, C.F.P., in her book *Financial Fitness for Living Together.* Worst of all, you lose your freedom to make spontaneous (and guilt-free) solo purchases. Can you imagine having to consult your partner every time you wanted to buy a cute pair of pants from Banana Republic? No, we can't, either.

Now, if you're looking for a way to simplify your household finances, you might want to consider opening a joint account to use for joint living expenses ONLY. Gayle and Dean of Wilmington, Delaware, are fans of this partial-share plan. "Every month or so, Dean and I each deposit a certain amount into our 'communal' account," says Gayle, twenty-nine. "We use that money for rent, utilities, groceries, cleaning supplies, and all other shared expenses." Personal expenses such as clothes, cell phone, gym membership, and dinner out with friends are paid out of their individual accounts, she adds. A "communal" account can make it easier to pay bills and purchase household essentials (like groceries and such). It can also mean less time spent writing each other checks or arguing about which one of you forked out for the Windex, garbage bags, and frozen pizza.

But let us remind you: There are risks whenever you commingle your money. If you decide to go the joint convenience account route, you can play it safer by keeping the amount of available funds at a minimum. In other words, only deposit as much cash as you'll need to cover about two months' worth of bills (plus a little buffer to prevent bounced checks). So neither one of you has instant access to cash, you can pass on the ATM option and get a debit card instead. You can also request an "and" designation on the account, which means that both of your signatures would be required in order for checks to clear. This way, you'd both have to participate in bill paying. In some cases, debit and ATM cards may not be an option on "and" accounts, so check with your bank. Also, be sure to open a non-interest-bearing account to avoid the hassle of accounting for earned interest at tax time.

One More Thing About Bank Accounts . . .

Before heading to your local bank, here's a quick primer on the three kinds of accounts that may be options for you. All three of these "ownership options" apply to anything with a legal title: houses, cars, savings bonds, stocks, mutual funds, and business interests. As you'll see, each one has its pluses and minuses.

1. **Separate.** If you open a separate account, the money belongs to you and you alone. If you die, the entire amount goes to your next of kin (not your significant other) unless you have a will specifying otherwise.
   The benefit: You have sole access to and complete control over your own cash.
2. **Joint tenants with a right of survivorship.** Unless you specify otherwise, this is the type of joint account you'll automatically be offered at most banks and brokerages. If you opt for it, you and your partner would be considered equal owners of the account even if you don't contribute to it equally. Either one of you could write checks, make withdrawals, or close the account without the other's knowledge. If one of you were to die, the survivor would become the sole owner of the account regardless of whether the deceased had a will. Requesting that all checks require two signatures to be cleared (done by asking for an "and" designation) would ensure that one of you can't write checks or close the account without the other's knowledge. This might make bill paying more time-consuming but would ensure that you're both aware of activity on the account.
   The benefit: Household purchases and bill paying made simpler.
3. **Tenants in common.** Generally, this type of ownership is available only on savings and brokerage accounts or title agreements. But you never know, so ask your bank. With this

type of joint account, percentage of ownership would be based on the amount that each of you contributes. In other words, if you deposit six thousand dollars and your partner puts in four thousand, the ownership split is 60-40. Unless you have a written OK from your partner, you can only withdraw your share of the account at any time. If you die, your share of the money goes to your next of kin unless your will specifies otherwise. Keeping copies of deposit slips, wire transfers, and cancelled checks is usually enough to track your individual contributions, but it can also be a pain in the you-know-what.

The benefit: Saving or investing as a team without running the risk of being totally wiped out.

Who Will Play Accountant?

To minimize confusion (and the risk of savings-draining late fees), it's probably better if one of you is in charge of paying household bills and, if you have a joint bank account, balancing the checkbook. Deciding who gets the job may be easy if one of you has more free time or is a financial wizard. Or if you both feel strongly about keeping the books, you could take turns on a bimonthly or semiannual basis. Either way, both of you should be kept in the financial loop and have quick, easy access to the records.

If you decide to open a joint checking account, you'll need to develop a system for keeping track of checks paid, ATM debits, and deposits. Peter and Laura, both thirty-one, use what they call the "candy dish" system. Every time Peter makes a transaction or writes a check from their communal account, he tosses an ATM receipt or written note into a crystal bowl that sits on Laura's desk. Then Laura, the household accountant, logs the transactions into their joint checkbook and the personal finance software program that she uses to monitor their money. "People tend to forget things, so I think it's crucial to have everything in writing," she says.

Don't forget: Only the accountants attending the Academy Awards have glamorous jobs. For the rest of the pencil pushers, monthly bookkeeping is usually quite tedious, and it can be just as time-consuming as washing dishes or folding laundry. So be sure that you factor it in whenever you start arguing about who does more work around the house.

Financial Faux Pas

Avoid these dollar don'ts to keep your bank account in the black *and* your relationship on the right track. You should never:

1. Agree to a household budget that requires you to live beyond your means.
2. Pay some or all of his expenses without a written IOU stating he'll pay you back in full.
3. Promise to cut back on your expenditures when you have no intention of giving up your fifty-dollar face cream or weekly massages.
4. Use your joint bank account to purchase items for your pad without consulting your partner first.
5. Contribute toward a major asset such as a car or a house that is in your boyfriend's name only. If you end up splitting up, it could be money down the drain!

Joint Retail Therapy (Cha-ching!)

Obviously, after you shack up together, you and your roomie are going to find yourselves at want for *something,* whether it's a new DVD player, set of matching dishes, coffee table, or place to sit other than his ratty, beer-stained sofa. Caution: Before you start slapping down your credit cards, we'd like to offer a piece of advice. As long as you're living in sin (as opposed to being lawfully bound), DON'T MAKE ANY MAJOR PURCHASES TOGETHER! By "major," we mean domestic goods (such as furniture, appliances, or electronic equipment) over two hundred dollars as well as big-ticket items such as a house, car, or motorcycle.

Our purposes for saying this may be fairly obvious, but we'll state them for the record. First of all, if your relationship collapses, you want to be able to split up quickly and without a lot of fuss over "who paid for what." Second, unless you have written documentation, you could have a hard time proving that you really did pay for part of your boyfriend's Jeep Cherokee or half of your new washing machine. Unfortunately for us, there are no state laws to protect unmarried couples when it comes to the division of joint property. Your married friends, on the other hand, have some legal guarantees. If they live in a so-called community property state, their joint assets would be split down the middle; in all other states, it would be up to a judge's discretion. But at least they would have Uncle Sam behind them.

If you have a bunch of things to buy, keeping your purchases separate shouldn't be too tricky. For example, you could purchase the kitchen table while he picks up the chairs. Or, you fork out for the DVD and he puts down his gold card for a new TV. Just be sure to keep a written record of who pays for what and save all of your receipts. Of course, all of this is assuming that you and your mate each have sufficient cash flow to make solo purchases. If you're both hurting for funds, there may be an essential piece of furniture or appliance that's out of the affordable price range of either one of you. In which case, you may have no other choice but to go in for it together.

If, for whatever reason, you decide to make any co-purchases, we strongly recommend drawing up a joint purchase agreement. This is a simple (we swear!) written document that states what will happen to the property if you break up or (God forbid) something happens to one of you. Sure, these sorts of dismal scenarios are a bummer to discuss. But doing so could save you a lot of vicious wrangling if your relationship were to come to a screeching halt. All you need to do is agree to your terms and document the basics—how much you paid for the item and who will get first dibs on it in the event of a split. No fancy language or law degree required! If you don't believe us, check out the joint purchase agreement sample on page 168.

If you don't have written agreements for joint purchases, be sure to keep a paper trail (i.e., receipts, credit card bills, and cancelled checks) to show who paid what. This is important not only in the event that you and your man end up going your separate ways; you may also need the information for insurance purposes if, say, a pipe bursts and destroys all of your new Crate and Barrel furniture and other precious belongings. Keep all the info together in a file for quick, easy access in the event of an emergency.

Joint purchase agreements are great for items that don't break the bank or require legal titles, such as sofas, coffee tables, TVs, and refrigerators. But what about major purchases, like a condo, house, or car? If you disregard our advice and decide to buy a major asset together, you'll need a more detailed co-ownership agreement to protect your investment. Detail to come in Chapter 6.

Shacking Up Tip

Have as many bills—for example, utilities, cable TV, and renter's or homeowner's insurance—as possible directly debited from your joint checking account. The fewer checks to write, the more time for fun!

Joint Credit Cards

No, no, NO!!! Please don't make the mistake of opening a MasterCard, Visa, or American Express account together. Here's the reason: With a joint credit card, you are both equally responsible for EVERY SINGLE CHARGE on the card. So if your boyfriend goes on a spree at Circuit City and can't pay up, the creditors could come after you. And, as we said previously, one bad credit patch could affect your credit history for years to come.

You Bought WHAT?: Four Ways to Stop Spending Spats

Maybe your motto is "Shop 'til you drop!" and his is "A penny saved is a penny earned." Or maybe it's the other way around–who knows? What we do know is this: If you and your mate don't see eye-to-eye on spending, your shacking-up lives could start to resemble an episode of "I Love Lucy." Remember how the Ricardos were constantly arguing about money (and Lucy's schemes to come up with bucks to pay for her spending sprees–*aiyayai!)?* And then there were their landlords Ethel and Fred Mertz. Fred was a total tightwad, and it used to drive Ethel crazy! Anyway, our point is, different spending habits can be the source of major tension in a relationship. Unless you address them, they could end up driving you in opposite directions. Here are four ways to minimize the financial friction.

Talk shop. No, we're not telling you to alert your boyfriend to the latest sale at Bloomingdale's or the fabulous blouse you spotted at Burberry. We're simply advising you to sit down and discuss your spending disparities. To avoid ongoing animosity, you must be clear with each other about your priorities and sore spots. What's important to you? What drives you crazy? Once you're aware of each other's needs and sensitivities, vow to accept and respect them, even if you question the logic.

Take a concession stand. As with most areas of disagreement, compromise is essential. For example, if your man is economically minded (read: a total Fred Mertz) when it comes to grocery shopping, you could make an effort to buy store brands and use coupons whenever possible. If you absolutely must have your favorite (and more expensive) brands of laundry detergent and shampoo, those could be your mate's concessions.

Set spending limits. An easy way to prevent spending arguments is to establish a dollar limit for shared expenses. Our friends Kelly and Ben, for example, agreed to check with each other before making any household purchases over $150. Or, you might decide to put a spending cap on things like restaurant meals or groceries.

Get a referee. If you and your mate have trouble discussing money or can't agree on a spending plan, you may want to get the aid of a qualified financial advisor. Many couples find it easier to hash things out in the presence of a neutral third party. A money manager can't teach you fundamental communication or conflict resolution skills, but he or she could help you establish an open dialogue, pinpoint problem areas, and determine common goals.

Your Financial Future

Once you and your man have decided that you're in it for the long haul, you'll want to start talking about your future financial plans and goals, like building your nest eggs, paying off your debts, or saving up for a house and possibly (good grief!) your future children's education. Or perhaps you've been fantasizing about buying a new SUV, renovating your kitchen, taking a leave of absence from your job and traveling around the world, or starting your own business. All those nifty things. There's so much that you're yearning to do. If only you had the dollars to do it!

We realize it can be hard to think about saving for the future when you're so overwhelmed with the "now." After all, unless you have a too-good-to-be-true salary, a cushy trust fund, or tons in the bank thanks to stock options, you probably (like most of the twenty- and thirtysomethings we know) feel perpetually strapped for cash. Every time you open your mailbox, all you see are bills, bills, bills! For starters, you have to fork over a big chunk of your paycheck every month for rent. Then there are your car and insurance payments. Your gym membership. Cell phone. Dry cleaning. Parking tickets (eek!). Hideous bridesmaid dress. The cost of going out for dinner, seeing a movie, or having margaritas with the girls. And let's not forget that cute pair of BCBG pants and leather jacket that you simply can't live without. The green stuff just seems to fly out of your pockets! It's enough to make your head spin like Meryl Streep's character in the movie *Death Becomes Her.*

There's certainly something to be said for living in the moment. But the reality is, if you don't plan for the future, you could spend more time worrying about money than enjoying your golden years. Without a clear financial road map, it'll be that much harder for you and your mate to get ahead financially, dig yourselves out of debt, and live your dreams. Bottom line: Whether you have aspirations of becoming the next Donald Trump (although we don't recommend it—could you live with that hair?) or simply living a low-key lifestyle in a small apartment, you need money to do it. That's why we're urging you to stop procrastinating and start taking control of your dough.

For many of us, retirement seems like nothing more than a very, very distant light at the end of the tunnel. But your financial future is about so much more than your far-off dreams of no longer working nine to five. It also relates to your hopes and dreams that are right around the bend—next week, next month, or next year. We're talking about saving up to buy "real" furniture (bye-bye futon), a plane ticket to your best friend's wedding, or a mai tai–filled Hawaiian honeymoon (so you can finally say you got lei'd in Maui). For many of you, we also mean working to pay off your debts and setting aside some cash for emergencies, and not the fashion kind.

Believe us, as two fun-loving, semi-reformed shopoholics, the last thing we want to do is give you something else to stress about. Instead, we want to help you stop worrying about your Visa bill or feeling guilty for not saving enough. By investing a little time and effort into learning how to manage your money, you can start making up for your sins and get your derailed finances on track. Now that you're sharing a roof and basic living expenses with your mate, there's more than your own bank balance and sanity at stake. Your financial transgressions and oversights could have an impact on his quality of life.

We're not trying to lead you to believe that this financial planning stuff is a snap. It can be kind of complicated, particularly if you and your partner have contrary financial attitudes and goals. That's why you may want to consider getting hands-on help from a certified financial planner or advisor. A savvy planner can help you identify problems, establish priorities, and develop a strategy for reaching your financial objectives. "Although a [financial] counselor can't be a therapist, a good one can be sensitive to the needs of each [person] and can try to find a middle ground on the financial issues you're grappling with," says Eric Tyson, M.B.A., in his book *Personal Finance for Dummies.*

However, you must be very careful when choosing a financial advisor. Tyson warns against those who earn commissions on sales of financial products or charge a percentage of the assets that are being managed or invested, mainly because he questions their objectivity. He believes hourly based planners are a better bet, though you should still be wary about who you're hiring. Word of mouth is probably the best way to find the right person for the job. Or you could try contacting the National Association of Personal Financial Advisors at (888) 333–6659 or www.napfa.org. (Fees can range anywhere from fifty dollars to several hundred dollars per hour.) But never accept anyone's recommendation blindly, Tyson urges. You should always do a background check to make sure a prospective advisor is up to snuff. Likewise, you should try to learn as much as possible about financial planning before talking to anyone. Otherwise, how will you know whether you're getting good advice?

Whether you're thinking of hiring an advisor or taking a do-it-yourself approach, your first step should be to do your homework. We'd love to tell you everything you need to know about saving and investing, but we'd need several hundred pages to do it. There are a ton of financial guides in the bookstores, but here are a few that we feel comfortable recommending: *Personal Finance for Dummies* by Eric Tyson; *Smart Couples Finish Rich* by David Bach; *The Road to Wealth* by Suze Orman; and *Get a Financial Life* by Beth Kobliner. Or, for the most up-to-date info, log on to a website such as www.moneycentral.com or www.ivillage.com/money.

Note: Unless you have a very long attention span and a generous supply of No-Doz, all of this financial mumbo jumbo can be hard to muddle through. There's a lot of information to absorb, and it isn't always easy to break down into bottom-line terms. In most cases, the material isn't geared toward shacking-up couples, either. To help, we've put together some basic guidelines for you to follow. We like to think of them as the Cliff's Notes version of financial planning for youngish, carefree cohabiting types like us. Here are the five things we think you and your partner absolutely must do to secure a rosy financial future for two.

DO Tell Each Other Everything

Now that you've established that you're fully committed life partners, should you reveal that rainy day account or amazingly large 401(k) from your last job? We think so. If you're planning on a long, happy future together, it isn't a wise idea to harbor *any* financial secrets. Can you imagine how you'd feel if you discovered your mate's hidden gold mine after you'd been chipping in extra because he claimed he was broke? Not good! Telling all doesn't mean that you have to dip into your cash stash or transfer your assets into his name. (And if he insisted that you do so, we'd worry!) In our opinion, there's nothing wrong with keeping your savings separate even if you decide to get married. Lots of couples choose to do this so they both have their own money to spend or in the event that they end up in divorce court. Personally, we like the idea of having freedom and a sense of security. But the decision is, of course, up to you.

DO Set Individual and Joint Goals

Talking about your financial plans and goals is important for several reasons. First, it can help you understand your partner better and clarify your individual priorities and objectives. Second, it may help you get your rears in gear in terms of saving and investing. (We've found it easier to pass on impulse purchases and day spa outings when we're picturing ourselves on the front porches of our beautiful, new houses!) Third, knowing your specific financial objectives and time frames for achieving them may help you determine what kind of investment strategy is best for you. All in all, goals can help you keep your eyes on the ball and your future plans on track.

We like to compare goal setting to planning a road trip. Your first task is to consider all the places that you could go and choose a destination. Then, you look at a map and figure out which routes to take (sorry—no option of using MapQuest or Yahoo directions). To do this, you must decide whether you want to take the slick superhighway (speedy but risky) or drive along back roads (safe but slow).

In terms of your financial goals, there are three degrees of planning that you and your mate need to consider: short-term, mid-term, and long-term. Short-term goals are those you hope to obtain in less than eighteen months, such as saving up for a state-of-the-art laptop, living room furniture, or one of those cool, new Vespas (an Italian motorscooter, in case you live in the boondocks). Mid-term goals are things you'd like to achieve in the next eighteen months to five years—think putting a down payment on a house, paying off a student loan, or buying a car. Long-term goals are no-time-soon big-ticket expenses like retirement at age fifty, paying off your mortgage, your future children's educations, or building your dream home.

Chances are, you and your partner will not have all the same financial objectives. Therefore, you will need two sets of goals—individual and joint. According to Elizabeth S. Lewin in her book *Financial Fitness for Living Together,* "Your goals reflect your value system—usually the attitudes you were raised with. For most of us, values are based on what is desirable and worthy." It's OK to want different things. For instance, you may both be eager to buy a home and build your nest eggs, but one of you may be more interested in renting a ski condo for the winter. The result: You'll have the same mid- and long-term goals but different short-term goals. But if your goals are drastically different or conflict with one another's, you must talk and come to an understanding to prevent a financial planning disaster. "If you have significantly different values and don't work through them, you probably won't stay together," warns veteran financial planner David Bach.

Once you've pinpointed your individual and couple goals, you should work together to determine time frames and specific dollar amounts for achieving them. To do it, ask yourselves the following questions. What do we want? How much money will we need? And when do we want to see it happen? For example, to buy a new computer, you'll need approximately three thousand dollars. You'd like to purchase it six months from now. That means you'll need to save five hundred dollars per month in order to do it. You may already have some money stashed in a savings account that you can put toward this goal. After you factor in those dollars, you can calculate how much more you need to set aside per month or paycheck.

Unless you have Katie Couric's salary or won the Powerball mega-jackpot, you'll probably have a limited amount of money to work with. Therefore, you'll need to prioritize. What are your primary goals? If you're getting married in a year and paying for a chunk of the reception, you and your partner may want to put that ahead of saving for a dream home. Or perhaps you'll decide getting the heck out of that tiny apartment and into a house is more important than buying new furniture or taking a romantic trip to Italy. Here's where your personal values will come into play again. You should both be clear about why you feel the way you do. That insight should help you be more accepting while you're debating how to spend (or not spend) your hard-earned bucks.

After establishing your goals and priorities, we recommend putting them in ink. For whatever reason, seeing our objectives on paper helps make them seem concrete and real. Besides, you'd have to be Alan Greenspan to keep all those numbers straight in your head. Be sure to sit down and review your financial objectives about once a year or so. And don't forget to modify it as your lives or priorities change and, one by one, you meet your goals.

DO Build a Crisis Cash Stash

A crisis cash stash means having enough readily accessible cash (or cashlike securities) to pay your living expenses for at least three months. (Note: Some finance experts recommend stashing away more if your job is unstable, you're bereft of other savings like a 401(k) or IRA, and you don't have friends or family members who could help you out in a pinch.) We think it's crucial for both of you to have this kind of backup in case you get sick, lose your jobs, or face any other sort of financial calamity. If you're splitting rent and other living expenses, you'll both have a big problem if one of you suddenly can't pay up. So before you start investing in long-term CDs or government T-bills, be sure to put enough cash aside to cover any emergencies.

DO Work on Paying Off Your Debt

Debt is one of those crazy words that brings fear to most of us ordinary mortals and joy to many CFOs. How come? Debt can be both good and bad. That's why, if you're in debt, you need to consider the type of debt. First, there is "good" debt—or the type used to finance a long-term investment, such as buying a house or paying for business school. This debt is OK because it usually has lower interest rates (say, 8 percent or less) and may be tax deductible. Plus, if you play your cards right, it can pay off in the long run. For instance, it could allow you to borrow money at low cost so you can invest other money at higher rates of return. For example, Jane gets an unexpected year-end bonus of ten thousand dollars. She could use it to pay off part of her mortgage (with a 5 percent interest rate). Or, she could invest the money in a high-performing mutual or index fund with an average return of 10 percent. The difference between the investment return (10 percent) and the mortgage rate (5 percent) is an additional 5 percent of income. A good trade-off.

Unfortunately, the majority of debt out there is what we consider the bad kind. In our book, "bad" debt includes anything with high interest rates (say, more than 14 percent) and no potential long-term advantages. Look at the interest rate charged by the bank issuing your Visa or MasterCard. We did and found rates as high as 18 percent. Look at a store charge card, and you might discover even higher rates. (For high-risk credit card customers, we've heard of interest charges up to 35 percent.) This kind of debt can be a huge financial drain if you don't pay it off quickly. Consider our friend Grace. After she got a preapproved platinum card, she went on a wild spending spree, racking up almost $10,000 worth of charges. Unfortunately, Grace only has $200 of expendable income to put toward the bill each month. So instead of paying $10,000 for her splurges, she'll end up paying a total of $22,800 over the next nine and a half years. How come? Ten thousand dollars at a 20 percent annual interest rate equals $2,000 per year. That means out of Grace's $200 monthly payment, only $33 goes to pay her original $10,000 debt. The rest are interest charges! If you said "yikes," we agree.

Clearly, if you have any high-interest debt, it makes much

more economical sense to pay it off as soon as humanly possible, even if you need to use your savings or borrow money at a low interest rate (think home equity loan) to do it. Why? The longer those big credit card bills keep rolling in, the more interest you'll wind up paying. Our suggestion: Pick up Suze Orman's *The Road to Wealth* or one of the other books we mentioned on page 145, and start learning how to effectively manage your debt.

Despite the depressing scenario we just presented, debt isn't the end of the world, especially if you and your partner work on tackling it together. So sit down and talk to each other about your debt problems, both past and present. Figure out a strategic plan for getting and keeping yourself out of the red. Debt is a demon that faces, or has faced, many of us. But a zero balance can be in your future if you band together and take a proactive approach.

DO Save and Invest for the Future (But Keep It Separate!)

After you've built your crisis cash stash and addressed your debt issues, it'll be time to talk about saving and investing. As we've mentioned (over and over again), we don't recommend combining your savings as long as you remain unmarried. It isn't that our glasses are half empty. We're merely trying to help you avoid unnecessary spats, protect yourselves from creditors and anyone who might sue you, and keep your taxes from getting unbearably complicated (as if you can imagine them being any more complicated!). No matter how much you trust each other, we feel it's best to keep the bulk of your bucks in your own names.

Since we've already beaten into your head the importance of keeping your savings separate, we'll skip ahead to the different investment options out there. As you know, procrastinating isn't going to help you achieve your goals. Nor is hiding your money under your mattress. To make your dollars grow, you and your partner both need to understand your options and learn how to get invested. Keep in mind that this isn't a how-to manual on striking it rich in the stock market. It's simply a quick cheat sheet to help you get started. For details on how to start building your fortune (or keep from falling any further behind), check out one of the previously listed books or websites. In the meantime, here's a rundown of the basic investment opportunities that you'll have to choose from, each with their own potential risks and rewards:

- Passbook savings and money-market accounts
- Certificates of deposit (CDs)
- Retirement accounts (IRAs, 401[k]s, and pension plans)
- Government securities or bonds
- Corporate bonds
- Stocks and mutual funds
- Real estate
- Small businesses
- Collectibles (stamps, coins, and the kind of stuff you see on the "Antiques Roadshow")
- Annuities (tax-deferred, interest-bearing "savings" accounts sold by insurance companies).

When deciding how to save or invest, you should consider your financial goals and time frames. Your short-term goals will require quick, easy access to cash, so you may want to invest in relatively risk-free, liquid assets like a money-market account, a shorter-term CD, or an easily redeemable mutual fund. Mid-term goals offer you a wider range of choices: mutual and other investment funds, stocks, short- to intermediate-term bonds, and longer-term CDs. As far as your long-term goals go, you might want to sink some money into a longer-term investment or try something slightly more risky (since you won't need the money anyway, you'll have time to try to recover from a loser investment). In any case, longer-term bonds, higher-risk mutual funds, stocks, real estate, small businesses, collectibles, and annuities are all options you could consider. Whatever you choose, don't put all of your eggs into one basket. Sure, Uncle Vinnie's new restaurant venture may sound like a sure thing, but if it goes belly up, you'll lose everything.

Which brings us to another key factor in deciding where to put your money: RISK. As a basic rule, the lower the risk, the lower the rate of return. That's why supersafe savings accounts, money-market funds, and government bonds generally offer much lower payoffs than other investment vehicles such as stocks or corporate bonds. Invest in a dot.com and you may see double-digit returns on your money, but you may also watch the stock price plummet before your eyes. When it comes to investing, everyone's risk tolerance is different. Just because you wouldn't hesitate to go rock climbing or bungee jumping doesn't mean you'll be comfortable taking chances with your dough. If putting your money into a high-risk stock will leave you tossing and turning at night, you may want to stick to safer options. Your best bet: Spread your investments around so you have a mix of risk or, as they say on Wall Street, a diversified portfolio.

Finally, even if you're saving and investing separately, you and your partner can still work together to sock some cash away. Presuming that you lowered (or will lower) your cost of living by moving in together, you can take the excess dollars and plunk them straight into your savings accounts. (If you start doing this from day one, you won't miss the money since the dollars never made it into your wallet.) Instead of feeling like you're sacrificing, you'll watch your bank balance go up with each passing month. If you can't resist the temptation to spend the extra bucks, consider having a portion (say, 5 or 10 percent) of your paycheck deposited directly into a savings or investment account.

Another (somewhat obvious) joint saving strategy is to cut back on your living expenses. Hold on—before you write off the idea of scaling back, hear us out. There are lots of ways to reduce your monthly expenditures without feeling like you're leading a no-fun, no-frills, impoverished existence. To figure out how, look at your monthly cash flow statement and determine where you can do a little trimming. Then, reconfigure your spending plans accordingly. To follow are eight painless cost-cutting strategies that have worked for us, and can work for you, too:

1. Cancel subscriptions to magazines that you can live without (and don't have time to read anyway).
2. Turn off the lights when you leave the room or house. (Trust us: This can add up, especially if you live in an energy-crunched state like California.)
3. Turn down the thermostat at night. Why pay for central heat when you have a male radiator to keep you warm?
4. Be a savvy grocery shopper. You can save big bucks by comparing prices and buying in bulk.
5. Ask your parents to call you back so phone calls home are on their dime.
6. Brownbag your lunch. We tried it and managed to save between three and six dollars per day. It doesn't sound like a lot at first, but over the course of a month, the savings added up to more than one hundred dollars. Besides, bringing lunch to work is so much healthier than eating fast food, cafeteria glop, or junk from a vending machine.

7. Smuggle candy, popcorn, and sodas into the movie theater.
8. BYOB. To up their profits, restaurants often jack up the prices on wine and booze—in some cases, they may be more than doubled. To avoid paying thirty dollars for a fifteen-dollar bottle of Syrah, bring your own and, if necessary, pay the small corkage fee.

Simple, Silly Savings

We all know the overwhelming joy of finding a five, ten, or *(ding, ding, ding! jackpot!)* twenty-dollar bill in a coat pocket. While we don't suggest hiding green stuff throughout your closet, we do have three super-easy savings schemes that you may want to try.

Coin toss: Every night, throw your change into a big bowl or jar. Count it after six months, and you may be surprised to find that you've got more than a hundred dollars' worth of coins. Stick them into a savings or investment account and watch them grow.

Dollar drop: Instead of change, set aside at least one "bill" every day. Make it a one-dollar bill, a five-dollar bill, or whatever is in your wallet. Tally it up after three months. You can think of this as "fun money" for a weekend adventure, his-and-her massages, or a new, battery-operated blender (so you can have frozen drinks wherever you go).

Team tariff: Name the one thing that drives both of you crazy. Is it dirty dishes in the sink? Foul language? Habitual tardiness? Charge the offender a tariff and save a few bucks while learning a lesson. Despite what they say, when money is involved, you can teach an old dog new tricks.

The Bottom Line

One of the best ways to prevent finances from becoming a relationship wrecking ball is to keep an open dialogue. "The reason couples fight about money is that they don't know how to proactively talk about it," says David Bach, author of *Smart Couples Finish Rich.* "They tend to discuss it at the worst possible times, such as when they're paying bills, in bed, or in the car." By planning "money dates," Bach says that you can avoid a lot of the arguments and resentment that dollar dilemmas can cause. So schedule a monthly meeting to confer about day-to-day issues such as bills, household purchases, and bank balances as well as future goals, saving strategies, and investment options. To minimize headaches and stress, get and stay on top of your financial games and don't stop communicating.

Oh, and one last thing before we get off our high horses. If you do decide to tie the knot, there will be a few more scintillating financial matters, such as a prenuptial agreement and taxes, to go over. Be sure to check out Chapter 8 if you and your partner hear wedding bells ringing. Remember, your financial future is in your hands. You can achieve your goals and overcome any pocketbook problems with planning and patience. So be sensible and savvy, and you and your mate will have smooth sailing over the silver, and gold, seas.

CHAPTER 6

Legalese for Live-Ins

We've tried, really we have, to make this chapter a page-turner. Please accept our apologies in advance if it isn't quite as riveting as a John Grisham novel. But boring or not, we believe the information on these pages is need-to-know shacking-up stuff. So pour yourself a supersize, high-octane cup of java and start reading. If nothing else, you could pick up some interesting trivia for your next cocktail party!

Whoa, slow down, some of you may be thinking. Part of the reason for living in sin is to *avoid* any messy, legal entanglements, right? Why do you have to worry about all this "Law & Order" and "Court TV" gibberish? Well, we probably should remind you that one of us is a lawyer. Therefore, we've seen what happens when people fail to consider the legal ramifications of their actions. On a positive note, the scales of justice can also help protect us. Knowing our legal responsibilities and options is the best way to ensure that we don't lose in the game of love.

Picture your handsome hunk carrying you over the threshold of your new place. Now, imagine the newlyweds across the street doing the same. You may think, *We're just like them! Only we don't have piles of wedding gifts to take back.* However, there are more important differences than having to stand in line at the return counter. Without a marriage license, you don't have all of the legal protections and rights that your smug married friends have.

In this chapter, we've provided you with the basic legal info you need to keep up with those newlyweds and protect yourself. We realize that, to some of you, it may seem like overkill. But keep in mind that we're looking out for your pocketbook and your future. So give our ideas some thought. Talk to friends and family members who are attorneys. Dig deep down inside to see if you have any qualms or serious concerns about your partner. While every suggestion may not appeal to you, you may be able to use the details provided to determine the legal avenues that best fit your unique relationship.

We touched on some of these legal issues in prior chapters: joint purchase agreements, leases, and who's-paying-for-what contracts. On the following pages, we'll expand on these points and provide sample agreements to work with. Common law marriages and palimony are two well-known (but rarely understood) living-together concepts that we'll define and clarify. We'll explain the importance of a shacking-up contract (a.k.a. a cohabitation agreement) and help you put pen to paper. Finally, we'll tell you about other legal documents that could help safeguard you in the event of a worst-case scenario.

Shacking Up Trivia

Believe it or not, fornication—that is, voluntary sexual intercourse between unmarried people of the opposite sex—is still against the law in twelve states. Cohabitation is listed as a crime in ten states. So have fun counting up the number of times you've engaged in an illegal act!

Shacking Up Contracts

One of the most important lessons we've learned throughout our lives is to "put it in writing." Whether it's a promise of employment or a rental agreement, you want to get it in black and white to be sure that you've sealed the deal. Why should your new living situation be any different?

As you know, laws exist to help dissolve a marriage and equitably divide a married couple's assets. The same laws rarely exist for couples who are shacking up. This could mean protracted legal battles and relying on the mercy of the court to do the right thing instead of having established legal guidelines to rely on. Does that mean you're left hanging in the wind should you and Mr. Not-So-Right split up? Not necessarily.

Maybe you remember the actor Lee Marvin from *The Dirty Dozen* and *The Caine Mutiny.* Anyway, he's famous in the legal world for a lawsuit with a former live-in girlfriend. Here's what happened: Lee shacked up with and supported Michelle for years. When they broke up, Michelle sued, claiming that Lee had promised to take care of her for the rest of her life. Because contracts between lovers were illegal at the time, Michelle lost in court. But the rest of us won since, as a result of the decision, the California Supreme Court later ruled that shacking-up couples could enter into enforceable written contracts. That's when cohabitation agreements came into being.

Today, these shacking-up contracts (our own term for them) are valid in nearly every state as well as the District of Columbia. The one exception: Illinois. If you live in the Prairie State, check with an attorney or legal aid office to see what your options are. Should you reside in a state that still lists cohabitation as illegal, check with an attorney or the bar association to make sure your agreement is worded in a way that will be enforceable.

Ten States Where Shacking Up Is Still a Legal No-No

Arizona	New Mexico
Florida	North Carolina
Massachusetts	North Dakota
Michigan	Virginia
Mississippi	West Virginia

So what exactly is a cohabitation agreement? It's a legal document that states both of your intentions with respect to property, purchases, and expenses while living together, and what would happen if you decided to move on. It's a way to add some structure to your live-in relationship and protect your property and interests in the event of a split. According to Debra S. Weisberg, Esq., a matrimonial attorney in Morristown and Short Hills, New Jersey, a cohabitation agreement can eliminate controversy and even potential litigation in case of a breakup. By putting everything in ink, you can part gracefully on terms you agreed to when you were level-headed, not frothing venom at the sight of the no-good loser.

You can also make sure you're clear with each other from the get-go. There's always a chance that you could miscommunicate your intentions—not with any ill will or malicious intent, but simply because you misunderstood one another. (Remember, there can be three versions of every event—yours, the other guy's, and what actually happened.) Putting it in writing before you move helps ensure that you're on the same page. Reality is, there's no such thing as a handshake agreement in business today. The same is true for love, romance, and shacking up.

But a cohabitation agreement is about much more than just you versus him. Having a written agreement is also about taking care of each other. Before September 11, we all had trouble imagining the deaths of so many twenty- and thirtysomethings. Unfortunately, we've all been awakened to the reality that horrible things can happen to anyone. Your shacking-up contract can serve as evidence of your wishes should the unthinkable occur. Example: Let's say you and your roommate purchased living room furniture together. If you passed away, you might like your beau to keep the couch and coffee table. Or, if you owned the place, you might want to be sure that he could continue living there until he found new digs. Without a written document or a will (which we'll talk about later), your family will have no way of knowing your desires.

While a cohabitation agreement may sound complicated, all you're really doing is putting on paper everything the two of you agree to verbally. Your agreement can be as detailed as you want it to be. If you've made a pact that your guy is solely responsible for his Labrador retriever, put it on paper. If you *love, love, love* your apartment, make it clear that you'll be the one to stay should the two of you split. If you've agreed to pay your man's living expenses for three months or until he finds a job, write it down. If it was important enough to discuss, it's important enough to document.

To make it enforceable in the eyes of Lady Justice, your shacking-up contract must be clear, unambiguous, and fair, and it should avoid any references to sex or "sexual services." You shouldn't enter into an agreement if one or both of you is still married. And you must tell all before signing on the dotted line. Fudging the truth about things like the size of your paycheck or the fact that your divorce isn't exactly final could invalidate your agreement. Once your cohabitation agreement is in final form, print out two copies and sign both (so you each have an original). Although it isn't necessary to have the contract notarized, it's always a good idea.

Please keep in mind that a self-drafted agreement isn't a substitute for legal counsel—it's merely an alternative. Get an attorney to review your document if you have any questions or want to avoid any loopholes. To be certain there are no conflicts, you should each have your own legal rep, especially if one of you is more in-the-know about legal contracts. For additional information, log on to www.nolo.com or pick up a copy of *Living Together: A Legal Guide for Unmarried Couples.*

Since this is a contract that would be personal to the two of you, it's impossible to give you an easy fill-in-the-blanks form. What we've provided on page 163 is the framework for an agreement—complete with ideas and special considerations.

COHABITATION AGREEMENT BETWEEN SUZY SHACKER AND RONNY ROOMMATE

The undersigned, Suzy Shacker and Ronny Roommate, make the following agreement and intend it to fulfill all aspects of their agreements and understandings with respect to their decision to live together:

1. We will be living together, but do not intend our relationship to be a common law marriage.
2. The separate property belonging to each of us will remain the separate property of each of us. [Note: You may want to list your separate property on an attached schedule.]
3. The income earned, from any source, by each of us will remain the separate property of each of us.
4. Anything either of us purchases or obtains from any source (including, but not limited to, gifts, inheritances, prizes, etc.) will be the separate property of the recipient or purchaser.
5. Should we decide to purchase any item or asset without a legal title together, both Suzy and Ronny will enter into a separate joint purchase agreement with respect to each item or asset purchase.
6. Should we decide to purchase together any asset with a legal title, both Suzy and Ronny will enter into a co-ownership agreement with respect to each asset.
7. Suzy and Ronny will each be responsible for his or her debts whether incurred before or after the date of this cohabitation agreement.
8. All joint expenses incurred, as listed below, as a result of our cohabitation will be paid as follows: ___% by Suzy and ___% by Ronny [insert the percentage you agree upon]:

    Rent/Mortgage
    Utilities

Insurance
Food
Other

9. All joint expenses will be paid by Suzy and Ronny, each depositing their respective share into their joint bank account no later than the first of each month.
10. The following outlines our other financial agreements: Insert any provisions of support, agreements by one party to pay for entertainment or travel expenses, and anything else you've decided on. [No matter how big or small, this is the place to include it in the agreement.]
11. Should we cease to live together, the separate property of each will remain with each respective party. We will abide by any joint purchase and/or co-ownership agreements for assets purchased jointly while we lived together. Any money held in a joint account will be split 50-50 [or whatever percentage split you agree upon] after the payment of any final joint expenses.
12. Suzy will have the first option of remaining in the residence.
    OR
    A coin will be flipped and the winner will decide who will remain in the said residence.
    OR
    Both parties will vacate the residence and split the costs associated with finding a substitute tenant.
13. All final expenses, including the expenses of the person moving out, will be split 50-50 [or whatever percentage split you agree upon].
14. If for any reason there is a dispute regarding the terms of this cohabitation agreement, Suzy and Ronny agree to obtain the services of a mediator or arbitrator and to split the cost of such service equally. The flip of a coin will determine who selects the mediator or arbitrator.

15. Both Suzy and Ronny intend that they, their heirs, and assigns will be bound by the terms of this agreement.

__________ ____________________

Date Suzy Shacker

__________ ____________________

Date Ronny Roommate

Throughout your shacking-up experience, your financial and other types of arrangements may change. You could get a raise, lose your job, or move to a less-expensive apartment. Or one of you might take some time off to regroup after a personal crisis while the other foots the bill for a few months. So be sure to review your shacking-up contract regularly and update it accordingly.

Common Law Marriage

You jokingly refer to him as your "hubby" at your annual girls' weekend. And even though you pretend to be mad, you secretly love it when his buddies refer to you as the "Missus." The problem? Legally you're not husband and wife. And in fifteen states and one district (Alabama, Colorado, District of Columbia, Georgia, Idaho, Iowa, Kansas, Montana, New Hampshire, Ohio, Oklahoma, Pennsylvania, Rhode Island, South Carolina, Texas, and Utah), a man and a woman who live together and hold themselves out as Mr. and Mrs. could be considered hitched in the eyes of the law. It's called common law marriage. What it means is that you'll have all the rights, duties, and responsibilities of a married couple—without a legal license, a big party, and lots of presents. Plus, you'll be heading to divorce court if you decide to part ways.

Could you wake up one day and "accidentally" find yourself married? Technically, yes, although it's extremely unlikely. To have a common law marriage, you must present yourselves as a married couple, using the same last name, calling each other "husband" and "wife," and filing your taxes together. You must also have lived together for a significant amount of time (each state's laws dictate how many years of shacking up qualify). If you reside in a state that recognizes common law marriages, you may want to take the time to type up and sign a short statement that says you don't intend to be married, especially if you don't plan on signing a shacking-up contract.

AGREEMENT BETWEEN SUZY SHACKER AND RONNY ROOMMATE NOT TO HAVE A COMMON LAW MARRIAGE

Suzy Shacker and Ronny Roommate, by signing below, jointly agree that their living together is not intended to, and does not constitute, a common law marriage in any state or territory of the United States.

____________ ____________________

Date Suzy Shacker

____________ ____________________

Date Ronny Roommate

Palimony

Palimony is the stuff of Hollywood tabloids. You've probably seen the headlines: "Mister Super Big Star Sued by Live-In Lover for Millions in Palimony Suit." But what exactly is palimony? Despite what many people think, it isn't a legal term. Instead, it's a catchy expression developed by the media to describe the assets or financial support given by one member of an unmarried couple to the other after a split. (Palimony . . . sort of like alimony. Get it?) Since the actual definition is so uncool, "palimony" has become the hip way to describe the outcome of a civil suit between domestic partners.

You may be wondering how a palimony lawsuit gets started. Our guess is that it's usually the result of a basic misunderstanding or a lot of pillow talk. Or perhaps it isn't words but actions that create the impression that Mr. Big Stuff will take care of Miss Understood (or vice versa) forever. For instance, Mr. Big pays for everything, including the mortgage, taxes, food, vacations, and even his sweetie's personal expenses such as clothing, spa days, and stylish haircuts. This goes on for years. Then, he dumps her for a younger, more attractive trophy, and she sues based on their implied agreement that he would support her indefinitely.

How do you avoid this inadvertent problem? By making your intentions clear in a cohabitation agreement. If one of you is going to be supporting the other while you're living together, you may want to add a line stating that this financial support will end upon termination of the relationship (no matter which one of you breaks it off). Or, if you've agreed to help support your mate for a specified amount of time (for six months or until he gets a job—whichever comes first), you should add it to your agreement.

Buyer Beware: Joint Purchase and Co-Ownership Agreements

When it comes time to furnish your new digs or purchase household appliances, we advise you and your partner to buy separately. As we noted in Chapter 5, a split could get very sticky if you own any major assets together. If you decide to jump into joint purchasing anyway, at least be sure to put the deal in writing.

In general, we see purchases falling into two categories. First, there are low-maintenance items without a legal title (such as sofas, chairs, dishwashers). Second are high-maintenance, big-ticket items that have a legal title and require upkeep (think cars, condos, and real estate). Each category requires a different type of contract. For those zero-upkeep, title-free items, we recommend a simple joint purchase agreement. Use the sample on page 169 as a guide or log on to www.nolo.com for ideas on how to personalize it.

For bigger, legal title purchases, we believe a co-ownership agreement is essential. A co-ownership agreement is nothing more than a detailed joint purchase agreement. Let's say you and your mate buy a house together. Your agreement would outline who paid how much for what and specify what would happen to the property should you go your separate ways. It should take into consideration who will pay the insurance, mortgage, property taxes, maintenance, utilities, and repairs. You should also include a method to determine final decision-making authority in case you disagree about the upkeep or whether or not to put out a "For Sale" sign. And that's just the beginning. Maybe now you understand why we advised you not to make any big investments together!

Joint Purchase Agreement Sample

Suzy and Ronny agreed on February 14, 2002, to purchase a Crate and Barrel sectional sofa together. The price of the sofa was two thousand dollars. Suzy contributed one thousand dollars to the purchase price and Ronny contributed one thousand dollars. Suzy and Ronny will each own 50 percent of the sofa. If either Suzy or Ronny dies while they are living together, the survivor shall own the sofa absolutely. If either Suzy or Ronny makes a will or other estate plan, this provision shall be reflected in that document. If the relationship dissolves, Suzy will have the first right to buy Ronny's 50 percent interest in the sofa. The value of the sofa at this time will be its fair market value. [In nonlegalese, what it's worth on the street.] If Suzy and Ronny can't agree on a fair price, they'll advertise the sofa to the public, sell it to the highest bidder, and divide the money equally. If any dispute arises out of this agreement, Suzy and Ronny agree to consult with and abide by the decision of a neutral third-party mediator or arbitrator. The flip of a coin determines who will select the mediator or arbitrator.

__________ ____________________

Date Suzy Shacker

__________ ____________________

Date Ronny Roommate

Since these co-ownership agreements can get complicated, we suggest you pick up a copy of *Living Together: A Legal Guide for Unmarried Couples* or click on to www.nolo.com for details.

Wills and Ills

OK, we know. You're probably thinking, "There's more? How can there be more?" Trust us, we feel your pain. However, we also want to give you as much information as possible to ensure your shacking-up experience is positive and beneficial.

In Chapter 8, we'll explain some of the rights you're granted when you say "I do!" Rather than having you skip ahead, however, we'll do a quick preview. First off, when a couple gets married, they become one another's "next of kin," which allows them to sign medical consent forms and visit their mate in the ICU. They're also granted certain property rights. For instance, if their marriage ended in divorce, they'd get an automatic elective share of their mate's assets (unless there was a prenuptial agreement stating otherwise). Likewise, they'd have a right to part of their spouse's estate (if there was no will) as well as his or her retirement and Social Security benefits in the event of a death. The following legal documents are for everyone, but are especially important for those of you who have made a decision to stay together without a marriage license. If the future of your relationship is uncertain, you should probably hold off on these documents until you're ready to sign on for life.

Powers of Attorney

By signing a power of attorney (a.k.a. general durable power of attorney, statutory power of attorney, and durable power of attorney for financial matters), you give another person the right to make financial decisions on your behalf. This power can be very broad and includes the ability to make gifts, buy or sell assets, create trust agreements, pay bills, and file taxes. Alternatively, the power can be limited to a specific time period or bank account. This is what is known as a limited or springing power of attorney. State laws generally dictate the extent of powers available to an attorney-in-fact under a power of attorney.

A power of attorney is a double-edge sword. On the one hand, it would be extremely important if you became incapacitated, since it allows you to appoint someone to pay your bills while you're laid up in bed. Otherwise, an expensive legal action might be required to appoint a guardian to take care of your financial affairs. On the other hand, unless you limit your power of attorney, your "agent" has the authority to withdraw all of your funds and, even though it would be illegal, skedaddle with all of your loot. So you may want to make it a limited or springing power of attorney. We agree, it's confusing. So we suggest consulting an attorney to find out which option is best for you.

Living Wills or Health Care Directives and Proxies for Health Care

A living will or health care instruction directive generally states your intentions regarding your health care should you be unable to make decisions for yourself. This document often outlines a desire to *not* be kept alive if you're in a terminal condition, brain dead, or if there's no likelihood of a meaningful quality of life. We indelicately call this the "pull the plug" or "don't keep me around" document. The fact is, however, you can issue *any* specific instructions—including a desire to be kept alive no matter how many tubes it takes—so your exact wishes are carried out.

The person whom you elect as your decision maker should be named in this document or in a health care proxy or power of attorney for health care (every state and attorney seems to call it something different). If you want your spousal equivalent to decide on your behalf, you must complete and sign a health care proxy. Since you're not married (and we're assuming that you aren't shacking up with a blood relative—gross!), your mate has zilch, zero, nada right to make medical decisions on your behalf. Who does? Your closest family member or next of kin, even if you haven't seen or spoken to him or her in years (tune in to old "ER" episodes to see what we mean).

Please keep in mind that you don't have to pick just one person with these types of documents. You can select more than one if you want to ensure a kind of "checks and balances" system. The critical factor is that you're comfortable naming certain individuals to make decisions on your behalf. So follow your heart and do what's right for *you*—not what anyone else thinks you should do.

Last Wills and Testaments

A will is the instrument you use to distribute your money and belongings to friends, loved ones, or charities upon your death. The assets you pass by will are those you own outright or as a tenant-in-common with another person. Any assets you own as a joint tenant with a right of survivorship will pass to the other joint tenant, whether or not you have a will. And if you completed a beneficiary designation for life insurance, an IRA, or 401(k), the person you named will receive that asset, again, no matter what your will says.

If you don't have a will, the laws in the state where you're living when you die determine who gets what, from your TV and toaster to your stocks and savings account. Technically, this means a bunch of faceless bureaucrats could pass your hard-earned bucks and personal belongings to a cousin you haven't seen since you were eleven. All right, maybe that scenario is a little far-fetched. The laws of intestacy generally start with a spouse and kids, then move on to parents, siblings, nieces, nephews, aunts, and uncles before resorting to cousins. However, notice that we didn't mention a partner, roommate, friend, or significant other. So if you want your boyfriend to get your car, photo album, computer, or favorite CDs, you need to be proactive. The only way to control the destiny of your dollars is to write and sign a will.

Don't fool yourself by thinking, "I barely own anything, so I don't need a will." In our opinion, it's important for *everyone.* (We could write volumes on the heartache and stress caused by the failure to have one.) You can pick up a will-writing software program for sample forms. Nevertheless, we recommend contacting a local lawyer to make sure your final wishes are stated in a manner that effectively distributes your junk and considers both your state and federal tax laws.

Miscellaneous Matters

IOUs

As Polonius said in *Hamlet,* "Neither a borrower, nor a lender be; For loan oft loses both itself and friend." We couldn't agree more. When the men we love are having financial trouble, it can be tempting to dig into our own pockets to help out. It's certainly nice that we want to be generous and aid a friend in need. But in our book, romance and handouts *definitely* don't mix. *Shacking Up* cardinal rule: Don't loan any money that you'd like to see again without having an IOU or other written agreement stating that you'll be paid back in full. Follow the quick-and-easy format on page 174 for an idiot-proof IOU.

Sample IOU

On DATE, for good consideration received, Suzy Shacker loaned to Ronny Roommate $1,000.00. Ronny Roommate promises to pay to Suzy Shacker the entire sum on or before DATE at an interest rate of ___% per year. If a lawsuit is necessary because Ronny Roommate fails to repay the entire sum by the due date, Ronny Roommate will pay all of Suzy Shacker's legal fees and costs. Should Ronny Roommate die prior to the payment of this debt, this note shall become a debt of his estate. Should Suzy Shacker die prior to the payment of this debt, the loan will (1) be forgiven or (2) become an asset of her estate.

_______________ _______________________________

Date Suzy Shacker

_______________ _______________________________

Date Ronny Roommate

And the Jury Finds . . .

After completing law school, we wonder how anyone could get through life without an understanding of the legal system and all of its complications, implications, benefits, and detriments. That's why we wanted to give you an intro to what we learned, what's important, and how to make the law work for you. You don't need to be a lawyer to profit from legal knowledge—you just require the smarts to think before you act. But hey, you picked up this book, so you're already on your way!

CHAPTER 7

Keeping the Connection

In the last six chapters, we've spent an awful lot of time talking about the hazards and unpleasantries of living together. So let's take a moment to reflect on the positive aspects of sharing your life with another person. Where shall we begin? For starters, you have guaranteed weekend plans and dates for weddings and major holidays—a plus! You have someone other than your creepy superintendent to help you deal with tragedies such as a stopped-up toilet or broken garbage disposal. You have a warm body to snuggle with on the couch and under the covers. You have a concerned roommate who will be alarmed if you don't come home and happy to see you when you do. You have a buddy to keep you company and laugh with whether you're watching videos or folding sheets. In a nutshell: All the things that you enjoy (or don't enjoy) doing can be that much better when you're with the one you love.

But as anyone who has been in a long-term relationship knows, there are no fairy-tale endings. Back in our single days, some of us naively believed in happily-ever-after scenarios. As we endured all of the dreadful dates, unrequited loves, and heart-wrenching breakups, we couldn't help but dream of the light at the end of the tunnel. We'd seen movies like *When Harry Met Sally.* If only we could find "the guy," our lives would be complete and the emotional turmoil would come to an end. Never again would we be lonely, feel rejected, or spend entire nights bawling our eyes out. Well, if you haven't wised up already, we're here to tell you: That isn't the way it happens. That's right—making the connection isn't the only hard part. Keeping the connection is just as tricky.

Like good and bad hair days, all couples have highs and lows. If you think that Hollywood's darling duo Brad and Jennifer (the Pitts, in case you aren't on a first-name basis) don't have their share of arguments or moments when they think "Oh my God, you are *so* annoying!," think again. Yes, it happens to *everyone,* including seemingly made-for-each-other twosomes. The problem is, the blissful, hormonally charged honeymoon stage can only last for so long. Once the lust wears off and reality sets in, our faults become glaringly obvious, and we begin to butt heads. It's how you handle the aggravations, disagreements, and tough times that determine whether your relationship sinks or swims.

That's where this chapter can come in handy. On these pages, you'll find a basic road map for navigating the ups and downs of your live-in relationship. It contains expert advice on how to hash out your problems and resolve disagreements peacefully. We've explained how to keep job upsets, financial difficulties, and other life crises from coming between you. You'll find out why your relationship could suffer if you don't spend quality time with your friends. We'll even tell you how to deal with a lagging libido and have maximum fun between the sheets.

If you talk to couples who have endured the test of time, they all tell you the same thing: Relationships take *a lot* of work. We're not just talking about piles of dirty dishes and extra vacuuming. We're referring to the compromising, sacrificing, sharing, and schedule coordinating needed on a weekly, daily, even hourly, basis. No, it isn't always a bed of roses. But if you're willing to put in the effort and learn how to get along, you can reap all of those amazing rewards. We think our friend Rachel sums it up beautifully: "Living together is one of the hardest things I've ever done, but it's also one of the best." So read on to discover the tools to make all of this work a whole lot easier and your relationship a whole lot better.

Communication 101

In case you haven't noticed, we live in a society that places a high value on communication. These days, cell phones, pagers, and e-mail allow us to stay in close touch wherever and whenever we go. But despite all these amazing technological advantages, many of us still have trouble communicating effectively with our mates. The reason? We haven't developed the most basic skills necessary to convey our fundamental needs and emotions.

What on earth are you talking about? some of you may be asking. *I'm a good communicator!* As far as your love life goes, anyhow, you think you're doing a decent job. Let's see . . . you're good about keeping your guy informed about new happenings in your life. You're always willing to blab about your feelings. And who's usually the one to initiate conversations about your relationship? You, you, you. But as any relationship expert will tell you, there's a lot more to good communication than that. And if you think "I speak, therefore I communicate," you don't know the half of it.

"Communication" can be defined as the ability to send and receive clear messages. To do it well, we must be able to express ourselves in ways that our partners can fully comprehend and won't cause them to withdraw or flip out. Likewise, we can't constantly swallow our feelings and pretend everything is OK when it really isn't. But good communication isn't just about lip service. It also requires us to be thoughtful listeners, which means paying close attention to what our mates say, trying to understand where their words are coming from, and responding in loving, nonjudgmental ways.

Like other animal species, we start developing our communication skills more or less the moment we're born. As babies, we learn how to cry to get what we want. Then, we slowly discover how to use facial expressions, gestures, and, finally, words and sentences to express our desires. During these formative years, we also pick up unhealthy verbal tendencies such as avoidance or passive aggressiveness from our parents and by watching shows like "Roseanne" and "The Simpsons," which become part of our communication MOs. But while we can get away with these dysfunctional behaviors among our families of origin, they can wreak absolute havoc on our romantic relationships.

Good communication is key to building intimacy and trust with our partners. Without it, we'll have forums for misunderstandings, hurt feelings, anger, and emotional distance that could end up blowing our special bonds to bits. Like improving our golf swings and shedding weight, communication is something most of us need to work on in order to be successful, notes researcher Catherine Cohan, Ph.D., assistant professor of human development and family studies at Penn State University in University Park. Fortunately, all it takes is some knowledge and practice to develop better speaking and listening skills.

Your Daily Dialogue

Whether you're exchanging "how-ya-doin' " e-mails or chit-chatting over morning lattes, the nature of your rapport may determine whether your relationship sizzles or fizzles. At least that's the theory of top relationships guru John Gottman, Ph.D., a psychologist at the University of Washington in Seattle. According to Gottman's studies, couples who respond to each other's subtle "bids" for connection are more likely to live happily ever after than those who tend to reject them. Here's an example of a bid: You're reading the newspaper when your mate (aargh!) interrupts to tell you about the impact of the fed's monetary policy on Midwest farmers. If you suck it up and listen thoughtfully, he'll feel appreciated and loved. If, on the other hand, you ignore him or act perturbed, he'll feel discouraged and dissed. When such emotional negation happens on a regular basis, your partnership is almost guaranteed to suffer.

Yes, we know. We're all subject to bad moods and episodes of stress-induced insensitivity. We're not saying your relationship is going to fall apart if you aren't a flawless conversationalist 365 days of the year. All we're suggesting is that you and your man try to be more conscientious and caring during your everyday interactions. After living together for a while, couples often take the importance of these seemingly small verbal exchanges for granted. You can start by making an effort to ask your mate questions about his day and lending an ear whenever he wants to share his feelings. Empathetic listening will help ensure that you're his go-to girl when he needs to get stuff off his mind. For mutually satisfying rap sessions, follow these communication dos and don'ts based on Gottman's best-selling book, *The Seven Principles for Making Marriage Work*.

Act interested. Whether your partner's rambling on about a virus on his hard drive or the giant striped bass he caught on his last fishing trip, give him your full attention. That means no flipping through the latest issue of *In Style* or surfing the Web while he's talking. Instead, look directly at him and lean forward to show you're totally engaged. Fire off a few enthusiastic quips like "What happened next?" or "I can't believe it!" And sound like you mean it.

Don't give unsolicited advice. You know how annoying it can be. All you want to do is think out loud or vent your frustrations when Mr. Fix-it starts jumping in with solutions to your problem. The moral: Unless your man asks for your opinion, try to keep your two cents to yourself. If you absolutely must share your brilliant insights, wait until he's finished telling his story and you understand all of the ins and outs before chiming in.

Be sympathetic. Even if you don't agree with everything your partner says, it's important to make him feel loved and accepted. Try saying something like "That totally sucks!" or "I can't blame you for being upset." If he feels judged or alienated, he's likely to clam up or look for a new confidante.

Take your mate's side. This can be challenging if you think your man's at fault or partially to blame for his predicament. But keep in mind that he's reaching to you for support, not reproach. So instead of criticizing, take the "team" mentality. Make it clear that you're 100 percent behind him, and it's "us" versus "them." No one's saying that you should lie, and you won't want to look the other way if he does something ethically objectionable, like steal a computer from work or cheat on his taxes. But if his mistakes are relatively minor (let's say, his boss yelled at him for being late for work), it's probably smarter to commiserate ("That's so unfair!") than condemn him ("Well, you shouldn't have been late!"). Get the drift? You're not his mother, so let him figure it out on his own.

Share the floor time. In general, you should try to take turns voicing your thoughts and problems, and aim to spend as much time listening as speaking. You'll never understand each other if one of you constantly does all the gabbing.

One final caveat: Under the right circumstances, talking to your significant other can be a great way to blow off steam and bring you closer together. But it can also create distance and tension if you catch him when he doesn't feel like communicating—for instance, when he first wakes up in the morning or walks in the door from work. So don't try to force a conversation if your partner's clearly not in the mood to chat. If you're dying to spill your guts and your man isn't in listening mode, call one of your friends and yak to your heart's content. You're not going to get the attention you're craving from your mate if he's grumpy or distracted. You can fill him in on the details of your life later, when he's feeling more conversational.

Friendship Talks

Early on in your relationship, you and your man probably spent a good deal of time talking about your feelings about the world and each other. Hit the rewind button for a moment. Remember how you rapped about politics, religion, literature, music, or your dreams for the future? These sorts of deep, meaning-of-life conversations are often part of the getting-to-know-you process and probably a major reason why the two of you fell for one another. In their book *Fighting for Your Marriage,* authors Howard J. Markman, Scott M. Stanley, and Susan L. Blumberg refer to them as "friendship talks." "Friendship talk builds and maintains intimacy, connection, attachment, and security—all the good stuff," they say. "If you stop having [them], you can lose touch with why you liked your mate in the first place."

Good heavens! You can't let that happen! Therefore, you and your beau should aim to spend some time (at least a couple of hours each month) gabbing about your relationship and life in general. This isn't the time to discuss the clog in the kitchen sink or what happened on last night's episode of "The Osbournes," but rather to share your feelings about each other as well as your fears, insecurities, and hopes for the future. "It's important to 'check in' regularly to make sure you're both feeling good about the relationship," confirms Heidi. "In my opinion, you won't grow as a couple if you only talk about surface things," adds Kristy. "To really know each other, you need to have meatier conversations about stuff that really matters." Scheduling a day and time for your heart-to-hearts probably isn't realistic (too much pressure). So look for opportunities to initiate them—for instance, when you're on a road trip or lounging in bed on a rainy Saturday morning.

Shacking Up News Flash!

Couples who live together before marriage don't communicate as well as those who move in after getting hitched. At least that's the conclusion of a study published in a 2002 issue of the *Journal of Family Psychology*. In the study, ninety-two pairs of newlyweds were videotaped as they talked about personal problems or dicey subjects such as sex and money. After reviewing the tapes, Penn State researcher Catherine Cohan, Ph.D., and her colleagues found that the former cohabitors had more trouble staying positive and productive during their discussions. Cohan isn't certain why, but she speculates that folks who shack up may feel tentative about the future of their relationships, and therefore may not try as hard to hone their communication skills. Hint, hint!

Tackling Touchy Topics

Inevitably, no matter how in love and right for each other you are, something that your partner does will start to drive you nuts, whether it's the way he leaves his dirty clothes on the floor, doesn't call when he's running late, or invites his buddies over without asking. "How can he be so inconsiderate?" your first thought may be, "I would never, ever do that to him!" Or perhaps you'll marvel at how anyone can be so incredibly clueless. "Does he have no common sense? Was he raised in a frat house?" Or "How many hints does a person need to give?" While all of these negative thoughts are swirling around in your brain, you're apt to react in one of two emotionally charged ways. By snapping and saying something angry or snide. Or, by keeping mum and continuing to let it boil up inside until your cauldron runneth over.

When we see them on paper, it becomes obvious that our typical coping strategies are highly counterproductive. Being bitchy or flying off the handle may be effective ways of dealing with pesky telemarketers that can't take "No!" for an answer (and whom we'll never, *ever* have to talk to again!), but they're likely to make our mates feel defensive or resentful. If, on the other hand, you fail to tell your man what bothers you, there's almost zero chance that he'll stop doing the stuff that annoys you. And by keeping your feelings bottled up, you're setting the stage for an explosion of anger and frustration that could do serious harm to your relationship.

Having grown up with role models like Mike and Carol Brady, many of us are under the false impression that good relationships don't involve conflict. As a result, we try hard not to disagree or rock the boat. Or, after past attempts to voice our feelings or concerns turn into brutal shouting matches, we fear that speaking up will only make things worse or start a nasty argument. Meanwhile, we continue to hope or expect that our partners will pick up on our oh, so subtle "You're bugging the crap out of me" signals, which is unlikely unless they're moonlighting for the Psychic Friends Network. But as we already established, ignoring the problem won't make it go away. Like a cavity, it'll only get bigger until you get up the nerve to deal with it or it becomes too excruciating not to.

Now, we're not telling you to get on your mate's case for every instance of less-than-desirable behavior. Nobody's perfect (including *you*), and you should always attempt to let the more trivial stuff slide. It's called cutting him some slack and picking your battles. But when you're faced with what you consider a flagrant infraction (i.e., he does something that really irks you and you'll eventually blow a gasket if it doesn't stop), try to get it out into the open as soon as possible, advises licensed psychologist Wes Patterson, Ph.D. "It's better to talk about the things that bother you before they turn into big problems," agrees Kelly, thirty-three, of Boston. That way, you can diffuse the tension before it becomes a dangerous time bomb.

So now that you've vowed to be more forthcoming, how do you speak your mind in a way that will get results, not start fires? The key is to be calm, clear, and compassionate as you communicate your needs and desires. Remember that your goal is to solve a problem, not punish or piss off your partner. In order to accomplish that, you need to make him feel accepted and understood. If he feels attacked, he's apt to tune you out or start firing missiles in your direction, says Bernard Guerney, Jr., Ph.D, director of the National Institute of Relationship Enhancement of Bethesda, Maryland. So aim to start the conversation when you're both in control of your emotions. "If I say stuff when I'm fuming, it never seems to have a positive effect," says Kelly. "I find that it's better to wait a few hours or even days until I've mellowed out." Once you have your anger in check (and your mate is tranquil, too), you can use this play-by-play guide to kvetch for success.

1. **Know the underlying issue.** Oftentimes, superficial conflicts are fueled by bigger, buried issues, says psychologist Catherine Cohan. So before laying into him, stop and ask yourself, "What's my real beef?" Are you miffed because he spends half his life at work, makes dinner plans without consulting you, or leaves the toilet seat up? Or is it about RESPECT? CONTROL? POWER? TRUST? PRIORITIES? "If you don't get to the latent issue, you're going to continue to circle around the problem and not get anywhere," Cohan says.
2. **Tell him what's bugging you.** How you start a conversation about a relationship problem can have a big impact on its outcome, communication experts claim. So watch what you say, because bitchiness and negativity could come back to haunt you. Here are five tips that should help you start your discussion on the right foot.
   - **Tame the shrew.** Always be sensitive and respectful when voicing a complaint. Use a neutral, nonthreatening tone of voice. Maintain an open body position (don't look away or cross your arms). Never be mean, insulting, condescending, or self-righteous, no matter how PO'd you are.
   - **State the facts.** Men aren't mind readers. If your guy is going to get the picture, you need to explain *exactly* what he's doing that upsets you. That means pinpointing specific scenarios, not

making vague, broad-based complaints. In their book *A Couple's Guide to Communication,* authors John Gottman, Cliff Notarius, Jonni Gonso, and Howard Markman recommend using "XYZ" statements to make your points. Here's how it goes: "When you do X in situation Y, I feel Z." All you do is fill in the blanks. Which brings us to our next tip.

- **Use "I" statements.** This pop psychology basic involves starting sentences with an "I" or "me" instead of "you." Examples: "When you didn't call me to tell me you'd be late, *I* felt hurt" or "It bothers me when you leave your socks on the bedroom floor." (Notice the "XYZ" setup.) In other words, focus on *your* needs and feelings. That way, it doesn't come off as an accusation, and your partner can't really argue with how you feel. Hopefully, anyway.
- **Don't be critical.** State problems as just that, not as accusations, criticisms, or overdramatized events. Instead of "You never remember to give me phone messages!" or "You've got to stop being so forgetful!" try "It bums me out that you didn't let me know that Amy called." "People tend to get defensive when they think they're being depicted in an unfavorable light," Guerney points out.
- **Butter him up.** Express appreciation or offer praise for other things that he's done well, suggests Stephanie, thirty-three, of San Francisco. A good rule of thumb: "For every complaint, I try to offer at least one 'thank you' or compliment," she says.

- **Keep it light.** Depending on the seriousness of your complaint, you can try using humor to get your message across. "My boyfriend used to get mad at me for not replacing the toilet paper roll, and it always seemed to turn into a fight," says Bridget, twenty-eight, of Camden, Maine. "Now, instead of acting irritated, he'll just sit on the toilet and jokingly sing, 'What do you do when you don't have a roll?' And I'm out of my chair instantly to bring him some. How can anyone get mad at that?"

3. **Listen carefully.** While he's responding to your lament, listen closely to your partner's words without uttering a peep. As he talks, you should be trying to step into his shoes and understand his feelings, Guerney says. If you disagree with anything he says, don't interrupt, make a face, or shake your head in disgust. When he's finished speaking, summarize what you *think* he's saying, then ask if you have it straight. This is a technique called "active listening" that can help prevent misunderstandings and show that you're paying attention. FYI: You don't have to parrot back every word he says, which would obviously be annoying. But do try to clarify his main points and anything that you're fuzzy on.
4. **Show compassion.** If you're totally ticked, you may not be in any mood to consider your partner's feelings (after all, you wouldn't be in this position if the dumb jerk had thought about yours!) But if you want to get your message across in a constructive way, you'll have to be the bigger person. Remember, even if he doesn't always vocalize them,

your boyfriend has worries, fears, and insecurities just like you. So factor in the stuff that he may be going through behind the scenes and show that you can relate (i.e., "I know things are tough for you at work right now" or "I realize that you're worried about your finances"). Trust us: A morsel of understanding can go a *loooong* way in solving problems.

5. **Propose a solution.** Instead of just complaining about what he *isn't* doing, tell him what he *can* do to make you happy. Again, be as clear, specific, and positive as possible. As a peace offering, you could volunteer to give something in return. For example: "Next time someone calls for me, it would be great if you could write the message down, and I'll do the same. I can put a pad of paper by the phone so neither of us forgets." If he doesn't like your suggestion, ask him what he thinks would be fair and try to come up with a compromise that works for both of you. A good solution should factor in your point of view as well as your boyfriend's, Guerney says. "Both of you should be 100 percent behind it."

If your approach doesn't seem to be working—your mate gets defensive, goes ballistic, or is turning a deaf ear—you'll clearly need to rethink it. What could you be doing or saying that's causing him to tune you out or turn against you? Is it your timing? Your tone? Your either blatant or subtle messages that he's a bad person or an incompetent failure? If you're not sure, ask him: "How can I phrase things so that you won't shut me out or get so mad?" "Do you feel like I'm being insensitive?" "What am I missing?" Bear in mind that anger is often a mask for pain, so if your partner's lashing out, he's probably feeling hurt.

Perhaps the best way to encourage your partner to be receptive to your complaints is to be receptive to his. When the tables turn, you'll get an unwelcome reminder of how it feels to be scolded or criticized. *Don't freak.* You may think that he's being hypercritical and you don't deserve to be picked on, especially after all the nice things that you've done! But as tough as it is to admit, there's probably a grain of truth in what he's saying. Plus, you should be glad that he's getting it off his chest and not harboring it inside. (Could you imagine learning that he can't STAND the way you eat your cereal after a year of living together?)

Even if you feel totally insulted, try not to get bent out of shape or start making excuses, which is likely to invite more criticism. If you feel like you've been attacked, take a deep breath and tell your partner why his approach sucked (only don't use the word "sucked" . . . try something more diplomatic). You can say something like "When you use words like 'stupid,' it makes me feel defensive." Once you've addressed his lame delivery, "acknowledge his complaint and let him know that you'll try to correct the problem," advises Kelly. Or, if you feel that you can't make the change, explain why and "keep talking until you find a solution that you both feel is fair and workable," says Guerney.

Having touchy discussions without one of you getting worked up will be challenging, to say the least. It can be difficult to express yourself calmly when you're feeling hurt or frustrated. Ditto on keeping your cool when you feel like your mate's stabbing you in the stomach. It'll require lots of Dalai Lama–like patience, awareness, and self-control on both of your parts. With practice, you should get better and better at it. In the meantime, don't expect every conversation to go perfectly. There are going to be times when your tempers flare and one of you forgets to hit the self-edit button. And that's why we've included the following conflict resolution info.

Say What?!?: What to Do If You and Your Man Speak Different Languages

We don't mean if one of you speaks English and the other Ukrainian–though that would obviously be a problem. We're referring to the major communication gaps that exist in some relationships and can turn seemingly harmless discussions into perilous minefields. "Everyone has a different style of communicating," the authors of *Fighting for Your Marriage* remind us. "Styles are determined by many influences, including culture, gender, and upbringing." Which helps explain why you and your sister or best friend may understand each other perfectly (sometimes without saying a single word), while you and your boyfriend occasionally find yourselves scratching your heads and thinking, "Huh?"

If you've read *Why Men Don't Listen and Women Can't Read Maps* by Barbara and Allan Pease, you may already know a thing or two about the gender differential. If not, here's the basic gist. Because of the way our brains are wired, we women tend to be indirect, dancing around issues and bouncing from one topic to the next. "Rather than explain exactly what they want, women often hint around it," Allan Pease explains. "Overall, their goal is to build intimacy and consensus." Men, on the other hand, typically get straight to the point, sticking to one topic and focusing on facts as opposed to feelings. "For men, conversations are negotiations in which people try to achieve and maintain the upper hand . . . and protect themselves from others' attempts to . . . push them around," the Peases say in their book.

As if the gender factor isn't enough, we also have the issues of culture and upbringing. Take our friends Shelly and John, for example. Shelly grew up in a reserved, never-raise-your-voice Southern home where "problems were either addressed in an unemotional way or were swept under the rug," she says. John, on the other hand, was raised in a big Italian family in which yelling was, well, normal. "That was our way of communicating," he explains. "If someone shouted at me, I shouted back. No one thought it was obnoxious or took it personally." To say that their first year of cohabitation was difficult would be an understatement. "Whenever John raised his voice, I would shut down or start to cry," says Shelly. "It frustrated him because he felt like we couldn't have a conversation without me getting upset. And I was afraid to say anything that might cause him to yell. We both felt like we were constantly walking on eggshells."

If you and your mate have clashing communication styles, everyday conversations that might otherwise unite you could send you into opposite corners. "The belief that sitting down and talking will ensure mutual understanding and solve problems is based on the assumption that we can say what we mean, and that we will be understood as we mean it," says linguistics expert Deborah Tannen in her book *That's Not What I Meant!* "This is unlikely to happen if conversational styles differ." One minute, the two of you could be getting along swimmingly. The next, you're arguing about God-knows-what and you have no idea how the fight started. You can't understand why your mate is turning on you and you feel as if you've been misinterpreted. You're frustrated because it all seems so unnecessary. You're also concerned about what it seems to say about the future of your relationship. As Bridget Jones would say, "Doooom!!!"

Fortunately, our communication experts tell us it is possible to shrink the gap and avoid needless miscommunications. The first step is to understand your individual communication styles. Start by analyzing your way of speaking, then study your partner's. (You can try using a tape recorder if it won't make your man feel like Richard Nixon.) Then ask yourself, how is your own conversation style contributing to the problem? What can you do to adapt to your mate's manner of speaking? In future conversations, try to tailor your approach to your mate's. If you hit a communication roadblock, "resist the impulse to do more of the same and try doing something different," Tannen advises in her book. "No matter what the effect is, doing something different will at least change the interaction and stop the spiral of clashing styles."

Duking It Out

Blame it on PMS. A bad day at work. The full moon. Temporary insanity. But sometimes, even when we know better than to lash out at our mates, we let our anger get the best of us. Maybe we're tired of being the "mature" ones or putting up with their BS. Or, maybe our mates say something so hurtful that we simply go off the deep end. Almost uncontrollably, our blood pressure rises, our faces turn a delightful shade of crimson, and we begin to hiss like notorious villainness Alexis Carrington from the TV show "Dynasty." "Intellectually, you know that you shouldn't take the bait," says Julianne, thirty, of Freehold, New Jersey. "But when your boyfriend says something nasty or is screaming at you, your natural reaction is to fight back."

Grrrrrr. Controlling our emotions when we feel like we've been wronged or attacked can be tougher than giving up chocolate for Lent. As Julianne suggests, it could be survival instincts that cause us to protect ourselves from perceived threats (but what do we know—we're not anthropologists). Not to sound sacrilegious, but even the Dalai Lama might get testy if he had a roommate who did unconscionable things like tell him his new robe makes him look "dumpy" or forget to tell him that Buddha called, again! BUT (and you knew there was going to be a "but," didn't you?) for the well-being of our relationships, we MUST make every effort to maintain our composure when we're seeing red. Otherwise, our tiny tiffs are likely to become big and explosive.

We're by no means suggesting that you be a doormat or lay down and play dead. Like we said earlier, if you try to suppress your anger, you could end up *totally* losing it one day (remember weenie whacker Lorena Bobbit?). It's important for us to stand up for ourselves and express our feelings, even if it creates friction. Remember, disagreeing isn't bad, and it doesn't mean that you're destined to become a shacking up statistic. In fact, a good verbal debate can help clear the air and bring the two of you closer together, experts say. That is, if you can keep it from getting nasty. "Fighting can be good as long as it's constructive, which essentially means sitting down and talking about your problems," Wes Patterson says. "It's seldom good in terms of shouting and throwing things, and it can be harmful if it leads to hurt feelings or continued resentment."

So the crucial question is, how can you keep your no-big-deal disagreements from turning into bloody brawls? You can begin by following the strategies for tackling touchy topics outlined a few pages back. Most melees can be prevented if you know how to discuss your relationship problems openly and effectively. In addition, you can learn how to stop antagonizing each other, avoid useless arguments, and find resolutions that make both of you happy. To that end, we've assembled eight top-notch, conflict resolution tactics. Take them with you to the front lines, and you could keep your relationship from becoming a casualty of war.

1. **Set ground rules.** To keep your altercations from escalating, it helps to set a few rules for engagement, Catherine Cohan says. Our suggestion: Sit down at a time when you're getting along well and agree on what constitutes a fair fight. Then, type up your "rules for the ring" and post them in a visible place (like on your refrigerator). Here are four fighting-

fair fundamentals that we recommend adding to your list.

- **Rule #1: NO unnecessary roughness.** Thou shalt not scream, yell, swear, make threats, punch walls, pull hair, bite, or exhibit any other kind of aggressive or intimidating behavior.
- **Rule #2: NO hitting below the belt.** Thou shalt not be insulting, sarcastic, undermining, disrespectful, hostile, condescending, or critical. Thou shalt never tell your partner that his or her thoughts or feelings are "stupid."
- **Rule #3: NO getting off the topic.** Thou shalt focus on one specific issue at a time. There shalt be no changing the subject or dragging in unrelated grievances.
- **Rule #4: NO storming off.** Walking out may be your way of lowering your emotional temperature and ending an unproductive discussion, but it's unfair to leave your partner hanging without any explanation. If you feel the need to flee, thou shalt tell your mate that you need some time to cool off and gather your thoughts. Then, thou shalt agree on a time to reconvene and finish the conversation.

2. **Don't try to prove you're right.** Many couples waste a lot of time arguing about who's wrong and who's right. In most cases, however, there's more than one correct answer. "When different belief systems collide, neither is right or wrong, even though you may feel that way," says licensed psychologist Steven M. Sultanoff, Ph.D. "The question shouldn't be 'Who's right?' " Bernard Guerney adds. "It should

be 'What can we do to solve the problem?' " As long as you keep trying to change your mate's mind or view him as an opponent, you won't be able to see his perspective, which will keep you from reaching a truce and widen the rift between you.

3. **See the other side.** We touched on this a few pages back, but it really bears repeating. When your mate presents his side of the argument, don't sit there planning your counterattack. Instead, listen closely to what he's saying, and try to understand his concerns and feelings. Attempt to look at the argument objectively, as if you're a neutral third party. Even if you think your partner is being illogical or selfish, respond with phrases like "I understand" or "I can see why you would feel that way." Maybe even nod your head to show that you understand him. Yes, that's it . . . just like Mother Superior in *The Sound of Music.*
4. **Count to ten before saying something stupid.** Ten seconds should give you time to think twice before you blurt out an inflammatory remark. You've seen what happens when Anne Robinson, the host of the TV show the "Weakest Link," starts hurling daggers. As you're counting to ten, we suggest doing some deep breathing to help take the edge off. *Calm, calm, calm.* If you absolutely cannot say something nice (or at least neutral), hit the mute button and wait a day—or longer, if necessary—to talk to him about it.
5. **Put out the fires.** Whenever sparks start to fly, do what you can to extinguish them. You might try showing affection (a big bear hug or playful, "Happy Days"–style noogie could do the trick) or

cracking a joke. Or, if the argument is really getting heated, you could call a time out. (Yes, like the kind that some politically correct parents use with their little monsters.) When you're furious, it can help to take a break so you can step back, cool off, and put things into perspective. Your TO should last at least twenty minutes, the minimum time it'll take your body to calm down. Try to spend the time doing something soothing, like listening to mellow music, walking around the block, or doing downward dogs. Do not sit around fuming or compiling a mental list of all the things he's done wrong.

6. **Take responsibility.** Resist the urge to blame your boyfriend for your pain or grief. If the two of you are going to patch things up, you need to recognize your own role in creating the problem and be accountable for your feelings. Your mate isn't *making* you feel sad, angry, or frustrated; you're *allowing* yourself to feel these things. By taking responsibility for your actions and emotions, you'll give yourself the power to change your situation. If, on the flip side, you see yourself a victim, you'll feel powerless and paralyzed.
7. **Know when to give in.** In a perfect universe, you would get your way on everything. But in the real world, healthy, lasting relationships aren't one-sided. According to Judith Coche, Ph.D., founder of The Couples School in Philadelphia, "You should try to get your way 50 percent of the time that you disagree—no more and no less." Sounds like a good rule to us. But how do you decide when to fight and when to cave? Simple. When you're faced with a stalemate, evaluate whether the issue is more

important to your beau or to you, Sultanoff says. If you think it means more to him, then you should probably give in. If it's more crucial to you, don't back down. Important addendum: Letting him "win" must be something that you feel good about. So look at it as a gift that you're choosing to give your partner, without expecting to get anything in return.

8. **Go for a win-win.** Whenever possible, try to find a solution that satisfies both of your needs. "Ideally, you'll come to an agreement that works 100 percent for both of you," says relationship coach David Steele. Example: If you're fighting about where to go on vacation—he wants to go skiing and you're craving fun in the sun—make a pact to hit the slopes for New Year's and head to Miami in March. Or, if you can't afford two trips, take separate vacations (your girlfriends have been dying to spend time with you anyway!). That way, neither of you feels like you're losing out. Remember, in a live-in relationship, an "It's my way or the highway!" attitude won't fly. So learn to follow the yield signs until you find a middle ground that you can both agree on.

Apparently, Tom Cruise and Nicole Kidman aren't the only ones who have "irreconcilable differences." According to relationship experts, every couple has disagreements that can't be negotiated. Some of them may be relatively minor, I-can-deal-with-it disparities, like sleeping with the window open versus closed. Others may be major and what we typically consider "deal breakers." For example, one of you wants to have children and the other doesn't. To have a great relationship, you certainly don't have to agree on everything. But if you want to avoid a Cruise-Kidman unhappy ending, both of you should decide what you can and can't live with *before* you take the next step and involve the law. While talking about your irreconcilable differences may not solve your problems, it should help you gain a better understanding of each other. Alternatively, it could alert you to the very real possibility that your relationship won't go the distance. If you're not able to accept or compromise on your discrepancies, you'll end up beating your heads against the wall until one of you cracks. Sorry to end on a pessimistic note, but that's the harsh reality.

Overcoming Obstacles

We all like to think that bad things will never happen to us. You know all those misfortunes that you read about in the newspaper or hear on CNN—people being laid off from their jobs, going broke, falling seriously ill, or losing loved ones in tragic accidents. Those things happen to everyone else, right? Not you or me! Don't we wish. The fact of the matter is, life is full of unexpected hurdles. From career curveballs to financial fiascoes to family woes, you never know what your future may hold. "The only constant that you have in life is that things are never constant," says Louisa, thirty-two. "Every time you hit a lull, sit back and enjoy it, because at some point soon, things are going to get bumpy again."

But there is one thing we DO know: How you and your partner cope during the inevitable down times could determine whether your love affair lasts. Stress from the outside world has the potential to tear apart your relationship. Or, it can make the two of you stronger and tighter than ever. It all depends on how you cope. So it's important to be mentally prepared for challenges and know how to react in times of crisis. Whether the bummer befalls you or your boyfriend, it will affect both of you, *especially* now that you're shacking up together. No matter how big or small the problem is, it can rock your boat unless you stick together and have the will to work through it.

We've been pretty lucky so far. Neither of us has endured any major calamities in our lifetimes (knock on wood!). But we have seen some of our friends suffer unimaginable tragedies, such as having all of their worldly belongings destroyed in a fire, being abandoned at the altar, and losing a beloved sibling in the World Trade Center collapse or at the hands of a drunk driver. We've learned a lot by watching the way they reacted in the face of adversity—in each instance, with amazing strength, dignity and life-must-go-on resolve. They didn't let their heart-breaking losses destroy them. Instead, they made the choice to rise above. We try to keep them in mind when we're coping with life's minor annoyances.

Hopefully, your relationship will never be tested by any truly dire disasters. But like all couples, you will face obstacles, if you haven't already. The following survive-it tips can help you surpass the smaller speed bumps (like a nightmare boss or a stolen car) as well as the Mount Everest–size mountains (the stuff we can't bear to think about). And if and when the time comes to put this emergency plan into action, try not to hit the panic button. Instead, take comfort in the fact that you have each other. And remember, if you and your mate can overcome THIS, you can overcome *anything*.

Give him space. In times of anguish, guys tend to internalize their feelings while women generally like to vent. If your boyfriend's under duress and doesn't want to discuss it, don't pressure him to open up. Instead, let him know that you're there if he needs you, then let him be. That's what Jordan, twenty-nine, did when her boyfriend got fired from his job. "It was hard because I really wanted to help him work through it," she says. "But it was obvious that he didn't want to talk to me about it. He just wanted to be alone." Eventually Mark came around, but it took a couple of days, she says. Her advice: He'll come to you when he's ready to speak. Until then, remember that this isn't about you and your needs!

Be extra cool and comforting. If your man's going through a tough time, do what you can to show that you love and care about him. Being a good listener (when he wants to talk) is step number one. Little gestures, like cooking him a special dinner or leaving Hershey's Kisses on his pillow, can also help a lot, says Tricia, thirty, who treated her boyfriend with TLC after he received a demoralizing 25 percent pay cut. Our recommendation: Try to make the home front a stress-free zone. That may mean pulling some extra weight or putting up with a little more crap until his cloud begins to lift. Home should be a safe haven that he feels comfortable retreating to. Adopt an attitude of acceptance, and he's more likely to turn to you, not away.

Tell him what you need (and why). If you're the one who's having a crisis, don't expect your beau to know how to console you. For example, since most men don't like to talk about their feelings as much as we do, he may not understand your need for overanalyzation. Rather than getting upset, explain to him that talking will help you process the issues and start moving forward, says Laura, who was crushed when her parents announced they were getting divorced—and whose boyfriend told her she was "dwelling" when she was still talking about it a few weeks later. If that doesn't help, don't push the issue. Instead, try turning to a friend or family member for emotional support.

Be proactive. When bad things happen, it's easy to get totally down on the world: "Why is this happening? It isn't fair! My life is ruined!" Bear in mind: As long as you feel helpless and hopeless, it will be difficult, if not impossible, to climb out of the ditch. "Focus on solutions rather than the stuff that can't be changed," Jordan suggests. Rather than seeing your situation as an insurmountable setback, try to look at it as a challenge.

Act like a team. Think of the problem as "ours," not "his" or "mine." If you put your heads together and operate as a twosome, it will be easier for both of you to pick up the pieces and get on with your lives. Gayle and Dean are good examples. When Dean was handed a pink slip, Gayle responded with, "Let's spend tonight working on your résumé." She typed while he recited, and the job was done within two hours.

Reach out to others. Yes, you want to be there for each other when the chips are down. But if you try to be your man's full-time Florence Nightingale or one-woman support team, you're bound to wear yourself out. Spending time with other people when your boyfriend's bumming isn't selfish. You need to take a break! Talking to a friend could help you gain a new perspective on your partner's problem. Or, it could be an opportunity to spend a few hours NOT discussing it. Either way, the social outlet should give you an emotional boost, which can help you stay strong and upbeat for your mate. Your beau will also benefit by seeking support from a friend or family member. As awesome as your company is, he probably could use another set of ears or guy time to help him get his mind off his problems.

Get help. Whether you've experienced a personal loss, a financial blow, or a career failure, you may want to seek professional help. Expert consultation can help you address the problem and get back on your feet faster. Or, if you've suffered an emotional trauma such as the death of a loved one, a serious injury, a violent crime, or mental or physical abuse, a therapist or support group may help you deal with your feelings of shock, grief, anger, or sorrow.

Keep the faith. It may be the end of the world as you (or your boyfriend) know it. But as the R.E.M. song goes, you *will* be fine. Can we tell you how many friends of ours have lost their sucky nine-to-fives only to find their dream jobs? Or managed to turn their personal tragedies into something positive? If you try to keep the right frame of mind, you will prevail and find a way to go on enjoying life. We promise.

Maintaining Your Independence

This may not be a terribly huge concern for some of you, especially if you've waited a long time to meet a man with whom you actually connect. If you're anything like us, you've had more than your share of lousy dates and lonely nights watching reruns of "Frasier." At long last, you're in love, and the feeling is mutual. You want to relish it. The fact is, you enjoy your togetherness, and you don't have as much fun when you're without him. Besides, with your absurdly hectic schedule, you only have so much free time. Whenever possible, you'd like to spend it hanging out with your guy.

There's only one problem with this attached-at-the-hip scenario: It isn't necessarily good for you *or* your relationship. We're not trying to rain on your parade, just trying to give you the benefit of our experience. As we see it, the best couples that we know don't feel the need to spend every single second together. Nor do they "complete" each other, as Jerry Maguire would say. "I always think of a good relationship as two complete individuals joining forces, not two needy halves feeding off one another," says our friend Diana, thirty. (If you remember *The Celestine Prophecy,* a book that was all the rage in the mid-1990s, her theory may sound vaguely familiar.) Our point: To have a healthy, fulfilling relationship, you need to be your own person, complete with your own friends and interests and with a strong sense of self. We've got three moves to help you hold on to your individuality.

Move #1: Don't lose your identity.

It's one thing to reinvent yourself, which we need to do occasionally to grow and evolve as people and keep life from becoming totally boring. It's quite another to be a relationship chameleon, completely changing your personality and interests depending on the guy you're dating. We think that it's healthy to accept some of your partner's influence. For instance, if he's a die-hard Yankees fan, it isn't a bad thing to watch games with him and develop a love for baseball. Or, if he's a tennis fiend and you haven't picked up a racquet since you were twelve, you might take lessons so the two of you can play together. But to protect your identity, you should never drop all of your favorite activities to make room for all of his.

One good friend of ours actually made this mistake. We're talking total *Invasion of the Body Snatchers*! When she fell in love with Jonathan, she changed everything from her eating habits to her favorite sports to her political views. All of a sudden, she loved sushi and car racing, and hated liberals. A complete 180. She did eventually regain her personality, but not until after Jonathan dumped her. (Not to be mean, but we think it's because she was acting so insecure and wishy-washy.) The lesson here is that you must keep up your individual activities and interests. In other words, be totally yourself. Otherwise, you'll just be an empty shell and a bystander in your boyfriend's life. Your partner should love you for the smart, interesting, unique person that you really are. If he doesn't, then you shouldn't be with him in the first place.

Move #2: Spend time with friends.

When you think back on the best times of your life, chances are your friends were often there. Oh yes, they were front-and-center for all those insanely fun parties, wild weekend road trips, and dorm room giggle fests. They helped you celebrate your victories, such as landing a sought-after job or finishing your first marathon. Come to think of it, your friends were there for many of the not-so-great moments, too. They comforted you when your ex-boyfriend forced you to break up with him after subjecting you to weeks of emotional torture. They came to your rescue when you desperately needed something to wear to an important interview or a formal event. They commiserated when your boss, otherwise known as Superbitch, made you work for the third weekend in a row.

Throughout the years, your friends have acted as life coaches, relationship advisors, sounding blocks, and trusty shopping companions. They've listened to you bitch endlessly about everything from your rotten boyfriends to your bad hair days to your backstabbing coworkers. You've shared clothes and lecture notes and (ugh!) frightful hangovers. Best of all, they've made you laugh—on countless occasions, so hard that you practically wet your pants. From first bras to final exams, your friends have served as an invaluable support system. Honestly, what would you have done without them?

Keeping all that in mind, it seems crazy that so many of us drop our pals like hot potatoes when we get intimately involved. OK, maybe the word "drop" is too harsh. Maybe "set aside" is more like it. Anyway, it isn't that we don't care about our friends. It's just that, well, we get wrapped up in our romances and the million and a half other things on our over-the-top to-do lists. But trust us on this one: You do not want to let your friendships slide! No matter how sensitive and evolved he is, there's no way your boyfriend can satisfy all of your emotional needs. No, you need other people to talk to. Friends who understand you and your need for constant kvetching. Friends who will listen to you for hours without questioning or judging. Friends who will offer moral support and make you feel sane, secure, and grounded. Without your friends, you could end up feeling lost and alone, without a single thing to wear.

In terms of the quality of our romantic attachments, we don't think it's a good idea to spend 24/7 with your boyfriend, anyway. If you and your man are together constantly, he's more likely to grate on your nerves—and vice versa. We all know the expression "Absence makes the heart grow fonder." We think it's so true! Without someone other than our mates to talk to, we would eventually run out of things to say or die of boredom. Besides, if something changes and you're on your own again, you'll want to have your friends to turn to. Unless you take steps to keep your friendships intact, you could ultimately find yourself in hot water.

Sure, some friends will be in our lives forever, no matter how much time goes by without talking to them. But the rest of our friendships need to be maintained and cultivated. We can't really blame our buddies for being mad if we suddenly disappear off the face of the earth—they need us as much as we need them! So we must, must, must continue to make time for our close pals. To keep your inner circle (and sanity) secure, we suggest planning at least one "friend date" per week. (We're talking friends *only,* no beau in tow.) Dinner and a movie, a long walk, or a trip to the mall all qualify, with a group or one-on-one. Phone calls and e-mails are good for staying connected, but face-to-face contact is always optimal. Don't get lazy and leave it up to your friends to get in touch. They could be put off by your new living-together status and be waiting for you to make a move. So pick up the phone and make the effort! Your pals will appreciate it, even if they don't say so.

Of course, now that you're old "married" ladies, some of you may feel like your single friends aren't on the same page. Perhaps they're still interested in going to bars, flirting mercilessly, and staying out all night. You, on the other hand, may be in "nesting" mode, preferring quiet evenings at home or hanging out and talking. You want to see your friends, but you're not psyched to participate in their after-hours escapades. The solution? Suggest activities that are more on *your* terms, such as meeting for Sunday brunch or a bike ride. If your pals complain that you never show up for girls' night out, try sucking it up and hitting the party scene occasionally. Or, propose a compromise. Let's say you join them for dinner and stay for one drink, then leave them to their own devices.

If you have recently relocated to be with your man, you may find yourself in the position of having to develop new friendships. This can be tricky, especially if you're unfamiliar with the area and trying to adjust to your new living arrangement. Forming new ties isn't an overnight process and can take a good deal of effort. Frequent calls to long-distance buddies can help you through the transition. But it's also important to have local playmates that you can lean on, confide in, and have a good time with. If you don't believe us, listen to Emily, twenty-nine. "I moved three thousand miles to be with Eric," she says. "I didn't have a job or know a soul besides him. In the beginning, it was OK, because we were getting along. But after a few weeks, the fighting started, and I had nowhere to go and no shoulder to cry on. It was one of the loneliest, most miserable times of my life."

So what's the new girl in town to do? Based on our own attempts to expand our social circles, we recommend tapping into the friend network. Get the phone numbers of any distant relatives or friends-of-friends who happen to live in the area, then dial them up one by one. As our mothers might say, be outgoing and persistent! If you're employed, you can try working the coworker connection. Taking a class or joining a club can also be a great way to meet people with similar interests. Or perhaps your alma mater has a local alumni chapter. If you're convinced that you don't have time to socialize, try multitasking. For instance, you could turn your workout into a social hour or have lunch with a work pal. Two birds, one stone.

We've both been blessed with amazing friends—both near and far—and can't stress enough how essential it is to have them in our lives. So even though it may interfere with your mating rituals, we urge you to work on developing and sustaining your friendships, especially that extracrucial inner circle. Couple friends can be awesome, but they shouldn't take the place of your single pals (the ones who have seen you through thick and thin and will be there for you again if you're thrust back into the single world). Getting out of the house and spending time with your amigos will do wonders for you and your relationship. Added bonus: You'll be delighted to see your man (and he'll be excited to see you) upon your return.

Move #3: Fly solo.

We're the kind of women who cherish our alone time. Or shall we say want, need, and would go crazy without it. Maybe we're hypersensitive, but we can only take the noise and static from our constantly whirring lives for so long. We must escape! When we're alone, we find it so much easier to think, reflect, and figure out how we truly feel about things. It gives us a chance to reconnect with ourselves, so we can remember who we are and what we believe in. Then there's the fact that we can be on our own timetables, not waiting or rushing or answering to anybody. Finally, we can *breathe.*

In our experience, venturing out into the world alone can also be empowering. Whether we're touring the rugged coasts of New Zealand or attending a local book signing, flying solo makes us feel strong, independent, and self-sufficient. By stepping outside of our comfort zones, we can prove to ourselves that we aren't afraid or timid. We don't need anyone to babysit us, hold our hands, or make us feel worthy.

While it's good to know all of these things when we're single, it can be even more important when we're romantically linked. In our opinion, we must be OK being by ourselves before we can have a healthy, balanced relationship. Yes, it's wonderful to have someone else to lean on, but we don't want to be too dependent on our mates or anyone else for that matter. We think you'll agree that there's nothing attractive about being insecure or needy. Plus, it could put too much pressure on your partner or make him feel smothered.

For some of you, the idea of flying solo may seem counterintuitive now that you've (finally) found someone to love and hang on to. If you wanted to be alone, why would you be shacking up with your boyfriend? If that's your attitude, we say, all the more reason to take some solo flights. Go to a café for lunch (table for one, please), treat yourself to the latest chick flick (he probably won't get the leg waxing jokes anyway), or, as intimidating as it may sound, go away for the weekend by yourself. We don't want to push you into doing something that frightens you. We're merely trying to encourage you to remain independent. In all likelihood, your partner will appreciate the time to himself, and you'll come back feeling refreshed and confident.

Preserving the Passion

Some couples have so much sexual chemistry that they continue to boff like bunnies long after they move in together and the honeymoon stage is history. We're talking about twosomes like Billy Bob and Angelina or Pamela and Tommy Lee who seem to have insatiable appetites and be totally in touch with their inner porn stars. And we're happy for them. Really. We should all have smoldering sex lives that other people are willing to pay good money to watch (not that we'd ever let THAT happen). But the reality is, in most long-term relationships, the passion, excitement, and orgasms don't, um, come quite so easily.

There are a gazillion reasons why sex can lose its sizzle over time. We don't have room to get into them all, so we'll stick to a few likely culprits. First, there are the basic bedroom blahs. Unless you make an effort to mix it up, things can start to seem same old, same old between the sheets. Second, you could experience hormonal changes (related to childbirth, menopause, or, for men, the normal aging process) that diminish your sexual desire. Third, you could gain weight, lose your hair, get wrinkles, develop acne, or suffer any other sort of self-esteem blow that all but levels your libido. Fourth, your relationship could have fundamental holes or flaws that cause you to disconnect sexually.

Last but not least, there's what we call the "big underpants" theory. Here's how it goes. As time passes, you and your partner become more and more comfortable with each other (a nice thing, if you ask us). You also get swept up in the whirlwind of day-to-day life—juggling jobs, friends, family, workouts, and, possibly at some point, children—and stop making time for romance. As a result, you begin looking at each other as fond companions rather than do-it-to-me-now love machines. Before you know it, you've swapped the sexy silk negligees and thongs for more practical flannel pj's and big cotton underpants. In other words, you become your parents, and we all know that they *never* have sex (never, never, never!).

Research shows that the frequency of sexual intercourse is significantly higher during the first two years of coupledom, then tends to taper off with the passing years. Depending on how long you and your man have been together, some of you may already be experiencing the deep freeze. But the good news is, a less-than-steamy sex life doesn't have to spell bad news for your relationship. Having sex once a week, month, or year is fine as long as you're both happy with the arrangement, says Deborah Caust, Ph.D., M.F.T., a certified sex therapist in San Francisco. "What's important is that you both feel like your needs are being met," she notes. Besides, "sexless doesn't have to mean loveless," points out Laura. "When my boyfriend and I started dating, we got busy almost every night. Now, it's more like a few times a month. But we're both totally cool with that. And there's still tons of affection, like kissing, holding hands, snuggling, and spooning in bed. I'm like, who needs the rest?"

If, on the other hand, you and your mate don't agree on the fooling-around frequency (i.e., one of you likes to go at it much more often), you could run into trouble. Ditto if you have wildly different notions of what constitutes "good sex"—for example, you're an experimental girl and he's strictly missionary. For the record, surveys show that sex is near the top of most lovebirds' what-we-fight-about lists. According to Caust, your sexual differences can become a big bone of contention if you fail to address them. "If one of you feels deprived, it can really create a lot of problems," agrees Jill, thirty-eight, who has cohabited twice. "The unsatisfied person is apt to feel rejected or resentful. If you don't do anything to solve the problem, he or she may start looking elsewhere for attention."

For most couples, sexual satisfaction is important for the longevity of the relationship, Caust says. "Sexuality is an important way that couples connect with one another," explains Michael Milburn, Ph.D., coauthor of the book *Sexual Intelligence.* "During sexual activity, neurochemicals that are associated with feelings of pleasure and euphoria are released. When the level of sexual activity goes down, that element of pleasure diminishes in a relationship." So if you and your mate aren't in sync between the sheets, you must, as Salt-N-Pepa say, "talk about it." "First, it's important for each of you to understand your own sexual needs and feelings," Milburn says. "Then, you need to communicate them to each other." Bear in mind that neither of you is wrong for feeling the way you do. But you should be sure to consider how your behavior is affecting your mate and have respect for his point of view. Honesty, understanding, and open-mindedness are words to remember in all of this. They are the keys to finding a compromise that (literally) satisfies both of you.

If this sort of do-it-yourself approach doesn't work for you, our experts recommend making a date with a certified sex therapist. We realize that talking about your sex life (or lack thereof) with a total stranger may sound like a horrifying prospect. But some open dialogue and expert counseling may be just what you and your partner need to overcome your sexual stalemate. Therapy may also help if you have serious psychological scars from an abusive relationship or fears such as giving up control, shame, or guilt. To find the name of a qualified sex expert in your area, log on to the American Academy of Clinical Sexologists' website at www.sexologist.org. And don't forget, you can always try e-mail or phone therapy if you're supersqueamish.

Speaking of professional counsel, if either you or your mate experiences a sudden drop in interest or a shift in your ability to get aroused or reach orgasm, you should really consult a physician (either a general practitioner, gynecologist, or psychiatrist, if applicable). Certain medical conditions like diabetes and thyroid disorders as well as medications such as certain antidepressants and antianxiety drugs can affect sexual interest and response, Caust explains. Also, you must—we repeat MUST—see a doctor if you're experiencing physical discomfort during intercourse. Pain is a sign that something is wrong and warrants a trip to the doc—STAT.

Because sexual issues are so intimate and emotional, facing up to them can be extremely difficult. You may feel uncomfortable verbalizing your sexual feelings, especially if you were raised in a family that was hush-hush about "those things." Or, you may be worried that the truth (whether it be that you have trouble climaxing or like being a little more kinky) will hurt his feelings or make him think you're a total slut. But trust us on this one: Getting the issues out into the open will be a very good thing for your relationship. "The process of negotiating sexual differences can make for an extremely strong, loyal couple," Caust says. "In most cases, it brings people closer together."

One final piece of advice before we start delving into the kinks in your *Kama Sutra.* When it comes to your horizontal activities, you and your man shouldn't compare yourselves to ANYONE, not your friends, the Billy Bobs and Angelinas, or the couples on shows like "Temptation Island." "Sometimes I look around and think, 'Oh my God, everyone else is having sex all the time and we aren't. What's wrong with us?" confesses Alex, thirty-three, of Boston. But "sexual satisfaction isn't dependent on how often you have sex, what type of sex you have, or what anyone else thinks is right for you," Caust maintains. "It's totally personal."

For you and your significant other, a good sex life may be

about flirting, touching, kissing, holding hands, and cuddling, not intercourse, oral sex, or orgasms. So don't worry about the Joneses or the steamy bedroom scenes that you see in the movies or on TV. All that matters is that you and your man feel like you're getting enough. If, on the other hand, one of you is singing "Give It to Me Baby!" and the other is humming "I'm All Out of Love," keep reading. We have some tips that should be useful.

If He Wants It More Than You Do . . .

Maybe you've never had a Kim Cattrall–like sex drive. Or maybe, due to special circumstances in your life, you're experiencing a temporary dry spell. In any case, you're not feeling so horny these days. In fact, there are times (quite a few of them, actually) when you'd just rather be getting your beauty sleep, making love to a tub of Ben & Jerry's, or watching an all-new episode of "The West Wing." "Sex just isn't a priority for me," says Bridget. "When my boyfriend and I moved in together, I remember thinking, if I can get away with doing this twice a week, I'll be psyched."

Technically, experts say, there's nothing wrong with wanting it less than your mate. It definitely doesn't mean that you're a cold fish or uptight priss (and for the sake of your mental health, you should banish those phrases from the back of your mind). "It's not unnatural to have a higher or lower libido than your partner," Caust says. "It may just be who you are." That said, if you're a Diane Chambers (from the TV show "Cheers") and your boyfriend's a Sam Malone, you obviously have a dilemma on your hands. Think you've got it bad? Consider Bridget and Bob's disparity: "If it were up to Bob, we'd probably have sex every day," Bridget says. "If I had my way, it would be more like a couple times a year."

If you're like most of the women we quizzed on this subject, you've been trying to duck the problem rather than approaching it head-on. You know precisely what we're talking about. Instead of being straightforward, you roll over and pretend to be sound asleep or come down with a sudden illness (along the lines of the old "Not tonight, I have a headache" trick). Or, in some instances, you may "put up and shut up" because it's easier to go along with him than say no. All the while, you keep hoping that your boyfriend will catch on and learn when to leave you alone.

Now, we suspect that some of you are reluctant to level with your mates because you simply don't feel like dealing with the issue. We agree: It seems much easier to look the other way than try to talk about your sexual discrepancies. However, "if you're in a monogamous relationship, it isn't fair to put your partner on a diet without discussing it," says certified sexologist Isadora Alman, M.A., author of *Doing It: Real People Having Really Good Sex*. You don't *really* want to make the poor guy paw at you or beg for a little action, do you? And even if you have Meg Ryan's *When Harry Met Sally* orgasm scene down to a tee, he's bound to clue into the faking thing eventually. Unless, of course, he has the IQ and machismo of Joey Tribiani on "Friends."

Anyway, here's the bottom line: If you and your boyfriend aren't on the same sexual spreadsheet, you're both going to have to do some giving and taking. In other words, he may have to rev down, and you may have to rev up. "Just because you're not hungry doesn't mean you don't want your partner to have dinner," Caust says. "Like everything else in the relationship, you have to try to satisfy your mate's needs," seconds Jill.

As we said earlier, the first step is to examine the reasons why you're not psyched to go at it. Then, once you've ID'd your feelings and hang-ups, you should discuss them with your man and talk about what you can do to overcome them. If you suspect that a physical or deep psychological problem may be causing your sexual dysfunction (sorry, but that's the clinical term for it), we advise seeking treatment as soon as possible. If you don't seek help, you may be putting your health and your relationship at risk. Like most of the things that you dread (like doing your taxes and going to the dentist), it probably won't be nearly as horrendous as you expect. In fact, after all is said and done, we bet that you'll feel a huge sense of relief.

For those of you who are on the self-help program, we've pinpointed three common roadblocks to a rockin' sex life—and explained how to bypass them—so both of you can start getting more in-the-sack satisfaction.

The problem: You're just too tired. This is an easy trap for busy career girls to fall into. When your days are constantly go-go-go, you may not have much mental or physical energy left for sex. Even on weekends, you may be too wiped out to get your sexual engine revved.

The have-more-sex Rx: It's important to realize that this is a choice that you're making. Right now, you're putting other things such as your job, family, friends, workouts, and maybe even cleaning the bathroom in front of your sex life. The only way that you'll find the energy for *amore* is by making it a priority, which means (yes, we mean it!) cutting back on your other activities and resolving not to let work rule your life. Eating right, exercising regularly, and managing your stress are also key to regaining your passion.

The problem: It takes too long to get aroused. You're either not getting enough foreplay or your man doesn't know how to push your buttons. As a result, you have trouble getting aroused and rarely have orgasms.

The have-more-sex Rx: Chances are, your boyfriend is eager to please you. He may just need a little help putting two and two together. If he doesn't know how to work the machinery, you need to tell (and perhaps show) him *exactly* what turns you on. Despite what we said earlier in the chapter about using "I" statements, you should start these sentences with "you." For example, "When *you* touch me like this, it feels amazing." If, after all this frank talk, you still find that you have trouble climaxing, try staying focused on what feels good—the smooching, touching, and stroking—rather than trying to go for the big "O." If you don't have an orgasm, no big deal as long as you enjoy the ride. By the way, faking will get you NOWHERE. It'll only make your partner think that his maneuvers are working (when they definitely aren't). Do you really think you can keep the act up forever? Do yourself a favor and get to the bottom of the problem.

The problem: You feel ugly. "Body image can have a significant impact on one's sexual feelings and responses," says Caust. If you feel self-conscious, you're going to have a hard time letting go. And if you can't let go, you won't have much satisfaction under the covers.

The have-more-sex Rx: First, need we remind you that YOUR BOYFRIEND WANTS TO HAVE SEX WITH YOU? If he found you so unattractive, wouldn't he rather be drinking a Heineken or in the bathroom reading the *Sports Illustrated* swimsuit issue? We understand that you can't just take our word for it. Therefore, you really only have one option: You must learn to make peace with the mirror. That means giving up the fantasy of looking like Elle MacPherson and accepting yourself the way you are, which looks a WHOLE lot better than what you see in those three-way department store mirrors. It also means getting your butt to the gym, since exercise (and weight lifting, in particular) is a research-proven way to boost your self-image. For help dealing with mental hang-ups that may be holding you back, we suggest picking up a copy of *The Body Image Workbook* by Thomas F. Cash, Ph.D. And don't forget: When your boyfriend undresses you, he isn't thinking, "Look at all that disgusting cellulite!" Neither should you. Nothing kills sexual desire faster than a mental snapshot of yourself looking like Gwenyth Paltrow in her *Shallow Hal* fat suit.

If You Want It More Than He Does . . .

Some of you may be rolling your eyes right now and thinking, "Come on—how many men (other than old geezers like Bob Dole) could possibly have lower sex drives?" The thought certainly defies all the stereotypes of guys as sex-crazed horn dogs that are controlled by their you-know-whats (and that bad boys like Hugh Grant and Mick Jagger help perpetuate). But according to the twenty- and thirtysomethings that we surveyed, the lagging male libido is more common than many of us think. Just ask Naomi, twenty-five, who has been living with Glenn for three months: "I get frustrated that our sex life has become less active," she laments. "I usually think it means Glenn loves me less or something totally emotional. He takes a more rational approach—he's too tired or stressed."

Yes, it happens. And if it happens to you, don't take it as a sign that your boyfriend is losing interest. Despite your fears, his lack of lust probably has nothing to do with you. As we touched on earlier, there are lots of reasons why both women *and* men can lose their mojos. If your man's been under a lot of stress, he may be too mentally or physically exhausted to perform. He may feel down on himself because of work stuff (think a botched project or rotten performance review) or because he feels out of shape (yes, guys have fat days, too). Maybe he's been partying too much (excessive drinking can be a real libido killer). Or, if his sexual appetite has taken an abrupt nosedive, he may have a medical problem that needs attending to.

If you've ruled out any physical or complex emotional issues and your relationship is otherwise rock solid, here are some sanity-saving coping strategies that could help.

Don't take it to heart. Like Naomi, your automatic assumption may be "What am I doing wrong? Am I not skinny enough? Sexy enough? Good enough?" Enough already! "Whenever I don't feel like getting busy, my girlfriend always thinks the problem is her," says Damian, thirty-two. "The truth is, my job is killing me. I have other things on my mind. In most cases, I just don't have the energy to get it going." So try, try, try not to question yourself or your sexual prowess. In all likelihood, this really is a case of "It's not you, it's *him.*"

Ask "What's up?" If your man doesn't offer an explanation for his lack of sexual interest, don't hesitate to ask for one. "If, all of a sudden, you're not getting love or orgasms or affection and you don't know why, it's OK to bring it to your partner's attention," Alman says. You don't have to make a big stink about it. Just say something sweet and concerned like "What's going on with you? Are you feeling OK? Is this about the pressure that you're under at work?" Or, "I miss the way we used to cuddle while watching TV or wake up in the middle of the night and make love."

Massage his ego. "If you want to make him look at you in a way that will arouse him, you have to make him feel like hot shit," vows Grace. Try to be subtle and sincere about it, not saccharine or gooey. "Drop a few casual compliments," she suggests. "Tell him he's doing a good job at work or how proud of him and happy in the relationship you are." Flattery *can* get you everywhere!

Show affection. Even if he doesn't feel like getting busy, your boyfriend would undoubtedly enjoy a back rub or scalp massage. In fact, a little TLC may be just what the love doctor ordered. Don't do it with the intention of seducing him but rather to help him relax and make him feel adored. No strings attached.

Take matters into your own hands. If your boyfriend isn't feeling amorous (and you are), it's up to you to satisfy yourself, says Jill. "To put it bluntly, if you have an itch, you need to scratch it," she says. "You shouldn't feel bad or guilty about it. Try to look at it as a way of solving a problem."

Six Ways to Keep the Flame Burning

If your love life has gone from hot-hot-hot to ho-hum, here are a few ways to light a spark and keep you from feeling like a couple of old (un)married farts.

1. Go on dates. Remember the first few months of your relationship, when you got dressed up in sexy, little outfits and met him for cocktails or dinner, then rushed back to his place (or yours) and ripped each other's clothes off? When you're living under one roof, it's easy to let passion and romance go by the wayside. "After we moved in together, little things like going on dates and him showing up with flowers really trickled off," attests Heidi. To keep the flame alive, she recommends putting several "date nights" on the calendar every month. Planning a special evening on the town or even a candelit dinner at home can help you stir up some of the excitement and lust that you had when you started dating.

2. Have fun together. It may sound hokey, but girls, and guys, just want to have fun. That's why "couples who live together need to build 'sweetheart time' into their lives," Alman says. By that, she means time when you're doing the activities that you love, laughing and bonding, not discussing where to spend Thanksgiving or who should do the laundry. "Do the things that bring you closer together," urges Alex, thirty-three. "Go hiking, shop for antiques, or attend poetry readings. It doesn't have to be sexual." It'll help you remember why the two of you hooked up in the first place, Alman adds.

3. Psych yourself up. There's nothing like an X-rated fantasy to get you pumped for nooky. So let your imagination run wild while you're driving home from work, getting sweaty on a stationary bike, or eating a sandwich in your cubicle. Just don't forget to give your boyfriend a "heads up" that you, ahem, have plans for him later that evening, Alman says. "If you're writing a script, it helps to have the cooperation of the person in it," she says. Excellent point!

4. Have a glass of wine (but not two). Disclaimer: We aren't trying to turn anyone into a lush. If you don't already drink, this isn't a good reason to start. But if you *do* imbibe, let us remind you that a little cocktail can help you relax and let your hair down. "It probably won't give you the courage to put on handcuffs or dress up in a French maid's outfit," says Jill, "but it should help you loosen up a bit." Of course, alcohol doesn't have the same effect on everyone. You may find that a glass of wine puts you straight to sleep or makes you shriek like a hyena, in which case you may be better off doing without. We also feel obliged to warn you that downing more than one alcoholic drink per day is considered unhealthy, and it could cause you to do something regretful like bag the birth control. So don't go back for more, OK? There, we feel better now.

5. Hire a trainer. No, not the kind of trainer that Tom and Nicole supposedly had while filming *Eyes Wide Shut.* We're talking about a certified fitness professional that can help get you into tip-top shape. The passion payoff? If you're feeling strong and fit, you'll feel better about your body. And as we noted earlier, a positive body image is key to maintaining your drive and enjoying your time between the sheets.

6. Just do it! Sex really is like chocolate. The more you have it, the more you want it. "Make an effort to fool around, even when you don't feel like it," says Jordan. "Otherwise, it'll just get harder and harder to get back on the horse."

Basic Relationship Maintenance

Relationships are like houseplants. In order for them to survive and thrive, they need constant attention and nurturing. We polled a bunch of happy cohabitants (both married and unmarried) to get their top "green thumb" love-life advice. Here's what seven of our "success stories" believe are the secrets to a perennial relationship.

Don't sweat the small stuff. If you allow the little things to get to you, you'll not only drive yourself crazy, you'll be unbearable to live with, says our friend Wendy, thirty-two. So whenever you feel yourself getting bent out of shape, ask, "Is this really worth getting upset about? Do I have a legitimate gripe? Or am I just feeling PMS-y?" If your answer to questions one and two is "No," then just let it go.

Accept the warts. We all have habits, traits, and flaws (such as snorting when we laugh or twirling our hair) that can rub other people the wrong way. You can let your mate's shortcomings become big sources of irritation. Or, you can look at them as strange or even amusing quirks that are simply part of the package. After all, isn't that how most of us view our own little oddities? As Cindy professes, "Successful cohabitation is about seeing the truth about your partner (even if he continually pees on the toilet seat) and getting into bed with him at night anyway."

Remember that it's not all about YOU. Don't assume that every comment, snub, or foul mood has to do with you, urges Bridget. If your man seems distant or grouchy, he could be troubled about work, a drop in the stock market, or an ingrown toenail. Likewise, if he lectures you on how to change a lightbulb or balance your checkbook, it doesn't necessarily mean that he thinks you're clueless; he may simply want to help or convey his expertise and wisdom. (Men sometimes like to do that, you know.) A good mantra to remember: What other people say and do usually stems from *their* problems and insecurities. So try not to take his slights so personally.

Try humor therapy. Laughter is a glue that bonds people together, says licensed psychologist Stephen M. Sultanoff, Ph.D. In daily life, a small dose of humor can produce a flood of positive vibes. You can also use comic relief to cut the tension and put things in perspective during a fight. To keep plenty of laughter in your days, Sultanoff suggests playing up your inside jokes as much as possible and sharing at least one funny story a day.

Check your baggage. Yes, we all like to think that we're perfect. But the truth is, the majority of us are hauling around some form of emotional Samsonite from childhood or former romances that we don't even know about. Sometimes, these psychological hang-ups can go undetected until we experience a major life change, such as moving in with our boyfriends or getting engaged. When they bubble to the surface, we're apt to behave in ways that sabotage our love lives. To add insult to injury, we then blame our mates for causing the rifts. "What you perceive as your partner's problem may really be *your* problem," says Kelly, thirty-three. That's why it's vital to identify and work on your own unresolved issues, weaknesses and sore spots, either on your own or in therapy.

Take a chill pill. Stress from other parts of your life (such as your crazy job or colossal to-do list) can easily poison your relationship. If you don't make an effort to find inner calm, your romance could go to pot as quickly as Drew Barrymore and Tom Green's. (For those of you who don't read *People* magazine, their marriage lasted 163 days!) Lowering your stress factor is a two-part process. First and foremost, you must be sure to get plenty of shut-eye, eat right, and exercise regularly. (We recommend mind-body workouts like yoga to help you relax to the max.) Second, you should try to determine the root of your anxiety and what you can do to feel in control. Resolve to get organized, stop overcommitting yourself, tell your boss that you need an assistant, or look for a new job—whatever it takes to make your schedule more manageable.

Make *yourself* happy. As a wise man (if you really must know, it was our dad) once said, you can't expect anyone to be happy with you unless you're happy with yourself. And you can't expect anyone else but yourself to make that happen. If you're dissatisfied with your life, you need to figure out what you need in order to feel fulfilled. Otherwise, your inner angst is bound to weigh you down and wear on your relationship.

CHAPTER 8

Do I Hear Wedding Bells?

No doubt you've heard this question a few thousand times since you decided to shack up—and trust us, we're not asking! In fact, one might wonder why any of us would even *want* to join the ranks of our miserable married friends. It's the twenty-first century, after all. We don't need husbands to take care of us. We've got fantastic jobs, credit cards, savings accounts, and the freedom to do as we please. We're having our cake and eating it, too. Do we *really* want to give it all up and say our "I dos"?

Apparently, yes, yes, YES!

Despite all of our nontraditional, who-needs-a-ring bravado, national surveys indicate that most of us still have matrimony on the brain. More than 90 percent of Americans say they want or plan to get hitched at some point in their lives, says sociologist Susan Brown, Ph.D. And the majority of couples who move in together do end up tying the knot, recent studies show. We suspect that some of you hopeless romantics have been dreaming of donning Vera Wang gowns and walking down the aisle for a very long time. It's not that we can't have true love and total commitment without making it legal. But for a number of you (and your friends and families), having a ceremony and signing on the dotted line will make your relationship seem permanent and real.

Diamonds. Flowers. Cakes. Parties. It's easy to get swept up in the excitement and magic of it all. However, before you start shopping for rings, we want to warn you: Marriage isn't the logical next step for every live-in relationship. Just because you have the ability to coexist in close quarters doesn't mean that you're prepared for the challenges of married life. Or maybe one of you is ready to commit and the other isn't—a stumbling block that many shacking-up couples encounter. As we know by watching movies like *My Best Friend's Wedding,* the path to the altar isn't always smooth or stress-free. There are lots of potential glitches that could trip you up along the way. We'll get into a bunch of them in this chapter. And for those of you who manage to waltz by them, we have some tidbits to help you make a graceful transition from girlfriend to wife.

Decisions, Decisions!

Unless you plan on living together for life like Goldie Hawn and Kurt Russell, you and your partner will eventually have to make a choice: Will you become husband and wife in the eyes of your families, your friends, and the law? Clearly, you both understand the magnitude of this decision. Otherwise, you would have skipped the shacking-up step and headed straight to the altar. But now that you're comfortably cohabiting, you and your significant other may not realize how getting hitched could alter your relationship. Or maybe you don't have the same notion of what the marriage vows mean.

Like fashion and music, matrimony isn't what it was fifty years ago. While many of us still see it as a lifelong commitment, not everyone in our divorce-riddled "me" generation views the "till death do us part" pledge as binding. "The permanence of the marriage vow is something taken lightly by many people," says one twenty-eight-year-old guy from New Jersey. "In my opinion, marriage isn't forever. You can get out of it at any time." What's more, shifts in gender roles have changed the way most marriages look. Today, many wives have full-time careers, and husbands are more likely to cook, clean, and change diapers. Our expectations are also different. Most of us seek strong emotional and spiritual connections with our spouses in addition to companionship and financial stability. We're determined to have something better than our parents had. We want to marry our best friends, soul mates, intellectual equals, and lovers all rolled up into one.

These days, marriage is a conscious choice, not a financial or moral necessity. We don't *need* to get hitched, but the majority of us still *want* to. Why? It seems we've been subconsciously programmed to do what society expects of us. Since the days of the Pilgrims, marriage has been an important part of our national culture. Though marriage rates have dropped over the last few decades, the institution itself is still highly valued by most Americans. To make sure it stays that way, there are countless books, workshops, organizations, and even government programs to support it. "I've always pictured myself getting married," says Stephanie, thirty-three. "I guess it's a value that was instilled in me by my parents." "When I was little, I remember thinking, 'Someday, when I get married . . .' " adds

Gayle, twenty-nine. "I had the fantasy of having a big wedding and tossing the bouquet. It was just something I planned and expected to do."

Despite what some of you may think, there is definitely a difference between living together and being lawfully wed. As Linda J. Waite and Maggie Gallagher say in their book *The Case for Marriage,* "Marriage is not only a private vow, it is a public act, a contract, taken in full public view, enforceable by law and in the equally powerful court of public opinion. When you marry, the public commitment you make changes the way you think about yourself and your beloved; it changes the way you act and think about the future, and it changes how other people and other institutions treat you as well." To put it another way: By tying the knot, you fuse yourselves legally and socially. As a married couple, you gain certain privileges as well as obligations. If you decide you'd be better off without him, you can't just call it quits and move out.

Is marriage a trap? To some, yes. But for others, it can provide the confidence and support needed to achieve their personal dreams and be truly happy. According to most of the currently betrothed couples we interviewed for this book, marriage helped eliminate the question marks and insecurities that they felt while shacking up. After saying "I do," they felt closer, happier, and more settled. Research also shows that married people live longer, are healthier, earn more money, and feel more content with their lives. However, as you know by now, long-term relationships require a lot of hard work. You need dedication, determination, and drive (and we don't mean sexual!) to make it last. Considering the sky-high divorce rates, keeping a marriage alive and strong may be one of the greatest challenges of the modern world. That's why we urge you to approach your decision like a yellow light—slowly and with caution.

The Legal Side of Matrimony

Some people say it's only a piece of paper. But when you sign a marriage license, you gain a brand-new legal status with a new set of rights and responsibilities. This can be good or bad, depending on how you look at it. The laws are complex and vary from state to state, but here's a rough idea of what you'll be getting and giving up by tying the knot.

Sex, sex, sex: In almost half of the United States, sex with anyone other than your spouse is prohibited by law (though offenders are rarely prosecuted). In almost every state, adultery is grounds for divorce. On the bright side, studies show that married couples have more satisfying sex lives than their cohabiting counterparts. Shocking but true!

Dollar signs: If you pledge your troth, you and your partner will be considered an economic unit by creditors and the law. Unless you have a prenuptial agreement stating otherwise, you'll have an obligation to share property, income, retirement benefits, and pensions with your spouse. You may have a duty to split some of your assets and pay spousal support if you divorce. Your taxes must be filed (either jointly or separately) as "married" and will be taxed accordingly. You can be held responsible for debts incurred by your partner after your wedding day. On the plus side, you can give or bequeath assets to each other without being taxed to death (pun intended). You'll be entitled to part of your spouse's assets, social security, pension, and other retirement benefits if he passes away. As a married couple, you can get a discount on homeowner's, renter's, and car insurance policies as well as a gym membership.

Company perks: Many employers extend benefits such as health and dental insurance as well as relocation expenses to their employees' legal spouses. If you exchange vows, you'll also be eligible for (paid or unpaid) sick and bereavement leave from your job.

Life-and-death decisions: Upon marriage, you become your partner's next of kin. This means you should have the right to make medical decisions for each other in an emergency. Prior to tying the knot, you would have needed a health care proxy to make life-or-death calls or possibly even to visit your ailing "roommate" in the hospital. Legal spouses also have the right to (gulp) dispose of their deceased partner's bodily remains.

Split-up protection: If your marriage were to end in divorce, there would be state laws regarding the division of your joint property as well as spousal support, child support, and child custody.

Testimonials: Not that you'd ever find yourself on trial. But if you did, you could invoke the marital communications privilege to keep your better half from talking on the stand.

Timing Issues

We confess: In our younger days, we thought we had soul mates. We believed there was one perfect man for each of us. Someday, when fate kicked in, he would—*poof!*—appear before us and fulfill our romantic fantasies. Now, after years of dating, we realize that there are lots of potential "ones" out there. Yup, that's right. There are myriad guys who could make great matches and life mates—none of whom is absolutely perfect, by the way. Which one we wind up with has much more to do with timing than karma, kismet, or Cupid.

In an ideal world, you and your boyfriend would agree with each other—and everybody else—on when, and if, to make the leap from "roommate" to "spouse." But in the real world, we all have different wants, needs, and internal clocks. The result: We aren't always in sync with our partners, our peers, or our parents when it comes to the subject of tying the knot. Here are four possible timetable problems that you may face—and some solutions to help you stay on track.

Scenario 1: You're Ready to Get Hitched and He Isn't.

What a bummer! We hate to say it, but we know quite a few women who have been in your shoes. According to their testimony, there are a number of reasons why you could be getting antsy. Maybe you're eager to settle down so you can start planning beyond next week. Maybe you feel the ticktock of your biological clock and want to start a family. Or maybe it's due to the fact that you've been to six weddings in the past six months. Whatever the impetus, you're ready to take the plunge and start moving forward with your life.

Based on conversations with guy friends and past boyfriends (the ones who are still speaking to us), we really don't think men are much different than we are. Ultimately, most of them seem to want the same basic things—love, companionship, and a house with a dog and two kids playing in the yard. They just don't always have the same time frame for achieving them. It's hard to say why men tend to cling to bachelorhood. Perhaps it's because they're not as mature (remember high school?) or they relish their freedom more. It could also be that they need to feel financially secure before they take on the responsibility of having a wife and family. Research conducted by University of Michigan sociologist Pamela J. Smock, Ph.D., indicates that employment and income, especially on the part of the male partner, are major factors in a couple's decision to marry. To put it differently, your man may want to have his career on track and green stuff in the bank before he gets down on one knee.

Unfortunately, if you and your mate have different timetables, you may get stuck playing the waiting game. Needless to say, this can be highly frustrating, especially the longer you're forced to wait. Even if you feel great about your relationship, you're bound to start questioning your partner's intentions. And rightly so. We certainly don't want to lump all men into one category, but some are happy to cohabit indefinitely. As long as they're comfy, cozy, and getting free housekeeping services, they may not see any point in changing a thing.

If matrimony is important to you, there's only one thing you can do: SPEAK UP. By this, we don't mean hinting or nagging. If you're going to get results, you must sit down and have a heart-to-heart. If your beau isn't thinking marriage, it's better to find out as soon as possible, isn't it? If he hasn't ruled out the idea of swapping vows, then you may need to give him a little kick in the pants. Yes, we know it sounds terrible, but marriage is a scary concept for some guys. If you don't make it clear that you won't wait forever, he could keep making excuses until you're swinging seniors shacking up in a retirement home.

When it comes to raising a sensitive subject like marriage, our first suggestion is be prepared. Before piping up, you should know what you want to say and how you want to say it. You should also try to anticipate his possible responses so you're not caught off guard. Finally, you should think about the timing of the chat. You don't want to broach the topic when he's getting ready for work or about to turn on a World Series game. Do it when you have his full attention and plenty of time to talk. Likewise, pick a location that offers privacy, such as your living room or car (with the TV, radio, and cell phone ringers turned off).

Without question, these types of face-offs can be nerve-racking. As a result, some women opt to put their feelings on paper. "I wrote a letter because I wanted to make sure I got to say everything I wanted to say," says Gayle. "If I brought it up in person, I was afraid I'd get flustered." By a similar token, Lindsey, twenty-six, thought a written note would be less intimidating for her boyfriend. "I wanted to give him a chance to think before he had to respond," she explains. Keep in mind that this isn't a conversation that your boyfriend will be anxious to have, so don't be surprised if he tries to weasel out. If you're met with resistance, be sure to stand your ground. You shouldn't apologize or feel stupid for wanting to walk down the aisle. If your man is going to take you seriously, you can't waffle or back down.

As you learned on pages 183–189 (Tackling Touchy Topics), you must be careful about how you approach the discussion. You should be calm and compassionate, not whiney, pushy, or judgmental. So he doesn't feel threatened, you can start with a positive—a simple "I love you" will do—and an expression of understanding for his concerns. For example, "I know that you're worried about money" or "I realize you want to focus on work right now." Next, spell out your wants and needs. You can try a statement such as "I'd really like to get married and have kids" or "Marriage is important to me because of X, Y, or Z." Then, if he's not already bursting at the seams, ask him to tell you how he feels about it.

Obviously, his responses could run the gamut. Ideally, he'll announce, "You're absolutely right. It's time to move things forward. Let's go ring shopping!" Miracles happen, but we wouldn't bet your shoe collection on it. More likely, he'll give an excuse such as "I'm not ready," "I don't see a reason to get married," or "I've got too many other things going on in my life." If that's the case, don't throw a fit, act hurt, or accuse him of stalling. Instead, stay strong, composed, and objective. Ask him whether he can see himself married to you. If he says "someday," you know there's hope, and you shouldn't hit the high road just yet. But you must make it clear that you won't stick around forever. Then, you should try to negotiate an engagement time line that works for both of you.

If you're living with someone who says he *never* wants to get married, all we can say is we're so sorry! You can keep praying that he'll have a change of heart, but there's very little chance that he will. And since we know you'll try to cling to that "very little" part of the chance, we'll just go ahead and say zero chance. True, people can change their minds, but they have to *want* to change. If he says he has no interest in tying the knot, then he isn't going to marry you. Do yourself a favor and take him at his word. If you eventually hope to take your vows, you probably shouldn't waste any more time with a guy who doesn't have the same goal.

Let's say you had an engagement time line, the time line is up, and your boyfriend *still* can't commit. Well, then you basically have two choices. You can tell him it's over. Or you could try to delve deep into his commitment-phobic psyche and figure out what the holdup is. If you think there's a chance he can overcome his issues (and he's willing to put the effort into doing so), consider setting a new time line, one that you swear to stick to. We believe in second chances, but it obviously depends on your situation and disposition. We assume that your boyfriend has some redeeming qualities, in which case the relationship may be worth holding out for. You don't want to be a pushover, but it wouldn't hurt to show some compassion and try to see his perspective. If the roles were reversed, we hope he would do the same.

What about giving him the old ultimatum? We don't recommend it. We want our mates to feel like they're excited to spend the rest of their lives with us, not like they've been pushed into it. Then again, if things continue to drag on too long, you'll have to draw the line. In which case, we suggest telling him that you care deeply about him, but you can't wait any longer. Give your reasons—you want to tie the knot and start a family or whatever—and explain that you need to move out so you can start moving on. If he begs you to stay and is ready to talk seriously about getting engaged, then you may want to give him another shot. Otherwise, pack a suitcase and stay with a friend until you can make new living arrangements. Many women find that breaking up is the only way to get a concrete answer. Whether that answer is yea or nay is another question altogether.

The Guy's Take: On Getting Pressure to Take the Next Step

- "I've made it clear to my girlfriend that I have no interest in getting married. I'm not religious. I don't want to have kids. I'm happy the way things are. If it comes down to an ultimatum, I'll tell her what I've always told her: If you want to get married, then you need to make the decision to move on. You need to do what you feel will make you happy. The ball is in your court."

  –***Derek, twenty-eight*** (status at press time: still living together)

- "My girlfriend needles me about marriage a lot. The pressure doesn't work. If anything, it makes me feel even less enthusiastic about it. It's not that I never want to marry her. I can see it happening someday. But right now, I just feel too young. I don't feel mature enough. If we get married, I know the next question will be 'When should we start having kids?' At this point, I want to be free to travel without worrying about having a family."

  –***Simon, twenty-nine*** (status at press time: engaged)

- "While we were living together, Megan would periodically bring up the marriage question, usually after we'd been in the car for a while. She would say, 'I know you don't like talking about these things, but we need to figure out what we're going to do.' The first time she said it, we'd been dating for a couple of years, so I

thought it was totally appropriate. But I wasn't ready, and I told her that. From then on, I kept trying to stall or avoid the issue. Finally, about four years into our relationship, she reached the end of her rope. I walked into the house one day, and she was packing up her stuff. She was ***so*** upset. She said, 'I need to figure out where my life is going. I can't do that while I'm living here.' I instantly knew that wasn't what I wanted. I told her that I couldn't imagine not having her in my life, and I would do my best to imagine what it would be like to get married. Five months later, I popped the question." ***–Nate, thirty-three***
(status at press time: married with a baby)

SCENARIO 2: HE'S READY AND YOU AREN'T.

Judging by the surveys we did for this book (and there were a lot of them), this scenario isn't nearly as common as the previous one. In fact, we didn't find one cohabiting couple that fit the "he's ready, she's not" profile. But we know you're out there! So we've decided to address your predicament based on information gathered from our not-prepared-to-take-the-plunge male intelligence pool. (Those of you dating guys who can't commit may also want to read this to try to get inside their heads.)

If your man's geared to get hitched but the notion of it makes you feel queasy, ask yourself these questions: *What is it that makes me nervous about marriage? Is the problem him? Me? Or does it have something to do with our relationship?* You may require some time to yourself or input from loved ones and trusted advisors in order to come to any conclusions. Meanwhile, in an effort to help, we've gone over some possible explanations for your uncertainty and attempted to offer guidance.

If you feel like you're too young or carefree to be tied down, then you should hold off on marriage for a while. As we said earlier in the book, it's important to know who you are and what you want in life before making a decision like this. You should also wait if you think you haven't known your partner long enough. If your mate seems to be rushing your relationship along, you'd be wise to question his motivations. Why the sense of urgency? Could he be insecure and trying to fill an emotional void? Or does he have a deep, dark secret that he's afraid will come to light if he doesn't hurry up and seal the deal? Yes, it would be nice to think that he's simply head-over-heels and wants to snap you up as quickly as possible. But unfortunately, no matter what a wonderful catch you are, this probably isn't the case.

Of course, if your parents had a rotten marriage, it's possible that you're petrified about following in their footsteps. This is a common hang-up for kids from divorced or highly unstable families. If you're questioning the sanctity (and sanity) of matrimony, you obviously have some issues to resolve before saying your vows. Keep in mind: You must believe your marriage can and *will* work in order to overcome the inevitable challenges that come with any long-term relationship. Addressing your fears and making peace with your parents' relationship is apt to take time and the help of a good therapist.

Speaking of your parents, perhaps your commitment phobia stems from the fact that they don't like your significant other. If so, you should sit down with them and have a truthful conversation. Talk openly with them and listen carefully to their concerns. Once you're aware of their specific objections, you can try to determine a course of action. Maybe they feel like they don't know your partner well enough, in which case it may just be a matter of spending more time with them. Give them a chance to get used to the idea and opportunities to get to know him better. If they're taking issue with your partner's race or religion, then you're in a real pickle. Hopefully, with time and exposure, your folks will come to accept your mate. For now, you will have to decide whether you can live without their support and blessings. Personally, we think it would be a real tragedy if prejudice prompted you to sacrifice a great relationship. But for some people, blood is thicker than water.

If, however, your parents have a problem with your partner's character (i.e., they think he's rude, irresponsible, or a slimeball), you should take their worries seriously. They may be able to see something that you can't. Consult your friends or other family members to get second, third, and fourth opinions. Or get some feedback from an impartial third party, such as a minister or rabbi. See if you get a group consensus. Don't forget: Having your family's approval will make your life easier and up your chances of having a successful marriage. But as long as you and your partner are deeply committed to each other, you can have a happy, lasting relationship without it. Ultimately, if you're over the age of eighteen, the choice is yours.

But maybe Mom and Dad aren't the ones with qualms about your mate. Maybe it's *you* who has doubts about him. If that's the case, you must take a step back and try to clarify your emotions. As we said in Chapter 2, it's normal to have some anxiety when making a life commitment. But if your stomach is doing flip-flops or you feel panicky, you should consider it a warning. Is your anxiety in response to the concept of marriage or the idea of being with *this* person for the rest of your life? In any event, you'll need time to sort through your feelings and possibly gather more data.

Once you've identified your fears and hang-ups, we suggest that you sit down with your partner and start discussing them. Assuming that you don't want to break up, you can begin by telling him you love him, but you need time to work through your issues. Give him a general time frame—you think you should live together for at least (fill in the blank) months/years before making a decision about marriage. Then, you should make a conscientious effort to determine what you want. Spending time away from your partner could help you be more objective. A long weekend or vacation by yourself may be what you need to figure it out. You could also consider taking a minibreak, which would entail staying with friends or family for a few weeks. Also, you should think seriously about seeing a therapist to try to deal with any commitment issues and emotional baggage.

What if he pops the question before you're ready to say "Yes"? Don't feel obligated to accept because he's kneeling before you with an enticing velvet box. Sure, he'll be hurt if you turn him down, but he'll be even more heartbroken if you back out *after* he's announced your engagement to the world. Whatever you do, don't get married just because you feel guilty, can't bear to hurt him, or are afraid his family will never forgive you. These are very bad reasons to agree to spend your entire life with someone. Our friends who have passed on proposals or broken off their engagements all agree that it was the best thing they could have done; they only wish they hadn't waited so long to pull the plug.

Seven Really Good Reasons to Just Say "No!"

- You're not asking the hard questions because you're afraid of the answers.
- You think your mate will change his ways or shape up *after* you're married.
- You have doubts about your partner, but if you don't tie the knot now, you may not get another chance.
- You don't feel ready to get married, but you can't take the pressure anymore. You want to get your parents and/or your significant other off your damn back.

- Your family adores your boyfriend. If you don't marry him, they'll be *crushed.*
- You and your mate may be like oil and water, but you love each other SO MUCH. In the end, isn't that all that matters?
- Your partner has a drug, alcohol, gambling, sex, or other type of addiction and isn't in the process of recovery.

Scenario 3: Neither of You Is Ready.

For some of you, this may not be a problem at all. Perhaps you're living in the moment, going with the flow, and (hopefully) having a fabulous time. Here's what we think: As long as you both feel comfortable with the arrangement, there's no reason for you to sprint to the altar. You have the rest of your lives to spend together! So take your time and swap vows if, and when, you feel the urge.

Others of you, however, may be stuck in a ticklish place called relationship limbo, which can lead to the emotional cul-de-sac and eventual dead end that we discussed in Chapter 1. Your living arrangement may not be bad, but it isn't great either. Perhaps you'd describe it as "fine," "OK," or "comfortable." Or maybe your relationship has had dramatic ups and downs. At certain moments you may think, "Yes, I can see us having a future together." At others, you swear, "This is *never* going to work!" Deep down, you suspect that something isn't right, but you can't quite put your finger on it. You're afraid to leave the comfort and security of your nest to look for something better.

A lot of couples who shack up for convenience or money-saving purposes (as opposed to wanting to spend the rest of their lives together) find themselves in this situation. If you're one of them, you have some serious soul searching to do. If it's the wrong thing (and it very well may be), you're only prolonging a dead-end relationship. Worse, you could make the mistake of marrying the wrong person. That's what happens to many cohabitants who feel pressure to make a decision and don't know what else to do.

It may be difficult to figure out how you feel as long as you're together 24/7. Our recommendation: Take time to yourself, get some distance, and ask yourself the following: Can you picture waking up next to him in forty years? Will you still have things to talk about? Does he have all of the qualities you're looking for in a life partner? Do you feel confident and secure when you're together? ARE YOU HAPPY? If you weren't living together, do you think the two of you would still be dating?

Last but not least, what is your gut telling you? No one can ever be 100 percent positive when choosing a life partner. But in our experience, the more agonizing the decision, the greater the likelihood that the answer should be no. Do you really want to settle for "good enough" just because you're scared to be alone? As painful as it is to end a live-in relationship, it's harder to get divorced. Here's your chance to take control of your destiny rather than being swept along by the current. Wait until you're truly excited about becoming a "Mrs." and having a future with someone. If there's one thing we know, it's that being alone is far better than being in a miserable marriage.

Is It Time to Tie the Knot?: A Readiness Checklist

To help explain the mystery of long-term relationships, researchers like Jeffrey H. Larson, Ph.D., of Brigham Young University in Provo, Utah, have examined why some marriages fail and others last. In his book *Should We Stay Together?,* Larson lists factors that predict marital success, which include the following:

- **You're over the age of twenty-five.** The divorce rates are much higher for couples who say their "I do's" at young ages. To up your odds for a successful marriage, Larson recommends waiting until you're in your mid-twenties or older to swap vows.
- **You've been together for at least one year.** You need time to get to know each other and see how your relationship holds up in times of stress and crisis.
- **You've finished most of your education.** It'll be hard to focus on your marriage if one or both of you is bogged down with classes and homework. Plus, the lack of a steady paycheck is likely to create stress.
- **You're on firm economic and employment footing.** There will be less to worry and fight about if you have stable, secure jobs and aren't scraping to get by.
- **Your family and friends have given their "thumbs up."** Apparently, what they think ***does*** matter! According to Larson, getting the nod of approval from your loved ones should make you feel more confident about your marriage and increase the chance that you'll get support when you need it.

SCENARIO 4: EVERYBODY ELSE IS READY.

Unless your boyfriend's an ogre or it's obvious you're a terrible match, you can plan on getting lots of knot-tying questions from curious family members, friends, or even casual acquaintances. In many instances, it may be purely a matter of "inquiring minds want to know." For example, you're at your cousin's wedding when your Aunt Betty corners you and says, "Soooo, are you two going to be next?" On other occasions, especially the longer you shack up together, you may find yourselves getting subtle or not-so-subtle pressure to wed. Most of the cohabitants we surveyed reported getting hints and nudges from their anxious parents. In Daniel's case, it sounded more like a threat. "My girlfriend's father said, 'You better hurry up or we're going to have to get out the shotgun,' " the twenty-seven-year-old says.

"I absolutely hated getting the marriage questions!" rants Alex, who lived with her boyfriend prior to taking her vows. "I think they're totally inappropriate. People sort of assume that if you're seriously dating someone, marriage is your ultimate goal. But not everyone is interested in getting married. Or one person may feel more strongly about it than the other. Either way, it could create a very uncomfortable situation." You said it, sister. Even if you're in no hurry to make it legal, these matrimonial probes can throw you for a loop, particularly when they happen in front of your mate. When the bomb drops, you may see the trickle of sweat on your boyfriend's brow or the pained look on his face. Suddenly, you could be hit by a wave of doubt and insecurity. *Why does he look so nervous?* you may wonder. *Does it mean that he doesn't want to marry me?*

If it's any comfort, lots of us have experienced these sorts of invasions of privacy. As confounding as they may be, try not to let them get to you. All that matters is how you and your boyfriend feel about your relationship status. The last thing you want to do is let someone else's time line influence yours. What a tragedy it would be if Aunt Betty's meddling caused you to make a move that wasn't right for you! If you do get married, it should be on *your* terms. Meanwhile, if and when you get hit with a marital missile, do your best to shrug it off. To minimize the awkwardness, have a response ready. And remember, the traditionalists in your life can't help themselves. They simply want you to do the "right" thing or presume that you plan to take the conventional path. Of course, it's none of their beeswax. But *c'est la vie!* It's an annoying by-product of being on the cutting cultural edge.

Our Five Favorite Comebacks to the "Sooooo, When Are You Two Getting Married?" Question

5. We already feel married, so what's the rush?
4. We can't afford to buy an engagement ring right now, but we *are* accepting donations.
3. We've decided to wait until after our love child is born.
2. We didn't think same-sex couples were allowed to get married!
1. My, isn't that a personal question! Would you mind telling me your bra size?

Making It Legal

Congratulations! Best wishes! Or whatever the heck we're supposed to say. Once a marriage proposal has been made and accepted, you'll certainly have cause to celebrate. You're engaged! Perhaps you'll pop a bottle of champagne and start calling family and friends with the delightful news. Chances are, your brain will be reeling as you move full tilt into wedding planning and struggle to remember to use your mate's new title ("fiancé"). But before you get sucked up in the matrimonial whirlwind, we have a very important bulletin: There's more to think about than reception sites and bridal parties. To prevent a postnuptial nightmare, you and your boyfriend (whoops—we mean fiancé!) ought to discuss (or rediscuss) some major relationship issues such as children, lifestyle, and finances. On the upcoming pages, we'll lead you through these crucial conversations. We'll also prepare you for potential wedding planning snafus that could turn your love nest into a war zone. Lastly, we'll tell you what changes to expect after you're legally bound.

Must-Have Discussions

Now that you've agreed to enter the state of holy matrimony, there are some important powwows you should have about your future. Even if you covered some of these topics prior to shacking up, you may want to reopen the dialogue. To follow are eight must-talk-about topics, in no particular order, with some sample questions to get the information exchange going. Not all of the questions may apply to you, so pick and choose as you see fit. If some sound forced or stiff, substitute your own words. This is intended as a rough guide, not a Hollywood script.

1. **Marriage**
   What does marriage mean to us? Does it mean a lifelong commitment? Sticking together through thick and thin? Working through our problems, no matter how difficult? Under what circumstances, if any, would we consider getting a divorce? Where will our marriage fall on our priority lists? Will we place it before or after our careers, families, and extracurricular activities? What, if anything, do we consider to be wifely and husbandly duties? Do we picture ourselves falling into traditional roles?
2. **Lifestyle**
   How will our lifestyles change after we're married? Is there going to be a new set of "house rules"? Do we still picture ourselves staying out all night and partying? Will we take all our vacations together? Or are getaways with the girls/guys still cool?
3. **Religion**
   How will we deal with our religious differences throughout our marriage? On holidays? Around our families?

4. **Children**

   Do we want to have children? If so, how many? When do we see ourselves having them? Would we both continue to work if we had kids? Would one of us want to stay home? Do either of us have any strong feelings about education? Public school or private? Would we want our kids to be raised within a certain religious faith? What if we couldn't have children? Would adoption be an option?

5. **Career**

   Where do our careers fall on our priority lists? If we had a career conflict (i.e., one of us got transferred), how would we handle it?

6. **Family**

   How much interaction will we have with our families after we get married? How frequently will we see them? How will we handle major holidays?

7. **Geography**

   Where do we see ourselves living in five, ten, twenty, or fifty years? City or small town? House, condo, or apartment? Do we want to be free to pick up and move at any time or are we anxious to settle down and establish roots? Would we both be open to relocating if one of us had a career opportunity?

8. **Personal History**

   Is there any important part of our personal histories that we've neglected to tell each other? What about any psycho ex-lovers, arrest records, former marriages, children from previous relationships, sexually transmitted diseases, financial, legal, drug, alcohol, or gambling problems?

More Legal/Financial Mumbo Jumbo

Before exchanging vows, you and your partner have a few financial and legal matters to sort out—and we're not talking about purchasing the rings, paying for the honeymoon, or applying for a marriage license. As we mentioned before, after you're hitched, the two of you will be joined together financially in the eyes of Uncle Sam. There are certain economic benefits that you may want to take advantage of and changes to prepare for (everyone's favorite—taxes!). You may also want to take steps to protect yourselves and your nest eggs in the event of a worst-case scenario. Let's run down the list one by one.

Bottom-Line Basics

If you haven't already done so, it's time to lay all of your financial cards on the table. At this point, we heartily recommend telling each other everything, from the good (loads of cash in the bank and a big IRA) to the bad (a defaulted student loan, a personal bankruptcy, or a history of wild shopping sprees). Remember, if one of you gets into financial trouble, both of you could be held accountable, even if you have separate credit cards and savings accounts. So you owe it to each other to be totally honest. Full disclosure is also essential if you're going to sign a prenup (more on that in a minute). Prior to the wedding, you should attempt to work through any unresolved dollar dilemmas that you have. If you tend to argue about money, you may want to consult a financial advisor or a marriage counselor for guidance. Chapter 5 covers all of these topics in more depth. So start talking, chatting, and hammering away at the issues. The more you communicate and plan, the better off you'll be when he slips the wedding band on your finger.

Prenuptial Agreement

The question of whether or not to have a prenuptial agreement can be a real sticky wicket. No one likes to think about the possibility of divorce when they're in love and about to get married! While neither of us has been in a position to sign one, we can tell you what many financial advisors say: In today's world, you'd be crazy not to have a prenup, particularly if one of you has a much higher income or owns a business or property that you'd like to hang on to. Here's the reality, ladies: About four out of ten married couples end up in divorce court, and we doubt any of them thought their marriages would fall apart when they said their "I do's." You can say that it'll never happen to you, but who can foresee the future? What if your husband has a near-death experience and decides to move to Nepal and become a Sherpa? What if you come down with a bizarre illness that sends you into a catatonic state and your hubby can't cope? What then?

Like a cohabitation agreement, a prenuptial agreement allows you to clarify how your finances will be handled after you're bound "for richer or for poorer." With a prenup, you can specify how joint assets would be divided if you were to divorce rather than letting a faceless court system decide for you. In other words, you and your partner can decide who gets to keep the house, car, furniture, IRA, stocks, pets, or any of the other things that you own together. You can include details on how you want your children to be raised as well as child custody and support for the stay-at-home parent. While finances are the focus of most prenuptial agreements, you can include almost any area of potential disagreement during or after your marriage.

We like to think of a prenup as an insurance policy. It's always smart to be prepared for the things that could go wrong in life. That's why we buy health and life insurance, right? A prenup can protect both of you, whether one of you has a lot more dough, you'd like to keep your grandmother's silver, or you want to guarantee that your children's college tuition will be paid. Putting your agreement on paper while everything's coming up roses could make it easier to part without a nasty scene. At the very least, it would be an opportunity to work together to clarify your expectations. It's beneficial for you, your fiancé, and your marriage to be clear with each other from the get-go.

While it sounds similar to a cohabitation agreement, a prenup is not the same thing. Prenuptial agreements must take into account state laws with regard to the dissolution of joint property. For an enforceable agreement, you and your partner must also disclose all of your financial assets and liabilities. Since the teeniest mistake could render your prenup null and void, you should probably have an attorney draft it. You should each get your own lawyers to make sure your interests are protected, and so you can put together a sound, fair agreement that reflects both of your wishes. Think twice if your mate asks you to sign a prenup without giving you a chance to have an attorney take a look at it.

While your cohabitation agreement can serve as a great foundation for your prenup, you will need to draw up a separate document. According to www.nolo.com, contracts regarding the way money and property are handled during or after marriage must be made with matrimony in mind. This means your cohabitation agreement will be invalid after you become "Mr. and Mrs." unless it is drafted shortly before your marriage and takes into consideration the upcoming nuptials.

How to Say "I Love You, but Please Sign Here"

1. "My parents threatened to cut me off if I didn't have a prenup."
2. "Since the cohabitation agreement led us to the altar, maybe the prenup will help us make it 'till death do us part.' "
3. "It's just another way for you to tell me you love me."
4. "You treat me like a star, so I want to act like Hollywood royalty with a fancy prenup."

Employee Benefits

Being "legally bound" may provide you with some employee perks you should consider taking advantage of. For instance, many employers extend benefits such as health and life insurance to their employees' legal spouses. Why spend $200 per month each on health insurance when it would only cost an additional $50 per month to add your husband to your company's plan? It's an easy way to cut down on your monthly expenses. Even if you don't save money, one of you may have better coverage, making a switch worthwhile. Check with your human resource departments to find out your options.

Health Care Proxy and Power of Attorney

When you marry, you automatically become your spouse's "next of kin." This *should* give your new hubby the power to make medical decisions on your behalf. But to make absolutely certain, you'll want to name him in a health care proxy. Same goes for financial decisions. If he's the one you want to pay your bills and deal with your dollars if you can't, be sure to prepare a power of attorney.

Taxes

After the nuptials, you and your partner will be treated differently by the IRS. No longer can you file as a swinging single. You will, however, have the option of filing as "married filing jointly" or "married filing separately." Which you choose is probably more of an economic decision than anything else. If you file jointly, you'll get a smaller standard deduction than you would if you both were filing as "single." (In 2001, $7,600 as a married couple vs. $4,550 each if you're filing as unmarried individuals.) Even worse, all of your earnings will be lumped together, which means more of your income may be subject to a higher tax rate. This inequity is the so-called marriage penalty you hear so much about and which is scheduled to be partially phased out in 2005 and fully phased out in 2009. (But Congress likes to change its mind, so don't bank on it.) If you file separately, you'll each get a standard deduction ($3,800 in 2001) that is smaller than the deduction for singles ($4,500 in 2001). However, you'll be able to use the lower tax rates for a portion of your income, which could mean thousands of saved dollars. Our suggestion: Do your returns both "jointly" and "separately" to see which provides a lower tax, and check with a tax preparer for advice. Please keep in mind that if you sign a joint return, you're stating that the *entire* return is correct and truthful—not just the information that applies to you. So stay informed and understand what it is you're telling the tax man. If your tax return is inaccurate or, worse, your husband is trying to pull a fast one on the IRS, you could be held liable for the full amount of the balance due as well as any penalties or interest.

Wills (If Death Do You Part)

Whenever you experience a major life change like marriage or the birth of a baby, it's a good idea to review and possibly update your last will and testament. If you don't have a will, you shouldn't procrastinate on writing one any longer. Writing your intentions with respect to your worldly possessions ensures that your dearly departed wishes are met. Without a valid will, the government decides who gets what under the laws of intestacy, which vary from state to state. For example, if you lived in New Jersey and didn't have kids, your spouse would receive the first $50,000 of your estate; the rest would be split 50–50 between him and your parents. If you want your betrothed to inherit everything, you must specify it in a will.

Beneficiary Designations

One of the easiest ways to make sure your last wishes are met is to change the beneficiary designations on your life insurance policies and retirement accounts. You can name your spouse as your sole beneficiary or select several beneficiaries if you'd like to provide for other loved ones after you're gone.

Wedding Planning Woes

There are some women who actually enjoy the wedding-planning process. Like Steve Martin's daughter in the movie *Father of the Bride,* they have oodles of fun picking out invitations, shopping for dresses, and sampling wedding cakes. Then there's the other 90 percent (our own unscientific guesstimate) of brides-to-be who find it a stressful and exhausting exercise. For some of you, the headaches may start within nanoseconds of getting engaged, when you and your fiancé start debating the nuptials. Summer or fall? Indoor or outdoor? Big or small? Unless you've been a bride before and know the ropes, you'll probably start freaking out about the details and the unbelievable amount of work that needs to be done.

Next come decisions, decisions, and more decisions. From the location to the bridal party to the guest list to the flowers, there are dozens of agonizing choices to make. Your fiancé, of course, needs to be consulted. But so do your family, his family, your bridesmaids, and others. Whether or not you ask, "everyone has opinions about what is supposed to happen," says Alex. That can mean tons of emotionally draining negotiations and compromises. And let's not forget the dollar issues. Weddings aren't cheap and, unless your maiden name is Rockefeller, you may find yourself under tight budget constrictions or in a perpetual sweat about dollar signs.

During this emotional joyride, you may try hard to make everyone happy, including yourself. In the meantime, no one will seem happy, including yourself. Try this scenario on for size: Your bridesmaids are secretly horrified about paying $250 for a pink satin dress and matching shoes that, no matter how much you wish, they'll never wear again. Your father, who is footing the bill, is having a heart attack about the fifty "close" friends that your future mother-in-law insists on inviting. Your own mother threatens to boycott the reception if you have a casual beach party instead of a black-tie soiree. Then, to send you toppling over the edge, an old college pal who didn't make the invite list calls and says "When's the wedding? I want to book my plane tickets," and you must figure out a polite way to tell her that she's persona non grata.

Whether you're trying to cater to everyone else's wishes or you've turned into the bride from hell, you and your fiancé are bound to butt heads throughout this ordeal. In fact, many of our friends say that they argued more during their engagement than at any other time in their relationship. "We fought like cats and dogs," attests Julianne, thirty. "It got so bad that, by the time we tied the knot, Brendan and I were in therapy and I had given the ring back twice." The stress is hard for any couple to handle, but it can be particularly trying when you're living under one roof. "You can't get away from it!" Julianne says. "It seemed like every time we were home, we ended up talking about the wedding or there would be some sort of underlying tension about it." "There's nowhere to run and hide," adds Gayle. Even if you've never been so sure about anyone in your life, you could start to question whether you're making the right decision. "When you're engaged, the fights seem more significant or symbolic," says Tara, who was in the throes of wedding planning when we spoke with her. "It can be scary. You can't help but think, 'If we can't agree on this stuff, how will we survive when we're married?' "

Of course, there are ways you can minimize or even avoid this prenuptial turmoil. For example, you could have a destination wedding, in which you invite a handful (or dozens, if you prefer) of your nearest and dearest to a fabulous tropical locale (still a lot of planning involved, but at least you're almost guaranteed good weather and a lovely time for all). Or you could skip the whole darn wedding thing and elope to Las Vegas, like Elvis and Priscilla Presley. But assuming that your hands are tied—you want a more traditional wedding (or your fiancé or mother or soon-to-be mother-in-law does)—we have some advice that may help.

First of all, no matter what anyone tells you, remember that the wedding is about you and your fiancé. According to modern etiquette books, regardless of who's paying for it, the bride and groom's wishes ought to come first. However, in the spirit of goodwill and out of respect, you should consider your family's feelings and compromise as much as possible. If your folks are financing the fete, you should also be sure to stay within their budget. It doesn't matter how much you want the ten-thousand-dollar dress or designer wedding cake, you shouldn't ask them to spend beyond their means. If your families' wishes strongly conflict with yours, you and your betrothed could consider cutting the purse strings and paying for the wedding yourselves. That should give you the freedom to, as Frank Sinatra would say, do it your way.

If you get a hard time from either set of elders, remind yourself that your wedding is a symbolic rite of passage. In their eyes, you or your partner may finally be "all grown up" and leaving the nest for good, even if you really flew the coop years ago. "It's an age-old parting of ways," says Cindy, thirty-five, who recently tied the knot. "You won't be their baby anymore." If your parents are interfering or laying on the guilt trips, they may simply be having separation issues. They don't want to let you go! Unfortunately, there is no easy fix for this. Your best bet is to make them feel loved, respected, and part of your life. If you're marching to the beat of a different drummer, explain that their feelings are important to you and you're not trying to insult them. You simply have your own taste and sense of style. If they're overbearing or critical, try not to let their disapproval get to you. By acting hurt or defensive, you only give them the power to upset you.

Make decisions as swiftly as possible and with minimal negotiation, advises Cindy. If you're criticized for your choices, try to be strong and firm. Decide in advance what's most important to you and what you're willing to be flexible on. In general, don't waste too much energy trying to make everyone else happy. It's a losing battle! This is one time when you can and should be a little selfish. Take our word: When the big day rolls around, everyone will be so overjoyed by the fact that you're getting married (and no longer living in sin) that they will forget to worry about whether the table linens are the right color.

You and your fiancé should be responsible for setting boundaries with your respective families. In other words, your mate should gently but firmly put his foot down with his folks, and you with yours. Make a pact to form a united front against all meddling or disgruntled friends and relatives. "Turn the wedding planning into an opportunity to bond rather than letting it drive you apart," says Louisa, thirty-two. If the two of you don't see eye-to-eye, work together to come up with solutions and compromises. According to Cindy, it'll be good practice for wedded life. "After you're married, it will be about Christmas and Thanksgiving and where you're living and how many kids and what kind of school they go to and don't even get me started on the religion stuff," she says. Whenever possible, try to see the humor in all of it. Laughter will help keep you sane and bonded together.

Finally, keep reminding yourself that your wedding is NOT the biggest day of your life. It's just a party! Or, better yet, look at it as the first day of the rest of your life together. When your stress levels start to rise, think of the bigger picture and don't let yourself get worked up over the nitty-gritty details. Likewise, don't worry about the things that you can't control, such as the weather. If the day isn't absolutely perfect, is it really that big of a deal? The important thing is that you've found a great guy to love and cherish forever.

Shacking Up Trivia

According to legend, an engagement ring is a symbol of eternity. As a circle with no end, it is thought to represent a union that will last forever.

How Will Your Lives Change?

One of the first things many couples notice after they get engaged is the powerful effect it has on their families and friends. "Everyone was *so* excited," says Tricia, thirty. "Jack and I were excited, too. But our engagement didn't seem as momentous to us. I guess we had felt married since the day we moved in together." "People treated us differently, like suddenly we were a *real* couple," adds Louisa. "My boyfriend's parents never really acknowledged me while we were living together. But as soon as I had a ring on my finger, our relationship seemed to become legitimate. They started calling and including me in their plans. All of a sudden, I was part of the family."

In terms of everyday lifestyle, you probably won't experience a dramatic change after the ceremony. After all of the fanfare, you'll simply go home and pick up where you left off. For some newlyweds, it can feel a little anticlimatic. "Because we were living together when we got married, it took some of the excitement out of it," says Bryce, thirty-four. "We just went back to our apartment, like always." However, many couples said they were glad that the big move was out of the way. "I don't think we could have handled the pressure of moving in after the wedding," says Stephanie. "Once we got married, it didn't feel like 'Oh my God, our lives are so different!' " Alex explains. "You plan this big party and it's stressful, then everything goes back to normal. But I don't necessarily think that you need to have all this excitement surrounding the wedding. If that's all you're concerned about, then you should reexamine your relationship."

In general, most of the couples we interviewed said they felt happier and more secure after tying the knot. "A couple of words and a ring changes the whole ballgame," says Tara. "It changes your confidence and perspective." "Now that we're married, our relationship feels much more solid," agrees Louisa. "It's comforting to know that we're definitely in this together. Now, I feel like we can plan ahead more. We can start thinking about longer-term issues like buying a house or starting a family. And we seem to deal with our differences better. If we get into a fight, I don't think 'Oh no, is this the end?' When you know that you have to work through things, you take a more rational approach and try harder to solve the problems."

Another big bonus: Once you're lawfully bound, you'll never have to hear the "Soooo, when are you two getting married?" question ever again. Instead, you'll be hit with a brand-new and equally disconcerting line of questioning: "Soooo, when are you two going to have a baby?" Then, if you get pregnant, it will be, "Do you know if it's a boy or girl?" "What will you name her?" "Are you going to breast-feed?" or, as your belly expands, "Are you sure it's not twins?" Hate to tell you, but IT NEVER ENDS! So try to smile and have a sense of humor about it. As our own mother advised us, it's much better to be noticed than ignored.

CHAPTER 9

Breaking Up Is Hard to Do

Odds are, many of you began your live-in relationships with great hopes for the future. You imagined what your life together would be like, and you saw decades of lasting friendship, undying romance, and constant companionship. Others of you weren't so sure about the future, but decided to give the whole shacking up thing a whirl anyway, figuring it would help you determine whether your relationship was meant to be. In any case, things haven't exactly worked out for the best. After a few weeks, months, or years living under one roof, you've started to fear that you and your mate aren't compatible or don't have the same commitment level. Or maybe after you moved in together, your Prince Charming began revealing his ugly side, and you discovered that he was mean, inconsiderate, untrustworthy, or a total boob. Regardless of the circumstances, your relationship is on the skids. You and your man have drifted apart, you're unhappy, or your partner's acting distant and you're getting worried. What now?

When Trouble's Brewing

All relationships have Wow times and not-so-Wow times. Face it: If sharing your life with another person was a walk in the park, there wouldn't be so many couples sitting on therapists' couches or ending up in Splitsville. But how can you tell whether you and your mate are in a temporary slump or something is seriously amiss? It's not always easy to tell at first. The early warning signs are often subtle and easy to overlook. But then, as time goes by, they get bigger and bigger until they become Las Vegas–style neon lights that are impossible to ignore. Just ask Sharon, thirty-seven. "It got to the point where Dylan and I were fighting all the time," she says. "I felt like I was walking on eggshells whenever I was around him. I was crying myself to sleep every night, and he didn't even realize it."

As alarming as they sound, warning signs can actually be a good thing. Once you're alerted to the potentially toxic problems in your relationship, you can try to fix them. That's why it's so important to pick up on the signals as early as possible. Wish all you want, but your troubles aren't going to vanish into thin air—in fact, they'll only get worse if you keep looking the other way. It's like finding a lump in your breast (something that we all hate to imagine). You can wait and hope that everything's OK. Or, you can see a doctor and discover the truth. Don't forget: If the lump *is* cancerous, your chances for recovery are much better if you catch it early.

Cracking the signal code isn't easy, so we consulted top psychologists to identify these eight signs that your relationship may be in danger:

1. **You're not being 100 percent "you."** The old "you" seems to have morphed into a new, not-so-improved "you." You're trying to be who your partner wants you to be rather than who you really are. You sometimes feel uncomfortable around him, afraid to say things, or stifled. You feel like you're losing your sense of self.
2. **You feel unloved.** You don't always feel special, appreciated, or important to your partner. When you're around him, you often feel lonely, unattractive, or incompetent. In general, you don't feel like he listens to you or is there for you when you need him.
3. **You have perma-PMS.** Your man annoys you more than he used to. Instead of cutting him slack, you pick fights or act bitchy. You complain about him a lot to your buddies, coworkers, or pretty much anyone who will listen.
4. **You're distancing yourself.** You've been spending more and more time away from home. Rather than turning to your boyfriend for comfort, support, or a good conversation, you find yourself reaching out to friends, relatives, or work pals.
5. **You've got wandering eyes.** It's not just that you find other men attractive. You've been encouraging their attention or feeling real temptation. Maybe you've been developing a close "friendship" with a male coworker, talking to an "ex," or sending illicit e-mails to a guy you met online. All the kinds of stuff you wouldn't want your boyfriend to find out about.
6. **You're bored with the relationship.** After shacking up, it's not unusual to fall into a rut. The mystery and magic

tend to dwindle whenever romantic partners turn into roommates. For some couples, the issue can be solved by busting out of their routine or reserving time for romance (by planning date nights and such). For others, the problem lies much deeper and requires more than a quick fix. Boredom can occur when your emotional needs aren't being met. You should be concerned if you're losing interest in your partner and you no longer feel like making an effort. If you feel like you're growing and evolving as a person—and your mate isn't—then you should also take heed.

7. **Your gut is saying "It's never going to work!"** You say these words to yourself on a regular basis but continue to disregard them—against your better judgment.
8. **There are more negatives than positives.** According to researcher John Gottman, Ph.D., author of *The Seven Principles for Making Marriage Work,* a healthy relationship should have a "positive sentiment override"—which means that your positive feelings about each other should outweigh the negative.

Can You Repair This Relationship?

So you've come to a dismal conclusion about the state of your union. What started out as a cruise on the Love Boat is starting to feel more like a Poseidon Adventure, and every SOS you send seems to go unnoticed. At this point, you figure that you only have two options. (1) Hang on for dear life and hope that things miraculously turn around. Or, (2) prepare to bail out—why keep torturing yourself or wasting time in a sinking relationship? But Wendy, thirty-two, of Portland, Oregon, who has experienced the demise of two live-in relationships, says you shouldn't give up so easily. "If you felt strong enough about each other to move in together, there are probably a lot of positive aspects to the relationship that are worth fighting for."

If you and your partner are both committed to working at it, experts say there's a good chance that you can salvage your relationship. "It *is* possible to break unsuccessful relationship cycles and make the changes needed to develop a solid partnership," says Sharon Glass, Ph.D., a family psychologist in Owings Mills, Maryland. It probably won't be simple or easy, she adds. But when you think about it, many of life's most meaningful endeavors—from learning how to play the piano to starting your own business to raising kids—require a lot of effort. "Real-life love is hanging in there when times get tough," says Bonnie Eaker Weil, Ph.D, author of the book *Make Up, Don't Break Up.* "It's the tough times that bring people closer together."

We wish that we could tell you exactly what to do to successfully patch up your relationship. Unfortunately, it's a complex topic and beyond the scope of this book. We recommend picking up a copy of *Relationship Rescue: A Seven-Step Strategy for Reconnecting with Your Partner* by Phillip C. McGraw, Ph.D. (We're big Dr. Phil fans, and we found his book very helpful.) But if you can't get your hands on it, try following these three expert-endorsed tips.

1. **Pinpoint your problems.** Before repairing the holes in your relationship, you must understand what's causing them. If you haven't already, you and your partner need to talk openly and honestly about your feelings; listen to each other carefully without being defensive or judgmental; and try to get beneath the surface and identify the underlying issues. As part of this process, you both need to recognize how your own thoughts and actions are contributing to the problems in your

relationship. If you don't make any headway on your own, you should try couples' therapy, Glass suggests.

2. **Learn to be a better partner.** Good relationship skills don't usually come naturally. Refer back to Chapter 7 for our lessons on communication and resolving conflicts (two extremely common stumbling blocks for couples). Or, even better, get thee both to a couples' education course for some hands-on help.
3. **Shake it up, baby.** According to Weil, a temporary breakup is a good way to breathe fire into a fizzling relationship. "Most relationships can be saved, but you have to wake up, shake up—and possibly even break up—before you can make up," the family psychologist says. Spending time apart (what Weil calls a "brush with death") can help you both decide how important the relationship is to you. "The separation can last a few hours, a day, weeks, or months, but it usually takes about six weeks for the 'emptiness' to set in," Weil says. Just be careful when and how you go about it. If you take a break too early in your relationship or go into it angry, your rekindling plan could backfire. (Before trying this at home, check out Weil's book to get all the details.)

When It's Time to Throw in the Towel

Even if you've dated (and consequently dumped) dozens of guys, it can be hard to know when to call a live-in relationship quits. In some cases—let's say, he refuses to try to work on your problems or he's been physically or emotionally abusive—it may be more clear-cut. More likely, however, you'll spend weeks, even months, agonizing over the decision. In all likelihood, there will still be some good feelings between you and your man. You'll be afraid to let go after investing so much in the relationship. Deep down, you'll know that there's no going back if one of you moves out.

Complicating matters may be what we call the "yo-yo" effect, which Yvonne, thirty-six, knows well. "There seemed to be a pattern of ups and downs in my relationship with Kurt," she explains. "Things would be OK for a while, then they'd get bad again. It was easy to keep fooling myself and making excuses." Because you're cohabiting, you may also have financial or logistical barriers that keep you from pulling the ripper. You may be tied into a lease or mortgage, and finding a new place to live may seem too difficult or expensive. Or, the thought of being alone simply scares the begeezus out of you.

Eventually, however, if you're in a no-win relationship, one or both of you will reach the point where you just can't take it anymore. You may decide that you're tired of trying to make it work. Maybe too much damage has been done and it's just too painful to continue. Or, you'll finally accept that you and your mate don't want the same things. "We never had any huge fights or anything," says Gretchen about the end of her time with live-in boyfriend Jerry. "The relationship just sort of dissolved, and we realized that we had nothing in common. By the end, our emotions were totally drained. We were so disconnected. I knew it was time to go."

Once the writing is on the wall, and you've done everything that you can to try to fix the problems between you, don't drag your feet. You may be tempted to wait until your lease is up, your boyfriend finds a job, or the holidays are over. But believe us: There will *never* be a good time to end it, and you'll only make it harder on yourselves by delaying the inevitable. "If you know that you're not right for each other, it's better to cut your losses," says Yvonne. "The longer the relationship goes on, the more emotionally invested you'll be, and the harder it will be to leave."

As unbelievable as it may seem right now (and as much as you hate to hear it), you're better off being by yourself than in an unhappy relationship. You may dread the thought of returning to the dating jungle or being single (again!). You may be nervous about what your family will say and hearing the horrible I-told-you-so's. You may fear the emotional pain and loss that most certainly is in store. Severing an emotional tie is never easy, but in the end IT WILL BE A GOOD THING. If you continue to cling to a hopeless relationship, you'll never know what else is out there. By closing this chapter in your life, you'll be able to open a rich, new one filled with possibilities. So try to see it as an opportunity for growth and focus on what you could gain rather than what you're losing.

"It definitely made me stronger," says Emily of her split from fiancé Eric. "I used to harbor my feelings inside. Now, I say what I want. I'm much more outspoken at work. I don't let people walk on me." "It was a great learning experience," adds Yvonne. "I just wish it hadn't taken five years of my life."

She Said: "I Knew It Was Over When . . ."

- "He ended up buying a beach house with his brother (rather than a 'real' home with me), and I knew the relationship was doomed." *–Sharon, thirty-six*
- "We couldn't summon up the energy to talk about things anymore or try to process the issues." *–Wendy, thirty-two*
- "We went on a trip to Hawaii, and it was obvious that we had completely different interests. I wanted to go snorkeling or read on the beach. He wanted to play tennis or watch TV in the hotel

room. I thought to myself, 'Do I want to take these kinds of vacations for the rest of my life?' The answer was no."

–Emily, twenty-nine

- "He reneged on our engagement time line. When we bought a house together, we agreed that we would get engaged within a year. About nine months later, he said he wasn't sure that he could make that kind of commitment. I wanted to have a family. I couldn't wait forever." *–Yvonne, thirty-six*

Going Your Separate Ways

Breaking up is never pleasant, no matter what the circumstances. But when you and your boyfriend share a bed and a mailbox, it can be especially traumatic. "When you're living together, you can't just avoid each other or say 'It's not working' and walk out," points out Yvonne. "Your lives are too intertwined." You may be used to seeing or at least talking to each other every single day. Maybe you have a lot of the same friends or you're close to each other's families. You may also own furniture, a car, or even a house together. It may sound a little cliché, but "it really is like a divorce without the paperwork," attests Gretchen.

Carole Honeychurch, M.A., coauthor of *After the Breakup: Women Sort Through the Rubble and Rebuild Lives of New Possibilities,* refers to the first phase of any breakup as "ground zero." Whether or not you saw the debacle coming, "it's like a bomb has gone off and your world has collapsed around you," she says. Once your life gets turned upside down, you'll probably feel lost. You may not know where to go or who to turn to. You'll experience a mixture of emotions, including sadness, anger, loneliness, and disappointment. You may feel like a failure or embarrassed to tell anyone what happened. In all likelihood, you'll be heartbroken, and all you'll want to do is curl up in a ball and cry. "It's a huge loss," Honeychurch explains. "In many ways, it's similar to a death. It's the death of your relationship as well as your dreams and expectations for the future."

In the midst of this Kleenex fest, there are a number of practical matters that you'll need to deal with, too. "If you're living together when you break up, you have the added pressure of figuring out what to do about your living situation," Honeychurch says. You may have to find a new place to live or a new roommate ASAP. You'll need to decide how to handle any outstanding expenses. You'll also have to sort through your belongings and determine who gets what if you made any joint purchases. In the end, one or both of you may end up taking a big financial hit, which is apt to make it that much more hateful. "We rarely fought while we were living together," says Gretchen. "But during the breakup, we argued over who got to keep the computer and a bunch of other stuff. After all was said and done, there was a lot of resentment on both sides."

Exactly how ugly the split is—and how long it takes you to get over it—will depend on the nature of the breakup (i.e., who ended it, whether there was any warning, and if there was any betrayal involved). Needless to say, it'll be a lot less agonizing if you're the dumper as opposed to the dumpee. But even if you're the one who pulled the ripcord, the splitting-up process is bound to be painful. "Most women find it really hard and horrible to go through," says Honeychurch. Her advice is the kind that you know is true but can be difficult to accept: "Remember that you're doing the right thing for yourself," she says. "In the long run, you will be much better off."

Unlike wedded bliss, there is no formal ritual or procedure for ending a live-in relationship. "When you get divorced, there's a legal process that you must go through in order to dissolve the marriage," Honeychurch notes. "But when you're cohabiting, there are no steps or rules to follow. You have to make it up yourself." Even more troublesome is the fact that you don't have any legal protection when it comes to splitting up joint assets or any money that you may have put into a joint account. If you're smart, you may have kept your dollars divided and signed a shacking-up contract, per our earlier suggestion. If not, you'll find pertinent info in the following postbreakup recovery guide. First, we'll discuss the practical details of the split, then we'll talk about your broken heart and what you can do to mend it.

Making the Split

All of the breakup survivors we spoke to stressed the importance of making a clean and speedy break. "One of you should move out immediately or as soon as humanly possible," says Wendy. "Stay with friends or family members if you have to." The healing process can't begin until you have some distance, she adds. "Normally, when you break up with someone, you retreat to your own space to try to heal yourself," she says. "If you're cohabiting, you don't have that space." If you're renting an apartment, you may be tempted to hang in there until your lease expires. Warning: Doing so may save you money, but it could cost you emotionally. Think of it as a Band-Aid: Ripping it off quickly is ultimately less painful than trying to peel the sucker off a little at a time. "If you try to continue living together after you've decided it's over, you'll only be prolonging your agony," Wendy cautions. "It can be extremely awkward and hurtful." (Ever see the movie *War of the Roses*?)

Who Keeps the Place?

This may be a question that's up for debate if you both like your abode and you live in a tight housing market. In some cases, there may be an obvious answer, and it may be dependent on who lived there first, your financial situations, or the circumstances surrounding your breakup. "Dylan wanted to keep the place, but he knew that he had no bargaining power since he was the one who up and left," says Sharon. Likewise, for Yvonne. "There wasn't even a discussion," she says. "I told him, 'I moved here for you. I moved in with you. We bought a house. And *then* you decide that you can't commit?' I wasn't going anywhere."

Before you start making any demands or negotiations, one caveat to keep in mind: Holding on to your former love nest—and all the memories it contains—may make it harder to let go of the relationship and hinder the healing process. Take it from Yvonne, who kept the house that she owned with Kurt for four years after their breakup. "In hindsight, staying in the house was a big mistake," she says. "Financially, it was fine. He continued to pay his half of the mortgage. But emotionally, I would have been better off getting rid of the house right away. It would have been easier for me to move on."

Of course, it's possible that both of you will choose to move out because neither of you can swing the rent or mortgage payments by yourself (or bear the thought of taking on a roommate). If you have an outstanding lease, read the fine print or talk to your landlord to see what your options are. You may be able to sublet or possibly even break your lease if you find a new tenant that meets your landlord's approval. Until your pad is rerented, you may be held accountable for the rent, but once the apartment is rerented, your legal responsibility should end. If your landlord threatens to keep your security deposit (despite the fact that you're leaving the place in perfect condition), contact your local tenants' rights association to find out what your legal options are.

Regardless of who stays or goes, you and your now-ex will

need to decide how to handle future rent as well as any outstanding bills. Likewise, if you own a home together, you'll have to determine how to deal with future mortgage payments and how to divide the property. If you're moving out of a rented apartment and he's staying, you should be sure to have your name removed from the lease and any utility accounts. Most likely, there will be bills incurred as a consequence of the breakup. Wendy suggests splitting the relocation costs, including movers and broker fees, no matter who's "checking out."

Dividing Your Stuff

Immediately after calling it quits, you should close all joint bank and credit card accounts. Then, you and your ex will need to sit down and decide how to split the remaining funds. You should also talk about how you're going to handle any future bills and expenses. Over the next few months, remember to keep a close record of how much you've spent. If he hasn't paid his share or owes you money, don't just leave him a nasty voice mail. Let him know in writing in case future legal action is necessary. (Don't forget: Judge Judy always asks for evidence!) E-mail is fine—just be sure to keep a dated copy.

Splitting up jointly purchased furniture and other household items may be tricky if you didn't make any agreements when you bought them. You may argue over who gets to keep the sofa, the dining room table, or the prized Barenaked Ladies CD. You can't expect to walk away with everything, so pick your battles. To keep it equitable, we suggest reimbursing each other for half the purchase price of each item. For example, if your ex wants to keep the two-thousand-dollar couch that you paid a thousand for, he should fork over a thousand dollars. Don't bother trying to subtract the cost of normal wear and tear; it'll only complicate things or cause another spat.

No matter how amicable the breakup, you may have trouble deciding how to divvy up your goods. Don't be surprised if you feel some tension or animosity. "There's definitely an emotional element to it," says Wendy. "You can't help but feel like you're losing things." If you co-own a lot of property and can't agree on how to divide it, you may want to call in a lawyer or professional mediator (details on page 271). Once all decisions are final, consider drafting a settlement agreement—a written statement that outlines your verbal contract and must be signed by both of you.

Moving Day

Ugh—the dreaded day! Part of you is anxious to get it over with so you can close the chapter and start moving forward. The rest of you wishes that you'd wake up and discover that it's all been a bad dream. But there's no point in thinking about the what-ifs. Right now, you just need to get through it. And regardless of who initiated the split, the final exit is bound to trigger an emotional tsunami. "When Dylan moved out, I was devastated," says Sharon. "Suddenly, the house was half empty and I thought, 'Oh my God, I'm alone.' I kept looking for him to pull into the driveway. There was a sense of relief, but there was also an emptiness."

Prior to the move, you and Mr. Wrong should plan to walk through your pad together and label who gets what. After the boxes are packed, take inventory to make sure that nothing's missing, advises Cindy. "I still regret letting my ex pack up the CDs," she says. "He took half of mine, including my favorites—Patsy Cline and Neil Young." To minimize moving-day agony, our breakup experts say it's preferable if only one of you is present. "I asked him to move his stuff out when I wasn't home," says Sharon. "I couldn't stand the thought of watching him haul away the boxes." If you feel the need to supervise (and guard your belongings), ask a friend to join you, and try hard to avoid any nasty confrontations.

Seeking Legal Counsel or Mediation

If you're deeply involved in each other's finances—say, you own a car, a house, or a business together—the division of property can be very sticky, Honeychurch notes. In the best-case scenario, you and your ex will be able to talk it over and come to an agreement on your own. If not, a lawyer or professional mediator can help. "It can be easier than trying to deal solely with your partner," Honeychurch says.

If you decide to go the attorney route, try to find a lawyer who specializes in divorce or family law. Be forewarned: Unless you're able to settle out of court, you may be facing an expensive and complex civil action. According to Elizabeth S. Lewin, C.F.P., in *Financial Fitness for Living Together,* lawyers may call upon you to prove your respective financial contributions, which means (good grief!) digging up old checkbooks, cancelled checks, credit card statements, and receipts. That's precisely why many couples end up pursuing mediation, which tends to be less costly and less adversarial.

A mediator is an expert in dispute resolution whom you can hire to help you negotiate a mutually acceptable agreement. These neutral third parties aren't allowed to play favorites or offer legal advice. "Mediators are trained to be aware of emotional issues and can create a safe atmosphere in which you can work out the details of your split," says Dolores Walker, M.S.W., J.D., author of *The Divorce Mediation Answer Book.* For more info on mediation, click on to www.mediate.com. Walker adds that it's wise to have any agreements drawn up by a mediator reviewed by a lawyer before signing on the dotted line.

Shack Attack!

What if he acts like the great Houdini and pulls a disappearing act—leaving you with a lease or mortgage, utility bills, and other financial obligations? If the amount he owes you is relatively small (the amount varies from state to state, but usually no more than a few thousand dollars), you can avoid the cost of an attorney by taking him to small claims court. Otherwise, you'll need a good lawyer.

Will You Ever Get Over This?

As the saying goes, time heals all wounds. However, it's impossible to say exactly how long it will take for the hurt and pain to go away. "The time frame differs for everyone," Honeychurch says. "It really depends on the kind of person you are, the nature of your relationship, and how it ended." Based on our own experience, we predict about three months of grieving for every year that you and your ex were together. But that's a very unscientific estimate. If you were betrayed—let's say, you walked in to find the bastard in *your* bed with his slutty, she's-not-even-PRETTY coworker—it may take much longer.

During the recovery period, you will continue to experience a range of emotions such as sadness, fear, anger, and hopelessness. Despite your best efforts to keep it together, you may break into tears whenever you spot his favorite cereal at the supermarket or hear "your song" (the one you were going to dance to at your wedding) on the radio. You may find yourself obsessing about what he's doing (and with whom), rehearsing what you'll say if you happen to run into him, or fantasizing about the day he comes crawling back with rug burn on his knees. You may ponder whether you're completely unlovable and destined to be alone until the day you die. You'll probably spend a lot of time asking yourself "Why?" or kicking yourself for being a fool. "I questioned a lot," says Sharon. "I kept playing the tape over and over in my head and wondering how I could have been so wrong about the person I thought I was going to marry."

The sad truth is, you're going to feel like absolute hell for a while. And just when you think you're starting to get over it, you'll get an e-mail from your ex or bump into his best friend and suffer an unwelcome relapse. "The emotions involved with grief tend to come in cycles," Honeychurch says. "You may think you're done with being sad or angry, but then the feelings flare up again." As you ride the emotional roller coaster, it's important to remember that THIS, TOO, SHALL PASS. Right now, the pain may seem unbearable, but you *will* get through it. You will be able to pick up the pieces, rebuild your life and, *yes,* find love again. There's no foolproof method for overcoming heartbreak, but here are some strategies that may help.

Be miserable. Now isn't the time to try to swallow your feelings. Ultimately, you will feel better and heal faster if you allow yourself to grieve and mourn. So go ahead and cry, scream, punch a pillow, buy a voodoo doll, and wallow in self-pity. Gradually, the pain should start to subside. If it doesn't, and you start to feel like you don't want to get out of bed or you've lost pleasure in the things that you used to enjoy, consult an M.D. to see if you're suffering from clinical depression, which isn't uncommon after a painful breakup, Honeychurch says.

Assemble a triage team. If you've read John Gray's *Mars and Venus Starting Over,* you may already know how crucial it is to share your feelings with people who understand what you're going through. So don't be afraid to tell your friends, relatives, and even coworkers how much you're hurting and ask for their support. "Try to surround yourself with people who will listen and make you laugh," Wendy says.

Don't be a hermit. Resist the urge to pull down the shades, crawl under the covers, and shut yourself off from the world like *Flowers in the Attic.* It's OK for a day or two, but after that, you should force yourself to get out of the house. Regular activity and contact with others will help lift your spirits and build your self-esteem. Try to make evening plans at least two to three times per week, Honeychurch advises. To fill up your social calendar, consider taking a class or joining a club. Better yet, volunteer. Helping the less fortunate will help you put things into perspective and feel good about yourself.

Stay away from you-know-who. Keep your distance from your ex for the next few weeks or, preferably, months. "The more interaction you have, the harder it'll be for you to let go," Wendy professes. Every time you want to call or e-mail him, make a mental pact to ring up one of your friends instead. Remember, ladies, no drinking and dialing. And whatever you do, DON'T HAVE BREAK-UP SEX! A postbreakup fling may fulfill an immediate sexual urge, but it doesn't mean that you will (or should!) get back together. Let's not forget: There are reasons why the two of you split up in the first place. A mash session isn't going to erase the past or solve your problems. If anything, it'll only stir up a lot of confusing emotions and send you hurdling back on the recovery time line.

Reconnect with yourself. Do all the things that you love and he didn't. Watch sappy movies like *Pretty Woman.* Eat soy burgers and giant dishes of frozen yogurt. Cut your hair. Paint your living room red. Go for long walks. Plan a bike trip or go rock climbing. Whatever it takes. Just keep focusing on getting YOUR life back and becoming whole again.

Get in killer shape. Remember, the best consolation (and sweet revenge) is looking and feeling great. "After Dylan and I split up, I started running and going to the gym a lot," says

Sharon. "It gave me something to focus on other than the breakup and helped me rebuild my confidence."

Redefine your life. Try to see your breakup as a fabulous, new beginning (who needs him?) rather than a tragic ending (my life is a disaster!). According to Honeychurch, who interviewed dozens of people for her book *After the Breakup,* many women say that splitting up ended up being a positive thing for them. "It makes a lot of women ask, 'What do I want in life?' And many of them ended up doing cool things like starting companies, making new friends, or going kayaking in the Sea of Cortés."

Examine what went wrong. To avoid repeating the same negative patterns in your next relationship, you'll need to understand what went wrong and why. What *really* caused the two of you to drift apart? How much was your responsibility and how much was his? Writing in a journal or talking to a close friend or professional therapist may help you sort through your feelings and identify the underlying problems.

Life Goes On . . .

If there's one thing Bridget Jones has taught us, it's that being single has its advantages. Let's see . . . you can be completely selfish, have your own schedule, and flirt without feeling an ounce of guilt. Total freedom! Then there are the spontaneous after-work get-togethers and hilarious girls' weekends. Even dating can be fun if you keep an open mind about it. So don't spend too much time dwelling on the past or beating yourself up for your mistakes. You kissed another frog. Big deal! Try to stay focused on moving forward and living life to the fullest. This is *your* time, and you should make the most of it. We know it sounds corny, but SOME DAY YOUR PRINCE

WILL COME. And when he does, you'll be ready because you know that much more about yourself and what you want in a partner.

Dealing with the I-Told-You-So's

We're quite pleased to report that not *one* of the breakup survivors we talked to got those four dreadful words: "I told you so!" Not even Emily, whose parents opposed her live-in relationship. "I expected to get some flack, but when Eric and I split up, my folks were surprisingly supportive," she says. "They really came through for me." If you aren't quite as lucky, we suggest the following cope-with-it strategy. Should a loved one rub salt into your wound, take a deep breath and say, "I realize that I made a mistake. Right now, I'm trying to move forward, not dwell on the past. And I could really use some positive support." If his or her tune doesn't change, try to limit your interaction with this person until you're feeling stronger emotionally. Meanwhile, look to your buddies and others for a shoulder to cry on or a badly needed boost.

CHAPTER 10

Live-Ins for Life and Other Special Circumstances

We can't tell you what a blast we've had writing this book. We're almost sad to be nearing the end! After all of our research, we've learned so much about ourselves and how to deal in our personal relationships. (We're much more direct and less it's-my-way-or-the-highway now, thank you very much.) We've had an excuse to spend hours on the phone with our shacking-up pals, getting the inside scoop, comparing notes, and laughing until we had tears in our eyes. We've talked to dozens of other women and men to learn about their living-together adventures and heard a lot of happy tales as well as a number of horror stories. While there were some common themes—battles over thermostats, toilet seats, and tubes of toothpaste, to name a few—no two shacking-up experiences were identical. Some couples began butting heads the moment the moving truck pulled into the driveway. Some didn't experience major power struggles until after they got engaged or bought a house together. Many said they would do it all over in a heartbeat. Others said it would take serious hallucinogenic drugs to get them to move in again without a ring.

Hopefully, after reading, perusing, and studying our tome, you'll be better prepared for the challenges of sharing a residence. Or if you're already living with someone, we hope it's comforting to know that the rest of us have similar qualms, concerns, paranoias, hot buttons, and melting points. We also hope that our warnings and cautions haven't left you feeling too freaked out. There are so many unknowns in life and potential risks when you open your heart to another person. You simply can't plan for every snag or predict what will happen next. There will be good times and bad times, so you need to keep changing and adapting. Like everyone else, you'll make mistakes. The key is making the most of those screwups and using them to transform yourself into a better friend and partner. In long-term relationships and in life, the learning curve is endless. If you keep doing your best and giving 120 percent, you'll know that you're doing everything in your power to make your relationship a success.

In this book, we've made some bold assumptions. For example, we surmised that (1) you're a woman in the twenty to forty age range. (2) You're living with someone of the male persuasion. (3) You'd like to tie the knot at some point in your life. And (4) you don't have any rugrats from previous relationships. We seriously apologize for making any gross generalizations or leaving anyone out. Since addressing every person's situation would have been impossible, we decided to let the majority rule. Fortunately, no matter what your gender, lifestyle, or romantic affiliation, most of the information in the previous chapters should apply to you. (You may simply have to switch the pronouns here and there.)

So what's left? On the next few pages, you'll find some bare-bones info for those of you who fall outside of the "majority." From kids to cats to messy moments, we'll also help you work through any special circumstances and challenges you may be facing. Because as the bumper sticker says, "#%!$ Happens."

Partners for Life

In recent years, we've taken great strides toward the acceptance of alternative relationships. Thanks to gay rights activists and celebrities like Elton John and Ellen DeGeneres, we're starting to break the barriers. According to a recent Gallup poll, 52 percent of Americans agree that homosexuality is an acceptable lifestyle—up from 38 percent in 1992. Despite the progress, however, same-sex couples *still* don't have the legal right to marry. Hopefully, that will change in the near future. Meanwhile, the fight to legalize homosexual unions rages on.

Oddly enough, while same-sex couples are lobbying for the freedom to wed, more and more opposite-sex couples are waiving their rights to do so. Some seek the comfort and companionship of a committed relationship but don't feel they need a marriage license to "prove it." Some have been through bitter divorces and refuse to make the same mistake again. Some don't want the government sticking its nose into their business. For quite a few, economics are a factor. Some wish to keep their money and property legally separate for tax or inheritance purposes. Or, in the case of a growing percentage of senior citizens, they don't want to lose any Social Security or their dearly departed's pension, which might happen if they tied the knot.

Whatever their reasons for remaining unhitched, couples in nonlegalized relationships get shafted on some valuable government benefits. The United States hasn't yet caught up with countries like Sweden and Canada, where domestic partners have almost all of the same privileges and protections afforded to married couples. Eventually, sociologists predict Uncle Sam will follow suit. Until then, you can take legal steps to gain many of the rights and advantages that your hitched friends have. By preparing the proper paperwork, you can protect your mate and your pocketbook instead of relying on the feds to do it for you.

To begin with, there are the basics that we discussed in Chapter 6. First, if you want your mate to inherit your belongings when you kick the bucket, you should name him or her as your beneficiary in a signed will and on life insurance policies and retirement accounts. If you die without a valid will and beneficiary designations, state laws determine who gets your goods, and your spousal equivalent won't be on the list. Second, to make sure your partner can make medical and financial decisions for you if you're incapacitated, he or she must be named in a health care proxy and a power of attorney. Third, you should have cohabitation and property agreements to help protect your assets in the event your relationship ends in a split. Last, you should talk to an accountant, a financial advisor, or a lawyer to find out the best ownership options for joint property and estate planning alternatives to minimize estate, inheritance, and income taxes.

Aside from that, you may want to check into domestic partner benefits at your place of work. More employers are beginning to offer health insurance and other perks to their employees' unmarried partners. According to the Human Rights Campaign, a national gay, lesbian, bisexual, and transgender rights group, more than 4,400 U.S. employers currently offer domestic partner benefits. Approximately two-thirds of them cover same-sex and opposite-sex couples; the remaining third provide benefits to same-sex couples only. Employers typically set their own requirements for coverage. But in most cases, a couple must have been shacking up for six months or more and share basic living expenses in order to qualify. If your employer is picking up the tab, the benefits may be considered taxable income by the IRS. This means that your employer must report the fair market value of your benefits as earnings on your W-2 form. Ugh!

Depending on where you live, you and your partner may also have the option of registering as domestic partners. As of early 2002, a total of fifty-eight municipalities in twenty-eight different states had instituted domestic partner registries. Most registries are open to all unmarried couples, while some are limited to same-sex partnerships only. The registry requirements vary from place to place, but in most cases, you both must be eighteen or older and be jointly responsible for common living expenses. To register, you simply fill out a form, pay a nominal fee, sign a certificate, and have it notarized. As far as we know, you don't gain any legal rights or benefits by doing all this, but it does allow you to make a public declaration of your love and commitment. There's also a possibility that your employer will consider the registry when deciding whether to grant domestic partner benefits. A quick heads-up: If you sign a document saying you and your partner agree to share expenses, you could be held accountable for his or her portion of the rent, utility bills, groceries, and cleaning supplies. Don't you just love all this legal stuff?

By the way, if you and your partner reside in Vermont, you can also consider entering into a civil union. The Green Mountain State is the first in our country to allow these types of legalized unions to same-sex partners. Couples who get "unionized" gain all of the state rights but none of the federal rights afforded to married couples. If the relationship were to break up, a family court would preside over the split following the same legal framework used for divorces. While nonresidents can register their unions in Vermont, you must live within the state's borders to receive the benefits (so there isn't much of a point if you're from out of state). For more details, log on to www.vtfree-tomarry.org. Similar benefits are available in Hawaii, too. Someday, if we're lucky, these civil unions will be available in all fifty states, so lovebirds of all genders can make it legal if they so desire.

If you're in a same-sex relationship or plan to remain unmarried, we suggest you continue your research with one of the following books: *A Legal Guide for Lesbian & Gay Couples; Legal Affairs: Essential Advice for Same-Sex Couples; Living Together: A Legal Guide for Unmarried Couples;* or *New Families, New Finances: Money Skills for Today's Nontraditional Families.* The Alternatives to Marriage Project website (www.unmarried.org) is a great clearinghouse of information for domestic partners, with links to other online sites that could be helpful. We also found some useful material on domestic partners financial planning (www.domparts.com) and unmarried couples and the law (www.palimony.com). For issues specific to same-sex couples, you may want to check out the sites for the Human Rights Campaign (www.hrc.org), the National Gay and Lesbian Task Force (www.ngltf.org), and GayLawNet (www.gaylawnet.com).

Kid Catch-22s

For those of you considering bringing children into a live-in relationship, we want to issue a very strong advisory: There's some convincing evidence that kids in cohabiting households don't fare as well as those in married homes. Why? First off, research shows that shacking-up relationships tend to be less stable and, unfortunately, don't last nearly as long as most marriages. This kind of instability can create a shaky foundation for kids. (Despite all the love you have to share, children appear to do better in homes with two biological parents present.) Second, children don't always receive as much economic and social support when their parents are unhitched. To put it differently, your kid may not get as much assistance from your mom, pop, and other family members when and if she needs it.

Of course, there are exceptions to every rule. We're sure it's possible for you and your mate to raise happy, healthy, well-adjusted kids without having rings on your fingers. In fact, marriage is certainly no guarantee that you'll be able to provide a picture-perfect upbringing. (Just think of all your screwed-up friends who were raised in so-called nuclear families!) If you ask us, what's most important isn't that you're legally wed; it's that you can provide a stable, loving environment for your children, with both of you serving as attentive, emotionally invested parents. Whether or not you're hitched, a home filled with conflict and hostility isn't healthy for anyone, especially a kid. Clearly, having a parade of would-be dads coming in and out of their lives wouldn't be so great, either. Children need lots of love, stability, and consistency, and they can get very emotionally attached. So you should be sure your relationship is rock-solid before you mix any little ones into it.

Needless to say, having an unplanned pregnancy while you're living together could put you in a very difficult position. Remember, even if you think that you're being safe, accidents can happen. In fact, research shows that one out of every ten couples that shack up have a baby while they're cohabiting. This could cause you to do something unfortunate, like marry the wrong guy or make a gut-wrenching decision to exercise your right to choose. Or you could wind up a single mom, with no promise of financial aid for your kid if paternity can't be proved. Even if you and your partner are deeply in love and make a terrific team, it could throw you into an extremely stressful situation before you were emotionally or financially prepared. Parenthood is a full-time job that will alter your lives dramatically. Between sleep deprivation, physical exhaustion and money worries, your relationship is bound to feel the strain. So take our sisterly advice: BE EXTRA CAREFUL WITH THE BIRTH CONTROL. No matter how spontaneous or tipsy you're feeling, don't take a chance that could mess up your lives or bring an innocent child into the world under suboptimal circumstances.

If you and your partner are thinking of getting pregnant or adopting while you're shacking up (or married, for that matter), be certain that you're both committed to each other *and* the child. Sorry to be so obvious, but we felt a disclaimer was in order. We suggest consulting a family law attorney to get a legal guarantee regarding child custody and support if you and your significant other were to split up. A written coparenting agreement is also a good idea. In the agreement, you can outline any financial arrangements as well as details regarding custody, visitations, vacations, holidays, access to school and social events, and anything else that might cause a problem down the road. Be sure to consult an attorney or do additional research before you put pen to paper.

After talking to our friends who have recently become new moms and dads, we've concluded that having a baby can be one of the most amazing experiences a person can have. Being a parent can give your life more meaning and a greater sense of purpose. "Suddenly, there's this tiny person who is completely dependent on you for support," says our friend Kelly, who gave birth eight weeks ago. "It changes your priorities and makes you realize what's really important in life." However, it can also be very emotionally, physically, and financially challenging and can cause major stress on your relationship if you aren't ready for it. Be smart and don't forget to stop at the drugstore so you can start a family on *your* terms, when you're able to provide all of the love and support your bundle of joy needs.

Shacking Up Stats

More than one-third of all cohabiting households include children under the age of fifteen, according to 2002 U.S. Census Bureau estimates. About two-fifths of U.S. kids are expected to live in a cohabiting household at some point during their childhood.

Pet Peeves

As far as we can tell, there are two types of people: cat lovers and non–cat lovers. We just so happen to fall into the second category. It's nothing personal against kitties. Obviously, if so many of our friends love them, they must be sweet, affectionate creatures, correct? No, there is another reason for our lack of feline affection. Here are a few clues: sneezing, wheezing, itchy eyes, runny noses. Yup, you guessed it. We're both deathly allergic. Sadly, this can make hanging out at the homes of our cat-loving pals nothing short of torturous.

Many people adore animals and get very attached to their cats, dogs, birds, and boas. They tend to think of them as children and, quite understandably, would do anything to protect them. If forced to choose, they might pick their pets over their significant others. Then there are other folks who aren't so crazy about animals, whether it's because they can't stand the smell of a litter box, have an aversion to hair, hate cleaning up poop, or (like us) suffer terrible allergies. Or perhaps they're partial to certain species—for instance, they may not dig cats, but they're absolutely nuts about man's best friends.

In the early stages of a relationship, some non-animal-lovers will try to feign affection for their significant other's pet. But the truth usually comes out when the couple begins talking about shacking up together. If that's the case and neither one of you is willing to compromise on the issue, you'll have to face the fact that you have a deal breaker. Animals aren't disposable objects, and you can't blame someone for refusing to send a beloved pet to foster care. If you're the animal lover, you should probably find a mate who shares your interests or, at the very least, respects them. If you're the antipet person and the problem isn't medical, you really ought to give it the old college try.

If one of you agrees to become a pet stepparent, you should discuss cost, care, and cleanup responsibilities. Will you split the cost of food, vet visits, beauty treatments (a.k.a. grooming), kennel stays, and other expenses? Who will pay to replace your favorite pair of Manolo Blahniks that the puppy so thoughtlessly chewed or your boyfriend's Brooks Brothers suit that Fluffy shredded in a fit of rage? Likewise, you should decide whether you'll both be responsible for feeding, walking, and cleaning up after Spot. Just like the common courtesy code you established in Chapter 4, you may want to set behavioral guidelines for the third member of your household (for example, no playing catch in the house, sleeping on the bed, drinking out of the toilet, or eating off your plate).

Then again, there's always a chance that, once you're cohabiting, you'll fall head over heels in love with your partner's pet. Sophie, thirty-five, says her boyfriend Garrett was less than psyched when she moved in with her cat. But within a few weeks, he had fallen head over heels for Princess. Unfortunately, the same couldn't be said about Sophie's affection for Garrett. About six months later, she ended the relationship. Garrett was so distraught that she was moving out and taking Princess with her that Sophie decided to leave the kitty behind to soothe her guilty conscience.

If you and your partner decide to purchase a pet together, we recommend having a written agreement stating what would happen if you were to split. A simple way to do this is to add a pet provision to your cohabitation agreement. If you don't have a cohabitation agreement, you should draft a separate compact. In your agreement, you'll want to stipulate who gets custody of the pet should you part. If you plan to share custody, you should make a deal regarding visitation rights. Ryan and Erin of Los Angeles were glad they negotiated a puppy pact before their relationship went south. According to their contract, Erin retained primary custody, while Ryan got to hang with the pooch every other weekend. Says Erin, "It's a good thing we talked about it while we were getting along. Our breakup was so emotional that I think we might have had trouble being civil and rational about it." Let's not forget how much you'll need the pup on those cold, lonely, lovelorn nights!

Sticky Situations

One bed or two at your parents' places? Should you try to pass yourselves off as Mr. and Mrs.? In the last few decades, attitudes toward cohabitation have shifted dramatically. To our more laid-back, liberal-minded generation, there's nothing shocking, risqué, or objectionable about shacking up. Yet it continues to be frowned upon by many older Americans and in some social circles. Since the living-together trend is still fairly new, there are no established "dos and don'ts" to guide us when things get sticky. In an effort to help, we've provided the following answers to questions about shacking-up etiquette and what-the-heck-do-I-do-now conundrums.

Q. **Should we sleep in separate bedrooms when we visit my folks?**

A. Well, it really depends on how your parents feel about it.

Shacking Up tenet: In your parents' house, your parents' rules go. If you're not sure what they think, try asking them. You could say something like, "Hey, where would you like us to crash?" Or let your mom show your boyfriend to his room. If she delivers him to the "guest" quarters, that should give you a clue. Keep in mind: Your folks may know you're living together but that doesn't mean they approve of it. So show respect for their feelings and beliefs, even if you think they're old-fashioned or stupid. A few nights apart over the Thanksgiving holiday won't kill you. Look on the bright side: Unless you're stuck on a lumpy pullout couch or in a room with your brother who snores, you may get a good night's sleep for a change. If you absolutely can't accept your parents' ultratraditional ways, make a reservation at Motel 6, where you and your honey can cuddle or do the wild thing to your heart's content.

Q. **My company is having a retreat in Hawaii, and spouses are invited to attend. Would it be appropriate to bring my partner?**

A. You can try asking around to find out whether your coworkers are planning to bring their spousal equivalents. Or go straight to the source and consult your human resources department. If it's strictly "spouses only," we suggest rolling your eyes and accepting the fact that your place of work is behind the times. The alternative is to try petitioning for a change in company policy. If your corporate culture is superconservative—they're still wearing blue suits and red-striped ties, even on casual Friday—you may have a rigorous uphill battle. You'll have to decide for yourself whether it's worth making waves.

Q. **Is it OK to refer to each other as "husband" and "wife"?**

A. No, no, no. Or perhaps we should ask, why on earth would you want to? We can't think of any good reason to mislead people, especially when doing so could have legal ramifications. Again, it's the whole not being truthful thing. It can only get you into trouble. Besides, one look at your naked ring finger, and they'll probably put two and two together. Not to be harsh, but if you're so concerned about what other people think, perhaps you should suck it up and tie the knot. Otherwise, stick with "boyfriend," "roommate," "partner," "significant other," "special friend," or "spousal equivalent."

Q. **I just found out that I'm being transferred. I love my job, and I can't afford to be out of work. What will this mean for my relationship?**

A. A situation like this is bound to bring commitment issues to the table. Step one is to ask yourself, *What's most important to me? My job? Or my relationship?* In order to have both, your partner must be willing to relocate, of course. If he's game to go with you, see if your employer offers job placement assistance to domestic partners (some do). If, on the other hand, your mate isn't able or willing to move, you'll have three basic options. First, you can opt for severance pay and start pounding the pavement. Second, you can kiss your uncompromising housemate good-bye and take off to pursue your fabulous career. Third, you could try doing the long-distance thing. Some couples actually find this works pretty well for a short time. Whatever happens, if one of you is going to be relying on the other for financial support, you should be sure to put the deal in writing.

Q. **I was invited to my friend's wedding sans date. Should I call and ask if my partner can come?**

A. If your friend doesn't know that you're living with someone, you may want to bring your shacking-up status to her attention in a casual way. For example, you might call or send an e-mail to wish her congratulations, then mention your own exciting news. Perhaps she'll exclaim, "Oh, my goodness! I had no idea you were dating anyone! You should bring him to the wedding." If not, don't ask or act like you're fishing for another invite. Here's the deal: Even if your friend knows you're in a live-in relationship, she still may have chosen to group you into the "singles" category. Some couples decide to make this sort of across-the-board cut in order to save money. Technically, this *is* a faux pas on their part. According to *Emily Post's Complete Book of Wedding Etiquette,* any guest who is married, engaged, or shacking up *should* be invited to bring his or her significant other to the nuptials. But then the book also says that you'd be out of line if you requested to bring a date. So sorry—looks like you'll have to fly solo this time. No, it isn't fair. But unless you've been a bride or thrown a sit-down dinner for 150, you may not know how hard trimming a guest list can be. If you're deeply offended or can't bear the thought of going alone, simply send your regrets (and re-gift that hideous vase your cousin Martha gave you, if you're really ticked).

A Farewell Toast to the Happy Couple

When we started writing this guide, it was hard to imagine that we could fill up three hundred pages. But as it turns out, there was a lot to say on the subject. As all of you now realize, a shacking-up relationship can be complex, challenging, and exciting at the same time. It's like a *New York Times* crossword puzzle. A Rubik's cube. A lifelong labyrinth. The ultimate enigma. Unfortunately, there isn't any foolproof recipe for success. It's all about trial and error. We hope the information on the previous pages will assist you in your quest and steer you in the right direction.

The undeniable truth is, none of us are perfect. And there is no perfect relationship. We'd all like to think that we'll get this relationship thing down pat. But in reality, we'll never *totally* figure it out. If you ask us, that's also what keeps it interesting. There is one thing that we *do* know for certain: You can't take love for granted. You must always continue to make an effort. Set a good example. Rise above. Roll with the punches. Take responsibility. Perhaps most important, TAKE CARE OF YOURSELF! Don't expect your mate to be the answer to your problems. Strive to be the best that you can be. If you feel good about yourself, all those little annoyances won't bother you nearly as much.

Before we put a lid on it, we want to leave you with a closing thought. The following tidbit of advice, which hails from our family lineage, is supposed to relate to first dates, but we think it also applies to live-in relationships and life in general. In the words of our Great-aunt Muriel: "If you tell yourself you'll have fun, you *will*. And if not, then go and get yourself a little drink." Not that Chardonnay should be the answer to our problems either, but you get the drift. Cheers!

Shacking Up Golden Rules

1. Don't live together until you've dated for at least one year.
2. If you're hoping to walk down the aisle, make it clear to your mate before moving in.
3. Don't merge all of your money. Otherwise known as KISS (keep it separate, stupid).
4. She who has the most clothes gets the largest closet.
5. Talk about little problems before they become big, ugly ones.
6. Don't be holier than thou. Recognize when you're at fault and be willing to admit it.
7. Forgive minor sins. Always try to cut your man some slack and let the little things slide. You aren't perfect; neither is he.
8. Focus on the positives. Whenever he pisses you off, reflect on all the nice things he's done for you lately.
9. Be considerate. If it drives him crazy when you leave dirty dishes in the sink, try not to do it.
10. Don't listen to Dr. Laura. She's mean!

Acknowledgments

Wow, we kind of feel like we're at the Oscars. We have a lot of people to thank, and it's hard to know where to start! First off, we'd like to say a big thank you to Ted for popping the "Will you move in with me?" question and providing inspiration for this book. All of your patience, advice, and moral support during the writing process (and periodic emotional meltdowns) was absolutely invaluable. We couldn't have done it without you! Ditto for Mom and Dad. We can't thank you enough for all your love, wisdom, support, and editing prowess—despite the subject matter. And let's not forget the steady stream of home-cooked meals . . . you're the best, Mom.

To our agent, Faye Bender, for being a first-rate advisor, sounding board, and strategist. To Ann Campbell, for your expert editing and encouragement when we needed it most. Thank you for believing in *Shacking Up*! To Jenny Cookson, for all of your editorial input, enthusiasm, and behind-the-scenes help. To Jen, Sara, SBS, Hop, Deb, T-bone, Karen, Amy, Gitte, Claudia, Ellen, Jamie, Christy, and all of our other friends (whose names we promised not to print) for sharing your shacking-up highs, lows, and everything in between. Special gratitude to Jen and Pat, for scrutinizing the first draft and giving us some good giggles. Thanks also to Debbie Weisberg, for your sage legal guidance, and to Michael Castleman, for the savvy counsel only an experienced author could provide.

Last but not least, to all the cohabitors we interviewed for the book, for telling us your war stories and baring your souls. Hopefully, your wise insights and tips will help ensure happiness for all current and future shacking up couples—so smart girls will *never* have to hear those four dreadful words, "I told you so!"

Index

S

PHOTO COURTESY OF THE AUTHORS.

About the Authors

A freelance writer for national magazines including *Glamour, Cosmopolitan,* and *Shape,* STACY WHITMAN lives in San Francisco with her huband, Ted. Her sister, WYNNE WHITMAN, is an attorney specializing in tax and estate law. She lives in New Jersey.

Printed in the United States
by Baker & Taylor Publisher Services